Child Care
and Development

Pamela Minett

John Murray

First published 1985
by John Murray (Publishers) Ltd
50 Albemarle Street
London W1X 4BD

Printed and bound in Great Britain
at The Pitman Press, Bath

British Library Cataloguing in Publication Data

Minett, P.M.
    Child care and development.
    1. Children — Care and hygiene
    2. Child psychology
    I. Title
    362.7   RJ101
ISBN 0-7195-4088-7

Preface

This book on child care and development is based on paediatrics — that branch of medicine which deals with the care and development of children. It is both an art and a science. It overlaps many other subjects but belongs to none. It includes those aspects of biological development, psychology, language development, home economics, social sciences and community studies, which relate to children.

This book is primarily intended as a textbook for students of subjects variously called Child Care and Development, Parenthood, Home and Family, and other similar courses. It is designed to cover examination syllabuses for CSE, O level, GCSE (16+) and NAMCW (National Association for Maternal and Child Welfare), but should also be useful for those parts of Social Studies, Community Studies and Home Economics which are concerned with children.

Courses in Child Care and Development are not always followed by an examination. The subject covers an area of study which has a strong appeal to many young people and can, therefore, provide an excellent vehicle for the encouragement of a wide range of related educational activities. In addition, it provides useful guidelines for the parents of the future, helping young people to understand what is involved in the rearing of children. Awareness of the effects of the care of children on their development can lead to a greater understanding of a person's own behaviour — and, it is hoped, to a greater tolerance of the behaviour of others.

Students of this subject in schools and colleges are mainly young people who are not yet parents, nor even contemplating parenthood. The book has therefore been written at this level and with this approach. A broad outline of the subject has been presented in a simple, straightforward manner. Technical terms have been explained or given an everyday alternative. Where controversy exists, I have attempted to give a balanced view.

Although written primarily for students, it is hoped that the book will be of interest to the many parents and others who are concerned with the care of children.

Acknowledgements

Preparation of a book such as this requires consultation with and advice from specialists and experts in many fields. I wish to express my gratitude to Professor Illingworth MD, FRCP, DPH, DCH, DSc, FRPS, an internationally recognised authority in paediatrics, for reading the typescript and providing considerable guidance. I also wish to thank the many people who have so willingly and freely given of their time and knowledge, in particular, Dr Pat Allington-Smith (Senior Clinical Medical Officer), Fred Ashford (Safety Officer), Sue Chapman (Social Services), Trevor Ford (Road Safety Officer), Elaine Guest (Director of Nursing Service, Midwifery), Robert Illingworth (Headmaster, Special School), Stanley Minett, Dr David Wayne (Consultant Physician) and Sir Edward Wayne, FRCP. Special thanks are due to Coleen Rowles-Chapman for her cooperation and skill in producing the many drawings that illustrate the text.

The opinions expressed in this book are my own and may not in all cases correspond with those of my advisers.

Pamela Minett

Using this book

The book deals with different aspects of the subject in self-contained Topics. This allows for flexibility both in the selection of Topics to be included in a particular course, and in their order of study.

Arrangement of the Topics

The 64 Topics have been grouped into 8 Sections, as the Contents list shows, pp. vii–viii. The book begins with sections dealing with babies, their development and childhood, in order to introduce students immediately to young children and the fascination of their development, and to allow them to make an early start on the Child Study element which is included in most courses. Sections covering parenthood and family matters are placed later because, by this part of the course, the students should have greater maturity and knowledge to help in understanding the responsibilities of parents.

Within each Topic

Each Topic contains:
Information — with clear headings and presented in a succinct manner to emphasise the important aspects of the Topic.
Questions — which can be used to check knowledge and understanding of the Topic and as a basis for notes.
To Do — containing suggestions which can be used to extend the subject for the more interested and advanced students.
Child Study — discussed in detail on p. vi.

At the end of each Section

Exercises — a selection of questions, many from examination papers, which relate to the work in that Section and earlier Sections.

Supplement

This contains information required by some examination syllabuses but which the author considers too detailed to be included in the main text.

Useful resources

Page 273 lists books, pamphlets, films, videos, etc., which the author has found useful as teaching aids and as material for further study.

Use of the word 'mother'

The person who has the main responsibility for the day-to-day care of the child is referred to in this book as 'mother'. However, it is acknowledged that other persons may fill this role, such as the father, grandparents, aunt or foster parents.

Use of 'he' and 'she'

Generally, throughout the book the child is referred to as 'he' and the mother as 'she' solely for clarity. Although the usage may be controversial, consistency and clarity of text are considered to be of prime importance at this level of writing.

Age-stages

When the following terms are used, they relate to children of the approximate age range shown:
New-born — from birth to 1 month
Young baby — the first 6 months
Older baby — from 6 months to 1 year
Toddler — from 1 year to $2\frac{1}{2}$ years
Pre-school — from $2\frac{1}{2}$ to 5 years

Child Study

A Child Study carried out by each student is an essential part of many courses and may be required for assessment as part of the examination. It usually takes the form of a folder of notes and observations of the way in which a child, or children, develop. The examiners will be looking for understanding of the reasons for child behaviour. The inclusion of relevant photographs and drawings can make the Child Study more interesting. Suggestions and ideas for the study are given at the end of many of the Topics.

The Child Study can be carried out either on one child over a period of several months or longer or, alternatively, on children seen in different situations. The former is usually preferred. The child chosen for study should be one who can be visited regularly, and the younger the better, because children pass through different stages of development more quickly at an earlier age. The study can begin by recording the name, age, and description of the child. Further entries should be made at regular intervals to record changes in development and behaviour as the child gets older. The age the child has reached should be noted at the beginning of each entry.

Another way of carrying out a Child Study is to observe children's behaviour in different situations, for example, playgroups, parks, shops, buses, children's libraries, and when children are deposited and collected from school. The interaction between the children can be studied; so too can the interaction between children and adults. The behaviour of children of the same age can be contrasted, also the behaviour of children of different ages.

A Child Study gives great scope for development of the powers of observation and descriptive recording as well as of imaginative presentation. The student should take every opportunity to meet, play with and care for children and to record the observations and experiences.

Contents

Section 7

Parenthood

Section 8

The family and home

Section 1

Babies

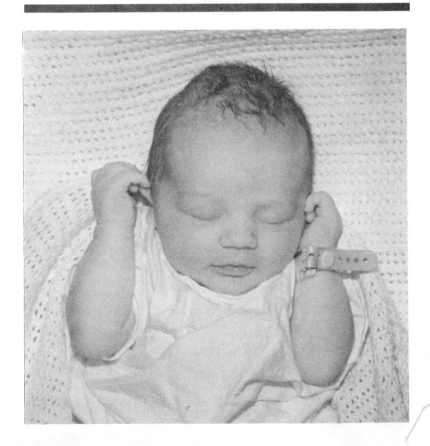

1 The new baby

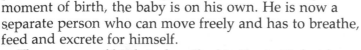

Until six hours ago, this baby had spent all his life inside his mother. She had provided him with food, breathed for him, removed (excreted) his waste products, kept him warm and protected him from damage and disease. Suddenly, at the moment of birth, the baby is on his own. He is now a separate person who can move freely and has to breathe, feed and excrete for himself.

The process of birth is described in Topic 53, but here we are concerned with the new baby now that he has arrived and **is doing well**.

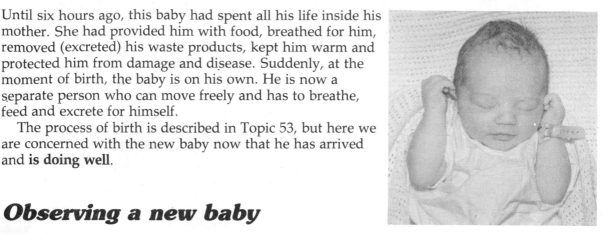

Observing a new baby

Size

People who are not used to looking at new-born babies are always surprised at their smallness. Three measurements are taken immediately after birth — weight, length and head circumference. They are used as the starting points for measuring the child's growth.

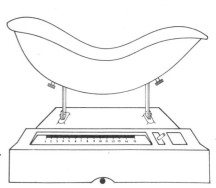

Weight   The birth-weight of full term babies varies considerably around the average of about 3½ kg (7½ lb). **Full term** means that the baby has completed nine months in the womb. Full term babies may weigh as little as 2¼ kg (5 lb), or as much as 6½ kg (14 lb). (Birth-weight is discussed further on p. 270.) Babies usually lose weight in the first few days of life and do not regain their birth-weight until the second week.

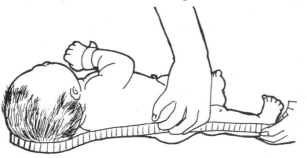

Length (height)   The length of a new baby is difficult to measure accurately. The average length of a full term baby is about 54 cm (21 in).

Head circumference   The average head circumference of a full term baby is about 35 cm (14 in).

Variations in size   Reasons for the variations in size of full term babies include the following:
    Small parents tend to have smaller babies and large parents tend to have larger babies.
    First babies tend to weigh less than brothers and sisters born later.
    Boys are usually larger than girls.

Shape

The drawing below shows the shape of the new baby. The head is very big compared to other parts of the body. The legs are very short. The abdomen (tummy) is large. A layer of fat under the skin of full term babies gives the legs, arms and body a plump appearance.

The stump of the umbilical cord can be seen. As it dries out, it will shrink and will drop off within a week to ten days after birth.

When resting on its back, a new-born baby lies with its head to one side. Often, the arm and leg on the face side are outstretched and the opposite arm and leg are bent. The soles of the feet are turned inwards.

Head

Hair   The amount and colour of the hair on the head at birth varies from baby to baby. Some babies have a lot of black hair — much more than the baby in the photograph on p. 2. Often the hair which the baby is born with falls out in a few weeks or months. The new hair which grows to replace it may be quite a different colour.

Eyes   Many babies have blue-grey eyes at birth, although babies with brown skins may have brown eyes. The baby will be several weeks old before the parents know for certain what colour the eyes are going to be.

Soft spot   There is a soft spot, **fontanelle**, on the top of the head where the four pieces of bone which make up that part of the skull have not yet joined together. Parents may notice that the soft spot pulsates (moves up and down) with the beat of the heart. This is normal and is caused by the blood being pumped through the artery underneath. There is no need to worry about touching the soft spot when washing the baby's head. It is covered by a very tough membrane which protects the brain underneath.

Skin

Vernix   At birth, the baby's body is covered with a greasy, whitish substance called the vernix which protects the skin whilst the baby is in the womb. It is also thought to give some protection against infection after birth. For this reason, in some hospitals babies are not bathed until they are several days old.

Lanugo   If the baby arrives early, the skin may be covered by a fine layer of hair called lanugo, which is normally shed during the last two weeks in the womb. It will come off by itself soon after birth.

Milia   Many new-born babies develop small, whitish-yellow spots on the face, particularly the nose. They are known as milia or **milk spots** and are the blocked openings of the oil glands in the skin. These spots will disappear quite quickly of their own accord.

Jaundice   At least half of all new-born babies develop jaundice on the second or third day after birth. The skin and eyes become tinged with yellow and remain yellow for three to four days. It is normal and harmless and no treatment is necessary.

Birth marks   There are different kinds of birth mark. Most are harmless, need no treatment, and disappear with time.

Red blotches on the skin of the upper eyelid, on the middle of the forehead, and on the back of the neck, will disappear within a year. They are often called **stork bites**. The old wives' tale is that this is the place where the stork's beak gripped the baby when he was being delivered to the mother.

Strawberry marks are another type of birth mark. They appear a few days after birth as bright red raised areas, and may get bigger for up to 6 months. They gradually fade and will be gone by 5 to 10 years of age.

Questions new parents ask

1. a What does 'full term' mean?
b For how long is a baby described as new-born? (See p. v.)
c Describe what is meant by the following: (i) fontanelle, (ii) vernix, (iii) lanugo, (iv) milia.

2. a What measurements are taken at birth?
b What are the average measurements of full term babies?
c What factors may account for the variations in size of full term babies?

3. Need parents be alarmed if their new baby:
a is covered with a fine layer of hair,
b is not bathed immediately after birth,
c has red blotches on the skin of the eyelids, forehead or back of the neck,
d develops jaundice a day or two after birth,
e develops milk spots,
f develops a strawberry mark? Explain why in each case.

To do

1. Draw a diagram of a new-born baby and describe its shape.

2. Find pictures of new-born babies to accompany your notes. Study them and make a note of any differences between the babies.

3. A baby's size at birth is dependent on many factors. Only three are mentioned here. Find out more about other factors which are known to affect birth size. Some information is given on p. 270 and the books listed on p. 273 may be of help.

Child study

(see p. vi)

If possible, ask the parents what the child was like when born and record the information.

2 What a new baby can do

Although basically helpless, new-born babies are able to do many things besides cry. There are times when they sleep and times when they are awake. They can move their arms, legs and head. They can stretch, yawn, hiccup, sneeze and make many other movements. They are also able to receive a certain amount of information from the world around them through the five senses — sight, hearing, taste, smell and touch.

Movements

Babies display a number of movements called **reflexes** or **reflex actions**. Movements of this kind are inborn and made automatically without thinking. The diagrams illustrate six reflexes shown by new-born babies.

A   Swallowing and sucking reflexes   When anything is put in the mouth, the baby immediately sucks and swallows — some babies even make their fingers sore by sucking them while still in the womb.

B   Rooting reflex   When gently touched on the cheek, the baby's head turns as if in search of the nipple.

C   Grasp reflex   When an object is put in the baby's hand, it is automatically grasped.

D   Walking reflex   When held upright with the feet touching a firm surface, the baby will make walking movements.

E   Startle reflex   When the baby is startled by a sudden loud noise or bright light, the hands are clenched, the elbows are bent to bring the forearms in, and the baby may cry.

F   Falling reflex ('Moro' reflex)   Any sudden movement which affects the neck gives the baby the feeling that he may be dropped. It makes him fling back his arms and open his hands, then bring the arms together as if to catch hold of something.

5

Some of these reflexes are necessary for a baby to survive, for example, sucking and swallowing. Others might have been more useful at an earlier stage of human evolution. For example, it is thought that the grasp reflex dates back millions of years to the time when our ancestors lived in trees. Grasping would have enabled the young animal to cling to its mother's fur or to a branch of a tree.

These reflexes mainly disappear by the age of three months and are replaced by actions which the baby has to learn. For example, the walking reflex disappears long before the baby learns to walk.

The senses

Sight   New-born babies can see. Their eyes focus at a distance of 20–25 cm (8–10 in), so they are short-sighted. They see most clearly those things which are near to them, for example, the mother's face when she is holding or feeding her baby. They also notice brightness, e.g. they will look towards a brightly lit window, or shut their eyes when a bright light is suddenly turned on. Sight is dealt with in greater detail in Topic 7.

Hearing   New-born babies can hear. They respond to sounds by blinking, jerking their limbs, or drawing in breath. They may stop feeding at the sound of a sudden noise. If crying, the baby may become quiet and appear to listen when someone speaks to him, and he soon learns to recognise his mother's voice. Hearing is discussed further in Topic 8.

Smell and taste   An unpleasant smell makes a baby turn his head away. He will also indicate if he finds a taste pleasant or unpleasant. When near his mother's breast he smells the milk and may try to get his mouth to it.

Touch   New babies can feel. They are sensitive to touch and pain and change of position. They will cry if the bath water is too hot or too cold. They will be comforted by contact with another human being, as happens when they are held close and cuddled.

Sleep

Many new-born babies spend most of their time asleep, waking at intervals to be fed. The amount of sleep varies from baby to baby, and often from day to day. Some sleep 20 out of 24 hours, whilst others spend much more time awake. It is also impossible to say how long a baby should sleep at any one time. Perhaps a baby will sleep for five hours, or perhaps only for an hour or two.

Very young babies cannot help falling off to sleep, and it can be difficult or impossible to wake them. But by nine months old, sleep has become more of a voluntary process, and they have some control over whether they stay awake or not.

Pattern of sleep   At first, new-born babies do not have a regular pattern of sleep. Gradually, as they become aware of daylight and the sounds of movement around them, sleep starts to fall into a pattern. They begin to sleep less during the day and more at night, although some babies decide that night-time begins at 10 p.m. or later. Most babies are sleeping through the night by the age of three months. They will still have one or more naps during the day, and may continue to need sleep in the day-time for several years.

Sleeping position   It is recommended that very young babies should be placed either on their fronts or sides for sleeping. If placed on their sides, they should be prevented from rolling on to their backs; this allows any milk which is brought up to trickle out of the mouth and not down the windpipe, which could cause choking.

After the first few weeks the sleeping position is of less importance. Many babies seem to prefer to sleep on their fronts. This position is a disadvantage when they are awake and all that can be seen is the side of the cot or pram. Other babies prefer to sleep on their backs. They lie with the head turned sideways, so the danger of choking is very slight. Also, normal healthy babies will always move their heads if anything prevents them from breathing. Babies placed to sleep on their sides rarely stay that way. They roll either on to their fronts or backs. By about five months babies are usually able to turn themselves over and can then change their position to suit themselves.

Questions

1. **a** What is the name given to movements which are inborn and automatic?
b Name six such movements shown by new-born babies.

2. **a** Name the five senses.
b For each of these senses, give an example which indicates that it is already functioning in a new-born baby.

3. **a** How much time does a new-born baby spend asleep?
b Does a new-born baby have a regular pattern of sleeping?
c By what age is a baby (i) likely to be sleeping through the night, (ii) have some control over whether he sleeps or stays awake?

4. For a young baby, compare the advantages and disadvantages of sleeping on its back or its front.

Child study

Find an opportunity to look at a very young baby. Describe the appearance and movements of the baby. If possible, compare this baby with other babies of about the same age.

To do

1. What is a new-born baby able to do? Make a list of as many things as you can think of. Add drawings or photographs to show some of these.

2. A reflex action can be defined as an automatic response to a stimulus. Continue the table below, describing the reflexes mentioned in this topic.

Reflex action	Stimulus (cause of movement)	Response (movement which follows)
Grasp reflex	something placed in the hand	it is automatically grasped

3 The needs of a baby

Every baby has certain needs. Some of these are essential for the baby to survive and to grow and develop physically. Others provide favourable conditions for emotional, social and intellectual development. Table 3.1 lists the needs of a baby and the main topics in which they are discussed.

Table 3.1

The needs of a baby	Topic number
Warmth	3
Food	18, 19, 33
Shelter	–
Clothing	22
Protection from illness and injury	40, 60–63
Fresh air and sunlight	3
Activity and rest	2
Love and comfort	10
Continuity of care	3
Security to make him feel safe	11
Training in habits and skills	9, 13
Stimulation from play to help in learning	24, 25
Praise and attention to develop self-confidence	–

As the child gets older, his needs increase. The additional needs of an older child are given in Table 3.2.

Table 3.2

Additional needs of an older child	Topic number
Discipline which is firm but kind	12
Companions to play with	9
The opportunity to become independent	–
The opportunity to be useful to others	–
The opportunity to be successful in some way	–
The opportunity to take responsibility	–

Body temperature

Normal body temperature of both adults and children can be anywhere between 36–37.5°C (97–99°F). It varies slightly throughout the day, generally being higher in the evening than in the morning. It is also affected by the temperature of the surroundings and by exercise. Crying, too, makes a baby hot and raises the body temperature slightly. The arms, legs or back are a more reliable guide to the baby's temperature than the hands or feet.

While in the womb, the mother keeps the baby at the right temperature. After birth, the infant is still dependent on her to protect him from becoming too hot or too cold. For the first month of life, a baby should be kept in a room temperature of around 20°C (68°F), day and night. As the baby grows larger and stronger, he gradually becomes more able to keep himself warm when in a cold place, but the room in which the baby sleeps should continue to be kept at about 20°C until the baby is several months old.

Effects of cold   Full term babies have some protection against losing warmth from the body as they are born with a layer of fat under the skin. This helps to keep the warmth in. The fat can also be used as fuel to supply extra heat when necessary. However, if a baby is kept in a cold place for too long, he loses more heat than he can generate and will suffer from **hypothermia** (low body heat). This condition may cause the baby to suffer from **cold injury** and can even kill. The smaller the baby, the more quickly heat will be lost from the body.

Effects of heat   If a baby gets too hot, he is not able to move away from the heat. In a very warm room, or in hot weather, an infant who is covered by too many clothes or blankets will become very uncomfortable and irritable and may develop a heat rash.

Tina at the seaside   Robert A. Smith

Fresh air and sunlight

Babies benefit from being out of doors for a while each day, as long as they do not become too hot or too cold. Being in the fresh air helps to make them lively, improves the appetite, puts a healthy colour into the cheeks, and helps them to sleep soundly at night.

Sunlight contains ultra-violet rays which kill bacteria and can also make the skin produce vitamin D (see Topic 33). As these rays cannot pass through glass, children need to be out of doors to benefit in this way.

9

Air pollution   The air near to some factories or to heavy traffic tends to be polluted with toxic substances. Factories give out smoke and sulphur dioxide as waste products, and cars produce carbon monoxide and lead compounds. Lead is added to petrol to improve the performance of motor engines and is expelled into the air with the exhaust gases. In some areas of heavy traffic, lead can reach dangerously high levels which may be a cause of brain damage in young children.

Continuity of care

It is better for a baby to be cared for by a small number of people who are familiar with him, rather than by strangers. These people provide a constant centre to his life and give him security — make him feel safe. A baby cannot cope with meeting many new people at the same time; he needs to get to know them one by one.

The mother is usually the main person who looks after the baby, but the more the father is involved the happier for all. He can help the mother with the continuous and tiring day-to-day care of their new baby. At the same time, he can share the fun and interest of watching the baby develop.

'The routine'   Most young babies soon fall into a pattern of times for sleeping, being awake, and wanting to be fed. The pattern varies from baby to baby and may change quite often as the baby gets older. Both mother and baby are likely to be happier when the mother follows her baby's natural pattern and does not insist on a 'routine'.

The new mother may be told that it is important to have a 'routine' — that is, set times for feeding and changing the baby and for bath-time, bed-time and so on. This is sound advice only if the mother fits the routine around the baby's natural pattern of behaviour. It can be a recipe for bad-temper for a mother to try to make her baby feed and sleep at certain times just so that she can keep to her routine.

When a baby becomes old enough to understand what is wanted of him, which will probably not be until at least the age of one year, then a suitable routine can be very helpful to family life.

Tim in a city street   Pat Winter

Questions

1. a What are the needs of a young baby?
b What additional needs does an older child have?

2. Compare the photographs above and on p. 9:
a Name five possible advantages to Tina of being in the fresh air and sunshine.
b (i) Name four substances more likely to be in the air being breathed by Tim than by Tina.
(ii) In what way can lead damage children?
c If the body temperatures of Tim and Tina were both normal, within what range would you expect them to be?
d The body temperature of these two babies will vary throughout the day. Name four causes of such variations.
e How may Tina behave if she gets too hot?
f What may happen to Tim if he remains outside in the cold for too long?

To do

1. Table 3.1 lists the needs of a young baby. Taking each item in turn, give a reason why it is necessary. Do the same with the list of the additional needs of an older child, Table 3.2.

2. Find out more about lead pollution. What evidence is there for thinking that lead may be causing damage to children's brains?

Child study

How many people help to look after the child? How does the child react to them? How does he react to strangers?

4 Why each child is different

Children come in an endless variety of shapes and sizes. Each can be recognised as an individual with his, or her, own unique appearance, character, and patterns of behaviour.

The way a child grows and develops depends on two factors:

1. genes;
2. environment.

Every child differs from all others because each has a different set of genes (except identical twins) and a different environment. From the moment of conception onwards, the genes and environment continuously interact to produce a person who is unlike anyone else.

Identical twins are an exception because they have identical genes. Nevertheless, they develop into different individuals because the environmental factors will differ. For example, they will be in different positions in the womb; one will be born first; they are likely to have different birth-weights; they cannot both be bathed or dressed at exactly the same time, or be in exactly the same place; they will have different accidents and illnesses and friends and so on.

Genes

A child inherits genes from his parents and they provide a set of instructions for growth and development. The baby's genes decide: the sex of the child; the general shape and appearance of the body; eye colour; skin and hair colour; shape of the face; blood group; etc. They also decide the age at which teeth appear, the size of the hands and feet, and the maximum height to which the child can grow, etc. More information about genes is given on p. 267.

Environment

Environment means the surroundings. The child's surroundings will affect his growth but they will have a much greater effect on other aspects of development such as social and emotional development.

Environmental factors include where the child lives, who looks after him, whether he is loved and wanted, the sort of companions he has, whether he is encouraged to learn, or is ignored, or prevented from learning by over-protection.

Other environmental factors are:

1 Food   A child needs not only enough food but the right sort of food in order to grow properly. **Malnutrition** (poor feeding) stunts growth and is often the result of poverty or famine. Sometimes it comes about because the child does not have a properly balanced diet. On the other hand, over-feeding will make a child uncomfortably fat.

   The brain grows fastest during the last weeks of pregnancy and the first three years of life. Malnutrition during this time may affect brain development and reduce the level of intelligence.

2 Illness   Severe illness may slow down growth, and the younger the child, the greater the risk of illness having a permanent effect. If a child's rate of growth is only temporarily slowed down by illness, he will afterwards adapt with a period of 'catch up' growth. Severe or prolonged illness may also affect emotional development.

3 Exercise   Exercise strengthens and develops muscles. Lack of exercise makes muscles flabby and, when it is coupled with over-feeding, encourages the growth of fatty tissue.

4 Season   The rate of growth in height is affected by the seasons, being fastest in spring and slower in autumn. Children gain more weight in winter than in summer since they are less active and eat more in cold weather.

5 Stress   Happy healthy children flourish. But those who are under severe stress for a long period of time, may not grow to reach their potential height and often become very thin, or over-eat and get fat. Stress may result from unhappiness, worry, loneliness or illness.

6 Smoking   There is some evidence that heavy smoking by parents may slow down their children's rate of growth and development both before and after birth. One investigation found that 7-year-old children whose mothers were smokers, were, on average, shorter and 3–7 months behind in reading ability when compared with children of non-smoking mothers. Another study found that the smoking habits of fathers can affect the birth weight of their children. Smoking in pregnancy is discussed further in Topic 49.

Twins

Twins are either identical or non-identical depending on whether they come from one egg or two.

Non-identical (fraternal) twins

Identical twins develop when a fertilised egg splits into two parts and each develops into an individual. These twins are very much alike in appearance and are always of the same sex as they have inherited identical genes. (See **A**.)

Non-identical twins (fraternal twins) develop when two eggs are released instead of one. Each egg is fertilised by a different sperm, so the twins will be no more alike than any other two children in the same family. They can be either the same sex or a boy and girl. (See **B**.)

In Britain, twins occur once in every 100 births, and about 7000 sets of twins are born every year. Identical twins are more likely to be born to a younger mother. The chances of having non-identical twins increases with the age of the mother, the number of pregnancies and when there is a history of twins in the family. The tendency to have twins is inherited through the mother.

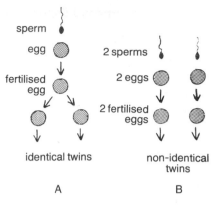

District General Hospital, Gorleston, Norfolk

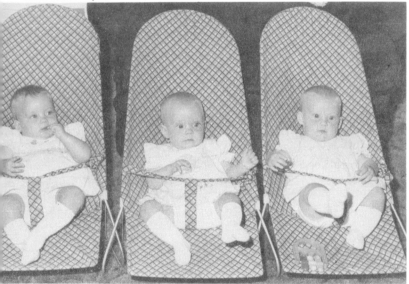

Triplets: which two are the identical twins?

To do

1. Study one family you know well, perhaps your own family or the family of the child you are studying. From your observations, list the ways in which a child in the family resembles each of the parents. Which of these resemblances are likely to be due to the genes the child inherited from the parents?

2. Suggest situations, perhaps in the home, which could give rise to stress in a child, for example, chronic (long-term) illness of a parent.

3. *Discuss* 'When food supplies are short, is it desirable to give priority to young children and pregnant women?' Give reasons.

Questions

1. What are the two main factors which affect a child's growth and development?

2. a Where do a child's genes come from?
b What is the function of genes?
c Give at least six examples of the effects of genes on the shape and appearance of the body.

3. a What does the term 'environment' mean?
b Give six examples of environmental factors which affect growth and development.

4. Twins can be of two types: identical or non-identical; which twins
a develop from one egg,
b are also called fraternal twins,
c are always of the same sex,
d are more likely to be born to a younger mother,
e are more likely to occur with a fourth pregnancy than a first one?

5. Name at least six examples of environmental factors which might help in developing differences in appearance and behaviour of identical twins.

Child study

Describe the child's home environment.

13

5 Growth and development

Growth is an increase in size and **development** is an increase in complexity (becoming more complicated). Growth and development go hand in hand and it is often difficult to separate one from the other.

All babies follow the same general pattern of growth and development, and the stages in which they learn to do things follow in the same order. This is because they need to master one stage before they can go on to learn the next. For example, their legs have to become strong enough to bear their weight before they can stand, they have to learn to stand before they can walk, and walk before they can run.

Each baby develops at his own pace

Although all babies follow the same general pattern, each baby develops at his own pace. The rate of development depends on a number of factors which include:
- the genes which the baby has inherited;
- the amount of encouragement and interest shown by the parents;
- the baby's state of health.

One baby is likely to be more forward in some aspects of development than others. When a baby is said to be 'slow' or 'late' in doing something, for example, walking, it is often because he is concentrating on some other aspect of development such as talking or using his hands — in which he is said to be 'quick'.

Growth

Growth can be measured in terms of height and weight. Generally, as a child grows taller he also becomes heavier, but not always, because weight also depends on how fat (or thin) the child becomes.

Finding the average rate of growth   The average measurement is worked out from the measurements taken from a large number of children of the same age but differing body build and social background. Graphs showing the average weight and height of children from 0–7 years can be found on pp. 271–2.

Joe Whitlock Blundell, 1984

A   B   C   D   E   F

Name	Weight in kg	Height in cm	Birth wt. in kg
A Cissy	24.5	121	2.95
B Susannah	24.3	119	2.13
C Amber	17.6	114	2.81
D Freya	25.2	126	3.29
E Georgina	22.2	122	2.89
F Rebecca	25.4	128	4.14

Individual variation   The photograph shows how greatly children of the same age can vary. These girls are all aged 7 years. Their measurements will spread over a wide range on either side of the average.

Gain in weight varies from child to child and from week to week. A weekly gain of about 170 g (6 oz) is to be expected in the first three months. As the baby grows older, the weight gain decreases. Between 4 and 6 months, the average weight gain is about 140 g (5 oz) a week. From 6 to 9 months it is about 100 g (3½ oz) a week, from 10 to 12 months — 70 g (2½ oz), and for the second year about 40 g (1½ oz) a week. Some gain more, some less.

As these figures show, a baby's increase in weight is greatest in the first six months and then gradually slows down. This is also true for increase in height. As a **rough** guide, the average baby doubles its birth-weight in the first six months and trebles it by one year.

How tall will a child grow?   The maximum height to which a child can grow depends on the genes he inherits from his parents, and nothing can be done to make him any taller. On the other hand, unsatisfactory conditions such as poor feeding can result in a child never growing to his full potential height.

15

Proportions change with growth

As a child grows, the different parts of the body both increase in size and alter in shape. Some parts grow more quickly than others. This has the effect of changing the proportions of the body as the child gets older. For example, at birth the head is about ¼ of the total length of the body, but by the age of seven years it is only about ⅙th, see below.

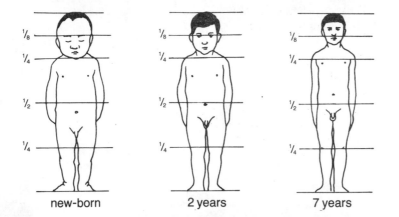

| new-born | 2 years | 7 years |

Growth and development of the legs   In the early stages, a baby is bow-legged. This condition gradually disappears and is often followed by knock-knees at the toddler stage. By the age of 6–7 years, the legs have usually straightened.

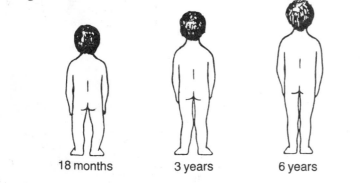

| 18 months | 3 years | 6 years |

To do

1. To your notes, add pictures of children to show the three stages of leg development.

2. a How does premature birth affect future growth and development?
b Are the girls' birth weights (p. 15) related to their weights at 7 years?

Child study

Measure, if possible, the height and weight of the child.
Comment on the child's growth and development and compare with other children of the same age.

Questions

1. Explain the difference between growth and development.

2. Find the average weight and height of the children in the photograph on p. 15.
a Make a table to record the name, weight and height of each child.

Name	Weight in kg	Height in cm

b To find the average weight of these children, add all the individual weights together, then divide by the total number of children, i.e. 6.
c In the same way, find the average height.
d Name the child whose (i) weight, (ii) height is nearest the average.

3. Study the diagrams showing the proportions of the body.
a Why do the proportions of the body change as the child grows?
b At what age is the neck very short and not visible in front view?
c At birth the head is about ¼ of the total length of the body. Is the head proportionately larger or smaller at 7 years?
d On the new-born, the eyebrows mark ⅛ of the body. What marks ⅛ of the body at (i) 2 years, (ii) 7 years?
e (i) At 7 years, what proportion of the body is that part of the leg from the knee to the foot? (ii) At 2 years, is the same part proportionately shorter or longer than at 7 years?
f At 2 years, the navel is at the mid-point of the body. Is the navel above or below the mid-point (i) when new-born, (ii) at 7 years? (iii) What have grown more quickly than the rest of the body to cause the level of the navel to rise?

6 Physical development

Topics 6–15 are concerned with studying different aspects of a child's development, one by one. All forms of development are taking place at the same time, but it is easier to study them separately.

This topic deals with physical development, that is, development of the body. Each of the diagrams is accompanied by the average age at which the stage occurs. It is usual for most children to pass through the different stages of development within a few weeks either side of the average age. But always remember, the age at which normal children sit up, walk and talk varies enormously.

Head control

Movement of the head is controlled by muscles in the neck, and in a new-born baby these are undeveloped and weak. Muscles need time to grow and develop. Also, the baby has to learn how to use them before he has control over his head movements.

New-born When the baby is picked up or lifted into a sitting position the head falls backwards: **A**; this is why the head must always be supported when the baby is being lifted:

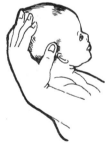

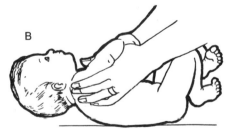

3 months The baby is beginning to control his head: **B**; there is much less head lag when he is pulled into a sitting position. When the baby is held upright, the head is still liable to wobble.

6 months The baby now has complete head control. There is no head lag; he is able to raise his head when lying on his back: **C**; and when in a sitting position he can hold his head upright and turn it to look around.

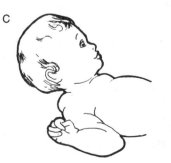

17

Learning to sit

New-born   When a new-born baby is held in a sitting position he appears to roll up into a ball: **A**. The back curves over and the head falls forward because, as yet, the muscles of the neck and back are not very strong.

3 months   The baby still has to be supported when in a sitting position but the back is much straighter: **B**. Although the head is still rather wobbly, he can hold it steady for a short while.

6 months   At six months the baby is now able to sit upright but still needs support from the chair or pram in which he has been placed. He can also sit for a short while on the floor with his hands forward for support: **C**.

9 months   The baby can pull himself into a sitting position and sit unsupported for a short while: **D**.

1 year   He is now able to sit unsupported for a long while and is able to turn sideways and stretch out to pick up a toy: **E**.

The prone position (lying on the stomach)

New-born   When a new-born baby is placed on his front, he lies with the head turned to one side and with the knees drawn up under the abdomen (tummy): **A**. By one month old his knees are not drawn up so much and he is beginning to be able to lift his head.

3 months   The baby now lies with his legs straight, and he can raise his head and shoulders off the ground by supporting the weight on his fore-arms: **B**.

6 months   He uses straight arms to lift his head and chest off the ground: **C**. Usually by five months, a baby is able to roll over from his front on to his back. It takes about another month before he can also roll over from his back on to his front, and when he can do this he can easily roll off a bed.

9 months   The baby can now move over the floor either by pulling or pushing himself with his hands or by rolling.

1 year   He crawls rapidly either on hands and knees, or like a bear on hands and feet: **D**, or he shuffles along on his bottom. Although most children crawl before they can walk, some miss out this stage altogether.

18

Learning to walk

The legs of a new-born baby need time for further growth and development before they can be used for walking. The muscles of the legs, hips and back have to strengthen. In addition, the baby has to learn how to co-ordinate all these muscles and also how to keep his balance. All babies love the opportunity to kick, and kicking is an essential exercise in the development of the muscles of legs and feet.

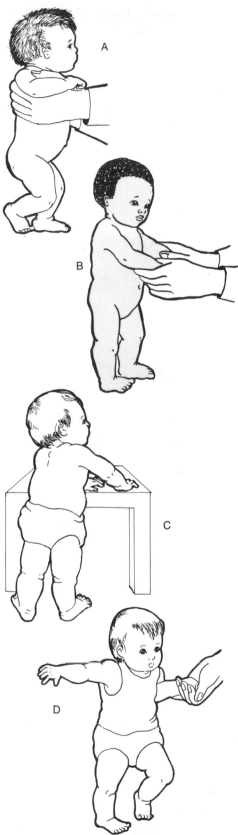

New-born When a new-born baby is held upright with his feet touching a firm surface, he automatically makes walking movements, especially if his head is pushed back a little by holding a finger under his chin. This stage is shown on p. 5; it is known as the walking reflex. The walking reflex disappears after a few weeks and it will be quite a while before the baby learns to make true walking movements.

3 months When the baby is held in a standing position, the legs are beginning to be strong enough to take a little weight although they tend to sag at the knee and hip: **A**.

6 months He can take his weight on his legs when being held: **B**, and enjoys bouncing up and down.

9 months The baby can pull himself into a standing position. From now onwards he will start to walk, either sideways holding on to furniture: **C**, or when both hands are held by an adult.

1 year He can walk with one hand held: **D**. At this stage he walks with feet apart and with steps of varying length; his feet also have a tendency to go in different directions.

15 months He can walk alone. Thirteen months is the average age at which babies walk on their own but some walk much earlier and others much later. At first they are unsteady on their feet and tend to hold their arms up in order to keep their balance; they cannot stop easily or turn corners, and if they look down they fall down.

   Once a child has learnt to use his legs for walking he can acquire other skills. By 15 months he is likely to be able to kneel and to crawl upstairs on all fours, but he does not yet understand that if he leans backwards he will fall down the stairs.

18 months He can walk upstairs by holding on to the rail and putting both feet on each stair.

2 years He can walk up **and** down stairs, two feet per stair, and can kick a ball without falling over. At 2½ years he can walk on tip-toe and jump.

3 years He can walk upstairs with one foot to each stair, but still places both feet on the same stair when coming down, and will often jump off the bottom stair. At this age he can also stand on one leg.

4 years By now he places one foot on each stair when he comes downstairs as well as when he is going up, and he is also able to hop.

5 years He can skip.

Using the hands

New-born babies keep their hands tightly closed for most of the time. The baby also shows a grasp reflex — if anything is put in the hand it is automatically grasped tightly (p. 5). The automatic grasp reflex disappears after a few weeks and the baby will only be able to grasp again when he has learnt to control the muscles of his hands.

3 months The hands are held open for most of the time now that the grasp reflex has gone. If the baby is given a rattle, he holds it for a few moments only. If his hands accidentally touch his clothes he pulls at them. This is the stage when he spends a long time looking at his hands: **A**.

In about another month he is able to clasp his hands together and play with his fingers; he learns what they look like, what they can do, and how to get them where he wants.

6 months He can now grasp an object without it having to be put in his hand, and he uses his whole hand to do so: **B**.

At this age, he picks up everything in his reach with one hand or two, passes it from hand to hand, turns it over, and takes everything to his mouth. When lying on his back, he likes to play with his toes; he loves to crumple paper, and to splash water in the bath.

9 months He is able to use fingers and thumb to grasp an object: **C**. He can also open his hands when he wants, and deliberately drops things on the floor.

By the tenth month he goes for things with his index finger and pokes at them, and can now pick up small objects between the tip of the index finger and the thumb: **D**.

1 year He can use his hands to throw things, and can point with the index finger to objects he wants.

15 months He can take a cup or spoon to his mouth — but his judgement is not yet very good. He is likely to tilt the cup too far when about to drink and to turn the spoon over before the food gets to the mouth. When playing with bricks, he can place one brick on top of another to make a tower.

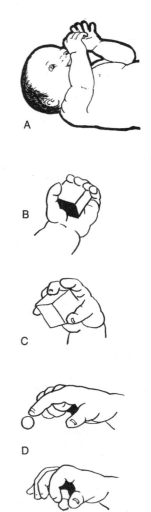

A

B

C

D

18 months He can feed himself completely, and make a tower of three bricks.

2 years He puts on shoes, begins to draw, turns door handles and unscrews jars. He can build a tower with six bricks.

2½ years He begins to be able to undress; builds a tower with eight bricks, and can thread large beads.

3 years He begins to dress himself but needs help with the buttons.

4 years He eats skilfully with spoon and fork.

5 years He dresses and undresses without help, and can use a knife and fork for eating.

Right-handed or left-handed?

When babies start to use their hands, they use both hands equally. Between 15 and 18 months of age it is usually possible to know whether the child is going to be right- or left-handed. Most children are right-handed, but a few can use both hands with equal ease (they are **ambidextrous**). Others use one hand for some types of activity and the other hand for the rest, and about 10 % of boys and slightly fewer girls are left-handed. Left-handed children have more difficulty in learning to write, in opening doors, and in using equipment designed for right-handed people.

Handedness is controlled by the part of the brain which also controls language — speaking, reading and writing. If a left-handed child is forced to use the right hand, it may result in stuttering and in difficulties in learning to read and write.

To do

1. Describe the stage of physical development which will have been reached by a new-born baby in
a head control,
b the sitting position,
c the prone position,
d use of the legs,
e use of the hands.
Draw or find pictures to illustrate each stage. Describe the progress made in **a–e** at 3 months, 6 months, 9 months and 1 year.

2. Carry out some research into left-handedness in children. For example, watch the children in a playgroup or classroom. How many are left-handed? Does being left-handed cause any difficulties? Are any of the children ambidextrous?

Questions

1. What is meant by physical development?

2. Why should a new-born baby's head be supported?

3. Although the legs make walking movements, a new-born baby cannot walk. Why is the baby unable to walk?

4. What is the usual age at which babies become able to
a roll off the bed,
b walk alone,
c play with the fingers,
d pick up small objects using the thumb and first finger?

5. a By what age does a child usually show whether he is right- or left-handed?
b Name two possible consequences of forcing a left-handed child to use the right hand.

Child study

Describe the child's physical development. What stage has been reached in head control, the prone position, sitting position and the use of the legs and hands. Is the child right-handed or left-handed?

7 Learning to see (development of vision)

Babies have some ability to see from the time they are born. As their eyes grow and develop and with experience, babies become able to:

understand what is seen;

alter the focus of the eyes to see things more clearly at different distances;

control the movements of the eyes and use both of them together;

recognise colours.

Development of vision

New-born   When new-born, a baby is probably only aware of vague shapes, darkness, light and movement. Babies of this age are very short-sighted because their eyes have a fixed focus of about 20–25 cm (8–10 in). They therefore see most clearly those things which are at this distance, with objects further away appearing blurred. When an object is placed about 20 cm in front of even the youngest baby, he will look at it for about two seconds. Babies look longer at patterns than solid colours — which indicates that they find patterns more interesting.

When a mother holds her baby in her arms, the distance between the eyes of mother and baby is the distance at which the infant can best focus. Babies are particularly interested in faces, and a few days after birth a baby is able to recognise his mother's face. Within a week or two, he will gaze at her face as she feeds or talks to him.

A new-born baby is sensitive to the intensity of light, and will shut his eyes tightly and keep them shut when a bright light is turned on. The baby also notices movement and will follow an adult or other large object for a moment. When an object, for example a bunch of keys, is dangled close to the baby, he will stare at it and will follow with short, jerking movements of his eyes if it is slowly moved from side to side.

3 months   Although still short-sighted, the baby now has a wider focusing range and therefore can see further. There is also much more control over the movements of the eyes. The baby is very interested in looking at everything around him and is able to follow people who are moving nearby. At this age, a baby spends much time in watching his own hands as he lies on his back.

6 months   The eyes have learnt to work together and the baby is rarely cross-eyed (unless he has an eye defect). He will alter the position of his head to see what he wants to see.

1 year   The baby is able to focus on objects which are quite a long way away, and he can easily recognise people at a distance. The eyes are also able to follow a rapidly moving object.

2 years   The child can now see everything which an adult can see.

2½–5 years   A child begins to show sense of colour from the age of about 2½ years. From then onwards there is gradual improvement in the ability to recognise different colours. Red and yellow are usually the first colours to be known, and blue and green are the next. Most 5-year-olds know four or five colours.

Eye defects

Squint   A child has a squint when the eyes appear cross-eyed or turn in the opposite directions. This means that the child is unable to use both eyes to look at the same object. A mild squint is normal in the first six months of life, but if it persists after that, the child's eyes need to be checked by an eye specialist. If a squint is not treated within two or three years, the child may go blind in one eye. Treatment includes the wearing of glasses and exercises for the eye muscles. The photographs below show a young child with a squint, and the same child wearing glasses to make her use her weaker eye to correct the squint.

District General Hospital, Gorleston, Norfolk

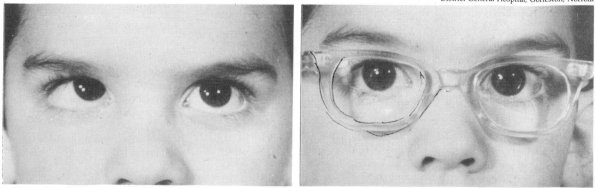

Short sight   A short-sighted child can see near objects clearly but everything further away appears blurred. Short-sightedness develops most often between the ages of 6–10 years, and it can develop quite rapidly. Short sight interferes with school work, for example, a child who is unable to see the blackboard may seem to be restless or slow.

Long sight makes objects near to the eyes appear blurred and fine details are missed. It is less common in children than short sight and may be more difficult to recognise. Long-sighted children have difficulty with writing and other close work and so they may seem to lack interest and be lazy.

Colour blindness is much more common in boys than girls. About 8 % of boys are affected to some degree compared with about 0.4 % of girls. The usual form is red–green colour blindness, and people with this defect cannot distinguish red from green.

Astigmatism   This defect of the eye makes things look crooked or out of shape.

Blindness   Babies who are born blind will grow in the same way as other children but their development will be hindered. Their lack of sight reduces opportunities for making contact with people and for play. This in turn reduces their opportunities for learning. Blind children will **not** be able to:

- make eye-to-eye contact with people (important in the emotional development of young children);
- gradually gain experience by seeing things and remembering what they look like;
- reach out for objects which look interesting in order to play with them;
- watch people and learn from watching;
- seek out people — they will always have to wait for people to come to them;
- move around on their own without being frightened or in danger;
- understand the meaning of a **green** field, or **red** shoes, or a rainbow.

Blind children learn mainly through touch and hearing. They therefore need specialist help and training from the earliest possible moment to reduce, as far as possible, the effects of their handicap. Parents also need to be taught how best to help their blind children develop.

Vision tests   Children's eyesight is given routine tests by health visitors, generally at six weeks old, between 6 and 9 months, and again at about 18 months. Their sight will also be tested when they start school. The aim of these tests is to discover any eye defects so that the correct treatment can be given to remove or reduce the handicap.

Questions

1. a When a new-born baby uses his eyes, what will he be aware of?
b As he gets older and gains experience of using his eyes, what will he become able to do?

2. a When does a baby become able to recognise his mother?
b How can you tell that a baby is (i) sensitive to a bright light, (ii) aware of movement?

3. a Give two ways in which a baby's vision develops between birth and three months.
b By what age can the eyes (i) work together, (ii) follow rapidly moving objects, (iii) see like adult eyes?

4. a Which colours are usually the first to be recognised?
b Which is the most usual form of colour blindness?
c Is it more common for boys or girls to be colour blind?

5. a Give an example of the way in which an eye defect can interfere with school work.
b What is astigmatism?
c At what ages do children have their eyes tested?

6. Give reasons why the development of blind children will be slower than that of sighted children.

To do

1. Read pages 107–109 of 'The First Years of Life' (see p. 273). Describe an experiment to discover what a baby finds most interesting to look at. If a large number of babies were tested, what would be the likely result?

2. Make a mobile for a baby's cot using everyday objects from around the house, or draw one that you could make.

8 Learning to talk (development of speech)

Speech is an important means of communication. Talking enables people to exchange information, tell others about their feelings and sort out problems.

Communication without words

Babies have an inborn desire to communicate with other people. Long before they are able to talk, they use other means of getting messages across, such as:

- **using the eyes:** contact with another person can be made in this way;
- **tone of voice:** a cry, scream or gurgle, all carry different messages;
- **expression on the face:** this can indicate pleasure, anger, contentment, etc;
- **using the hands:** a baby tries to make his wishes known by pointing, clinging, throwing, pushing away, pulling and so on.

Before they have learnt to talk, some babies become very cross and frustrated when they cannot make adults understand what is in their mind or what they want to do. Much of this bad temper disappears when they can use words. Being able to talk also makes life much more interesting.

How children learn to talk

In order to be able to talk, children have to learn how to make the right sounds and to put them together in a meaningful way. This ability comes with lots and lots of practice over several years. The following activities all play a part in learning to talk.

1 Other people talking to them   Most mothers and other adults seem to know instinctively that it is important for them to talk to a young baby. When they hold or look at a baby who is awake they nearly always speak or 'coo', often using a high-pitched tone of voice. It does not matter if the adults talk sense or nonsense at this stage. What is important to the baby is that someone is speaking to him.

2 Listening   A baby is very aware of voices. He likes being spoken to, gazing up at the speaker and keeping quite still as he listens.

As the child gets older he learns to make sounds which mean words. He does this by copying the sounds made by adults when they speak to him. A child cannot learn to talk merely by listening to the radio or television. He needs to be spoken to in a way that a young child can understand.

3 Practising making sounds   Babies get pleasure out of using their voices and often spend hours making noises (babbling) to themselves. They make noises to attract attention, and they enjoy holding 'conversations' (without words) with anyone whose attention they can capture.

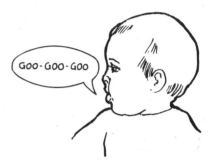

4 Copying sounds made by other people   Babies make a great variety of different sounds as they babble. Only some of these sounds are used when they reach the stage of copying the language of the people around them. If they are spoken to in English, they will copy English sounds and words. If they are spoken to in Chinese, Spanish or any other language they will copy the sounds and words of that particular language. If children hear a lot of swear words, then they will learn those too. If no one bothers to talk to them, then they will not be able to speak very well at all.

5 Learning what the sounds mean   Young children understand the meaning of words long before they can say them.

Pattern of speech development

Speech development follows a general pattern. However, there are great differences in the speed at which individual children learn to talk — greater than in any other field of development. Some children will be in advance of, and others much behind, the average ages mentioned here. Girls tend to talk earlier than boys.

New-born   The baby uses his voice to cry. He also makes other noises when he hiccups, sneezes and 'burps'.

By the age of one month, the baby is making little sounds which come from the throat (guttural sounds). At 5–6 weeks he is beginning to use his voice (vocalise) to coo and gurgle in response to someone speaking to him.

3 months The baby can make more sounds now that he is beginning to learn to control the muscles of his lips, tongue and larynx (voice box). He gurgles and babbles to himself, and also likes to hold 'conversations' with other people. A 'conversation' takes place when the baby makes a noise and then waits for the other person to make a noise.

6 months A great variety of sounds can now be made such as 'goo', 'der', 'adah', 'ka'. Much time is spent practising these sounds. The baby also laughs, chuckles and squeals in play, and screams when annoyed.

9 months The baby says 'dad-dad', 'mum-mum' and 'bab-bab', often repeating the same sound many times. He is beginning to learn to copy the sounds made by adults.

1 year The baby is beginning to understand that some sounds have definite meanings. It is usual, at this age, to say two or three words with meaning, for example, 'dad-dad', 'mum-my', 'bye-bye'. As the baby comes to understand the meaning of words he can obey simple instructions, like 'Give it to Daddy'.

Baby's first words are nearly always labels for people, animals or things. For example, 'dog' can be used for all animals. The next words are likely to be for food and clothes.

During the next year the child continues to learn more words. He practises making the sounds by talking to himself, at times continuously. At this stage a child may use a language of his own (jargon), which no one but his parents can understand.

18 months He says 6–20 words.

2 years He uses 50 or more words and may be able to put two or three together to form a simple sentence.

2½ years He uses pronouns — I, me, you — and is continuously asking questions. (See also Topic 14.)

3 years He can carry on a simple conversation and talks incessantly.

4 years A child's speech is usually easy to understand at this age because most of the basic rules of grammar have been acquired.

Pronunciation

Young children make many mistakes as they learn to speak. They may mispronounce words (say them incorrectly) because they have difficulty in making the correct sounds.

When they find a sound difficult, they substitute an easier one. For example:

- th for s (yeth for yes) This is called **lisping** and it is quite common in young children.
- f for th (fin for thin)
- v for th (fevver for feather)
- w for r (wed for red)
- l for y (lellow for yellow)

Difficulties in pronunciation have usually disappeared by the age of five or six years.

Stuttering (stammering)

Children aged 2–4 years may sound as though they are beginning to develop a stutter. Sometimes words or parts of words are repeated, almost as if the child is filling in time as he sorts out his thoughts. At this age there is much that children want to say, they are in a hurry to say it and they stumble over words as they try to do so. This is not a true stutter. It is a temporary stage that children pass through as they learn to speak.

Most children pass through this stage quite quickly. It is only likely to become a problem when parents make a fuss about it and try to correct the child's speech. The child then becomes self-conscious about talking and a real stutter may develop. A child who develops a real stutter may need the help of a speech therapist.

Slowness in learning to talk

Slowness in learning to talk has a number of causes including:

1 Inherited pattern of development   It may be the family pattern to be late in talking.

2 Concentrating first on other aspects of development
Learning to walk or use the hands may come first.

3 Not enough individual attention from adults
Children learn to talk from adults rather than other children. A young child in a large family may not get enough attention from adults. This can also happen to twins and in families where young children are close in age.

4 Lack of encouragement   If no one shares the baby's pleasure in the sounds he is making, then he will not be encouraged to produce different sounds.

5 Deafness A child can only learn to speak if he hears the words spoken by other people. He also needs to be able to listen to himself so that he can improve his own attempts at words.

Deafness

Some children are born deaf. Others may become permanently deaf through an ear infection or other cause. Temporary deafness can sometimes occur as a result of a bad cold.

Deafness can be total or, more often, partial. Partial deafness means that some sounds are heard but not others. Sometimes only low notes are heard, and not those of a higher pitch. A baby cannot then make sense of the sounds people make when they talk to him. In other cases only loud noises or angry voices can be heard, but not normal speech or the gentle, loving voice which a happy mother uses when she talks to her baby. So these babies link noise with unpleasantness.

When deafness is unrecognised, a child may be wrongly labelled as lazy, difficult to manage or subnormal. In fact he is confused and frustrated. He has great difficulty in understanding what is said to him and any slight changes or new instructions are a cause for worry.

Deafness prevents a child from learning to talk Up to the age of six months, a deaf baby uses his voice to gurgle and babble in the same way as other babies. The parents may not realise that their baby has a hearing problem because the baby is responding in other ways. Children respond to the vibrations of a slammed door as well as to the loud noise it makes. They respond to what they can see — facial expressions, gestures and the movement around them.

After about the first six months, speech development of a deaf baby does not progress any further. A child needs to listen to meaningful sounds in order to copy them, and a deaf child does not hear sounds which have any meaning. So he is unable to learn to talk. Instead of using his voice more and more like other children, a deaf child uses his voice less and the variety of sounds decreases.

Discovering deafness

It is extremely important to recognise deafness in children at an early age, preferably in the first year. The right training and treatment can then be given to reduce the effect of the handicap. A child who does not hear sounds until the age of three years will be slow in learning new sounds. If he cannot hear them by the age of seven, it will be very difficult or impossible to teach him the sounds.

Parents are often the first to notice that something is wrong with their child's hearing. They can obtain advice from their family doctor or Child Health Clinic.

Infant welfare clinics   Deafness may be discovered if the child is taken regularly to the clinic. Routine tests carried out there include the **startle reflex** to sound at six weeks.

Screening tests   In some areas, children are given more thorough screening tests, usually carried out by health visitors.

The first screening tests take place at between six and nine months old. By this age, the average child is able to sit up and has control over the movements of his head. He is tested for response to a low pitched sound, a high pitched sound, the 's' sound, and quiet speech. If the child can hear the sound he will turn his head in that direction.

The children are usually screened again at $3\frac{1}{2}$ years, and later on when they go to school.

Questions

1. Explain the meaning of these words:
a babbling, **c** vocalise, **e** jargon.
b guttural,   **d** larynx,

2. Give four ways in which babies communicate with people before they have learnt to talk.

3. Name five activities that must take place so that children can learn to talk.

4. The drawings on pp. 26-7 show children at different stages of speech development. Place the eight stages in the correct order of development, giving the average age at which each stage occurs.

5. a What is lisping?
b Give four other examples of the ways in which children substitute easy sounds for ones they find more difficult.

6. a Give a reason why some babies become very frustrated at times before they have learnt to talk.

b Which comes first, a young child's understanding of a word or the ability to say it?
c (i) Why may a 3-year-old appear to be developing a stutter? (ii) When is it only likely to become a real problem?

7. a Do girls or boys tend to be more slow to learn to talk?
b Give five other reasons for being slow to talk.

8. a Why may parents not realise that their young baby has a hearing problem?
b Although a deaf baby can use his voice, why can't he learn to talk?
c What can parents do if they are worried about their child's hearing?
d When a child's deafness is unrecognised, what may he be wrongly labelled?
e When a young child is tested for deafness (i) what sounds will his hearing be tested for, (ii) how will he respond if he can hear the sound?

To do

1. Talk with children of different ages and stages of speech development. Tape record the conversations. Discuss and compare the results.
a How many different words did each child know?
b List the different phrases of (i) two words (ii) three words.
c Sort out the words in your lists into nouns, verbs and pronouns.

2. *Discuss* 'Placing a child in front of the television for hour after hour is no substitute for a real live person to talk to.'

3. Find out about the types of treatment and training that can be given to deaf children.

Child study

Talk to the child, listen carefully to what is said, then describe the stage which has been reached in learning to talk. Give some examples of what is said. Make a list of the words the child knows, adding more examples during the course of the study. Note any surprising statements the child comes out with.

Exercises

1 a Give the approximate age (in months) at which children usually become able to:
- (i) walk with help,
- (ii) turn their head to watch something of interest,
- (iii) get into a sitting position unaided,
- (iv) take delight in dropping toys and other objects from the pram,
- (v) prop themselves up on their forearms when placed on the floor,
- (vi) point to an object they want.

b By what age should it be noticeable whether a child is right-handed or left-handed?

c Describe two ways in which a baby may move around unaided before he begins to walk.

d If a 4-year-old child is not yet talking, there must be a reason for it. Give two possible explanations.

e Who would be the right person to help a child who has difficulty in speaking?

f State any two causes of deafness in a young baby.

g Give two reasons why fresh air is important to a child's health.

2 a Describe a typical new-born baby, including the following information. (i) Average weight in kg, (ii) general appearance, (iii) reflex actions and abilities.

b Describe ten ways, apart from changes in size, in which the baby would be expected to have changed by the time he is three months old. (*YHREB*)

3 a List six important needs of a baby during the first six months of life.

b Choose three of these needs and write a paragraph about each to explain how it may be satisfied. (*EAEB*)

4 Gary is an average bright two-year-old. He has a vocabulary of about two hundred words. This means that he uses about two hundred different words himself, though he understands many more. By the time he goes to school at five, he will probably have a vocabulary of about two thousand words. He will have learnt a great deal. Using the following headings, describe how this learning takes place:
People.
Play.
Stories. (*SEREB*)

5 It has been claimed that one child in ten is hard of hearing and that many children are falling behind with their schoolwork when their only problems are minor hearing defects.

a Describe ways in which deafness in children can be detected.

b Why may a child with a minor hearing defect be wrongly thought to be backward?

6 The graph on p. 271 shows the average weight of boys and girls from birth to 7 years.

a Use information from the graph to complete Table 1 and Table 2.

b On graph paper, draw a graph showing the average weight of girls from birth to seven years (copy the graph for girls but *not* that for boys). Add to this graph another to show the weight of a girl called Nina. To do this read the following, mark Nina's weight for each year on your graph paper and then draw a line to join all the marks together.

When Nina was born she was a strong, healthy baby of 3 kg. During the first year she gained weight steadily and on her first birthday weighed 9 kg.
At 2 years she weighed 11.5 kg, 3 years — 13.5 kg, 4 years — 15.5 kg, and at 5 years — 17.5 kg. Then Nina started school and developed the habit of eating lots of sweets, chocolates, ice-cream and crisps. At 6 years her weight was 22 kg and at 7 years — 25 kg.
- (i) Was Nina's birthweight above or below the average?
- (ii) At what age did her weight equal the average weight for girls?
- (iii) By how much was her weight above the average at 7 years? What may have been the cause of this?

Section 2

Development

Howard Jay

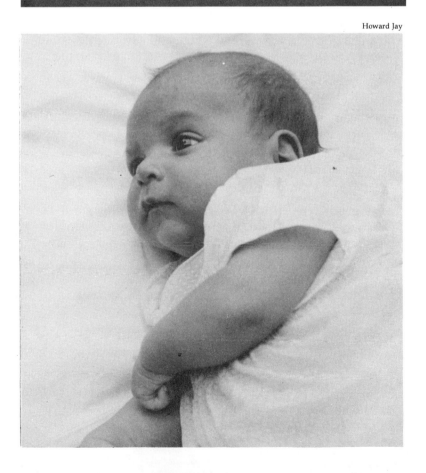

9 Social development

Social development is the process of learning the skills and attitudes which enable individuals to live easily with other members of their community.

Social development follows similar patterns all over the world although customs vary in different countries and even between different groups in the same country. Variation can be seen in eating habits, standards of cleanliness, forms of greeting, attitudes to dress, religion and morals.

Social skills

Children (and adults) are healthier and happier if they get on well with the people around them. It will be easier for them to do this if they are trained in social skills. **Social skills** are those skills which make a child more socially acceptable to other people. They include:
- the ability to meet, mix and communicate with others;
- knowing how to share, take turns, and accept rules;
- having standards of cleanliness acceptable to others, e.g. washing, using the toilet;
- eating in a manner which does not offend others.

Children are not born with a knowledge of these social skills. They have to learn them. If the parents do not teach them, how will they learn?

Pattern of social development

New-born babies are social beings right from the start. They have an inborn need for the company of other people. They cry if they are lonely and can be comforted by being held close to another person.

The baby begins to interact with other people

2 weeks The baby watches his mother's face as she feeds and talks to him and he soon comes to recognise her.

4-6 weeks The baby begins to smile. He will then smile to show pleasure when people look at him.

3 months When an adult speaks to him, he will respond by making noises, and he likes holding 'conversations' with people.

6 months The baby is beginning to understand how to attract attention, for example, by a cough. He learns how to make people do what he wants — at least on some occasions.

The baby learns that he is part of a family

9 months He recognises strangers from people he knows, and needs the reassuring presence of a familiar adult to overcome shyness and anxiety.

The child learns to co-operate as a member of a group

1 year He understands and obeys simple commands.

15 months He copies and 'helps' adults in the house and garden.

2 years He likes to play near other children, but not with them, and defends his possessions with determination. He will show concern for other children in distress.

3 years He plays with other children and understands sharing.

4 years He needs other children to play with but his behaviour is alternately co-operative and aggressive.

5 years He co-operates with his companions and understands the need for rules and fair play.

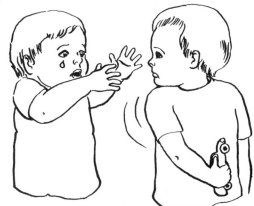

Learning to say 'thank you'

When people say 'thank you' they are expressing their gratitude for something which has been done for them.

Young children have no understanding of the efforts of others and it is not natural for them to say 'thank you'. But if they are taught to be grateful for what other people do for them, and to say 'thank you', it will make them more pleasant to live with.

Loneliness

The child who does not have sufficient social contact, that is, does not have enough people and friends to talk to and play with, will feel lonely. Feeling lonely over a long period of time can make a child unhappy and slow down development.

Adults who are cut off from sufficient contact with other people can also feel lonely and perhaps depressed as well.

This sometimes applies to mothers of young children. The remedy is for the mother to find ways in which she can meet and mix with more people. If these people also have young children, then her own child will benefit from more company as well as from a happier mother.

Development of social play

Between the ages of one and five years, children show gradual development from simple to more complicated forms of social play. Most children pass through the following stages as they learn to play together in groups.

Solitary play   Playing alone.

Parallel play   Playing alongside others but not with them: drawing **B** below.

Looking-on play   Watching from the edge of the group as other children play: drawing **D**.

Joining-in play   Playing with others by doing the same thing as everybody else, for example, running around together, or playing with dolls as in drawing **D**.

Co-operative play   Belonging to a group and sharing in the same task, for example, doing a jigsaw together, or cooking, or playing with a rope, as in drawings **A** and **C**.

Questions

1. a What is meant by social development?
b What is meant by social skills?
c Give some examples of the social skills which children need to learn.

2. List the stages which come under the heading 'Pattern of Social Development'.

3. List the five stages in the development of social play.

To do

1. Find pictures to accompany your list of the stages in the pattern of social development.

2. *Discuss*
a 'How do children learn the necessary social skills?'
b 'The effects of loneliness on a child's development' (see also — Topics 11, 16 and 29).

Child study

Describe the stage of social development which the child has reached.
   What social skills has the child already learnt?

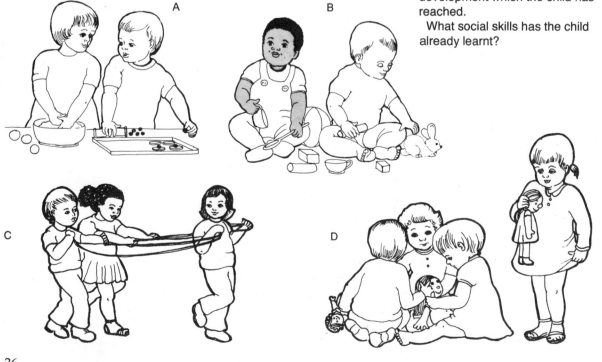

A   B

C   D

36

10 Emotional development

Emotions are feelings such as excitement, love, happiness, worry, sorrow, anger, contentment, pride, jealousy, shyness, and frustration. Young children show all these emotions and many more.

Emotional development

Emotional development is influenced by two factors.

1 Inborn temperament

This depends on the genes the child inherits. Children vary considerably in the strength of their emotions. For example, some children are naturally very excitable, others less so. Some children are very shy, others are rarely shy. Some are great worriers, others seem almost care-free.

2 Environment

This means the surroundings and conditions in which the child grows up. Environmental factors which have a marked effect on emotional development include:

A   The home   This includes the home conditions, the conduct of the people in the house and the effects of the fortunes and misfortunes which occur as a child grows up.

B   Training   The type of training children receive from adults will affect the amount of control they develop over their emotions (**self-control**). For example, control over temper; whether they are able to overcome feelings of jealousy; how they learn to deal with worry and frustration.

C   State of health   There is a strong link between a child's state of health and his feelings. When a child is ill, he will have different feelings from when he is well. Long-term illness or handicap can have a marked effect on a child's emotional development. What sort of effect it will have depends on the child's inborn temperament and the care and training he receives.

Bonds of affection

Emotional development will be affected by the extent to which infants form **bonds of affection**, that is, strong feelings of affection for the people who have the most meaning to them.

Being held close to another person gives a baby feelings of comfort and security. These feelings are strengthened by:

- **skin-to-skin contact** — as happens when the baby breast-feeds;
- **eye-to-eye contact** — when the baby gazes into his mother's eyes;
- **familiar smells** — a baby learns to recognise the smell of his mother's breast within a few days of birth;
- **familiar sounds** — a baby soon learns to recognise the voice of his mother and responds more readily to it than to other voices.

As the infant becomes familiar with a person who stimulates feelings of comfort and security, a bond of affection develops. The baby's first emotional bond will be with his mother or the person who looks after him most of the time. The more the baby is cuddled and loved, the stronger the bond is likely to be.

Love

Love is one of the basic needs of every child (and indeed every adult). Babies thrive on an abundance of love. Parents who truly love their child accept him for what he is. They let him know they love him by cuddling and talking to him and by giving him their time, attention and companionship. Their love is continuous and undemanding.

Not all babies are loved and wanted. Lack of love and interest tends to make a child feel insecure and unhappy. Often, such children do not thrive physically or learn to deal satisfactorily with their emotions.

A loving home affects a child's emotional and social development because it allows strong bonds of affection to be formed between him and other members of his family. He will not then be afraid to show affection for other people. Whereas a child who is not loved by his family may not learn how to love others, because he is unable to form long-lasting bonds of affection with them.

Smother love All children need plenty of love. They also need to be allowed to do things in their own way and to make mistakes so that they can learn from them. When they are over-protected and prevented from becoming independent as soon as they are ready, then the love

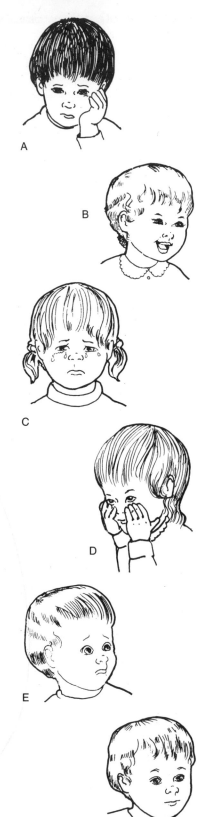

A

B

C

D

E

F

becomes 'smother love'. Smother love may show itself in the following ways:

- constantly picking the child up when he is not crying;
- not letting him play as he wants and always interfering;
- being over-anxious about every movement;
- constantly worrying about the child's bowels and toilet training;
- constantly worrying about the amount he eats and sleeps.

Shyness

Children have phases of shyness, often for no apparent reason. At six months old, a child is still friendly with strangers but occasionally shows some shyness. By one year old he is likely to hide behind his mother when a stranger speaks to him, or cover his eyes with his arm. Even when older, some children may become silent and shy in the presence of people they do not know.

Some children are by nature much more shy than others. The shyness is increased when the child is in a strange place with new people, whereas the presence of a parent helps him to feel much less shy.

Giving the child plenty of love and security and many opportunities to meet other children helps to prevent excessive shyness. Saying to a child 'Don't be shy', or 'Have you lost your tongue', or teasing him about it, will make him more shy. Shyness usually disappears with time.

Questions

1. a The six faces on p. 38 show the emotions of happiness, fear, worry, sorrow, contentment, and shyness. Sort out which face shows which emotion.
b Other emotions are mentioned in this topic. Can you find ten more?

2. a Name two main factors which influence emotional development.
b What does the inborn temperament depend on?
c Name three environmental factors which have a marked effect on emotional development.

3. a With whom will the baby form his first bond of affection?
b (i) What feelings are produced in a baby by being cuddled and held close to another person? (ii) What strengthens these feelings?

4. a How can parents let their child know they love him?
b How may a child who lacks love be affected (i) physically, (ii) emotionally, (iii) in learning how to love?
c Name five ways in which 'smother love' may show itself?

5. What may help to prevent excessive shyness in a child?

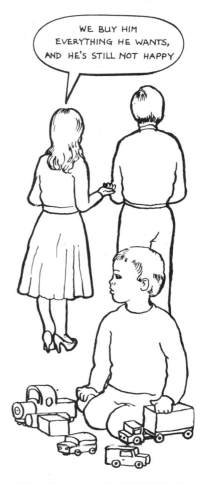

WE BUY HIM EVERYTHING HE WANTS, AND HE'S STILL NOT HAPPY

Child study

What different emotions have you noticed in the child? For each emotion mentioned, describe the occasion when you noticed it. Suggest a reason which, in your opinion, may have produced the emotion.

11 Security and insecurity

A child's feelings may affect his development in many ways, and of special importance are the feelings of security and insecurity.

Security

A secure child is one who **feels** safe. He knows that there is always someone who cares and always a place where he belongs. He feels safe not only from being hurt but also from being lonely, unhappy, rejected and afraid. Knowing that all is well with his world helps him to continue to develop normally.

Fiona Pragoff

Insecurity

An insecure child is one who **feels** unloved and unwanted. In general, children who feel insecure will either become timid and withdrawn or (more likely) indulge in bad behaviour in order to attract attention. Children soon learn that bad behaviour makes people notice them, while to 'be good' results in being ignored.

List A
Insecurity in children will be reflected in their behaviour.
It may be expressed as:
- jealousy;
- fear;
- rudeness;
- spitefulness;
- aggression;
- destructiveness;
- bad-temper;
- nervousness;
- extreme shyness;
- stutter;
- clinging to the mother;
- stomach ache, headache, or other symptoms of illness.

List B
Insecurity may be due to many reasons. The list below gives some suggestions.
- loneliness and boredom;
- excessive discipline and punishment;
- too little discipline;
- a new baby in the family;
- the mother feeling depressed because she is unhappy or unwell;
- fear of starting school;
- too much worry on the part of the parents over such things as feeding, cleanliness, tidiness and potty-training.

Regression

Reverting to an earlier stage of behaviour is called **regression**. It is particularly likely to happen when a child feels insecure. For example, a child who is toilet-trained may revert to wetting his pants. It is no good scolding or smacking the child. What is needed is extra love and attention until he feels secure enough to go back to his normal behaviour.

Jealousy

Jealousy is a natural human feeling common to all children, but it is not a happy feeling. It can show in many ways including:
- hitting and biting another child;
- snatching toys away from another child;
- demanding attention;
- moping (listlessness).

A new baby in the family   Jealousy is often a problem when a new baby comes into the family. The feelings of an older brother or sister are likely to be a mixture of affection for the baby and jealousy arising from fear that the new baby is a rival for the parents' affections. Thus, the older child feels insecure. This type of jealousy is known as **sibling rivalry** (sibling means brother or sister).

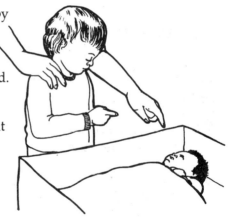

The jealous feelings of the older child cannot be prevented. But, if the parents handle the situation well, jealousy can be kept to a minimum. It will gradually disappear when the older child no longer fears that the baby is a rival because, at this stage, the insecurity disappears.

How parents can help   Parents can help to reduce the amount of jealousy in the older child by:
- preparing him for the new baby's arrival;
- reassuring him often that he is loved and wanted (even when behaving badly);
- encouraging him to feel more grown-up and independent;
- avoiding comparisons with the new baby in his hearing.

Preparing for a new baby   It is a good idea to prepare the child for a new baby's arrival. He will notice that his mother's tummy is getting bigger, and she can tell him that there is a new baby inside. She may let him pat her tummy and feel the baby kicking, but should explain that the baby needs to grow a little bigger before it is ready to come out. The mother should tell him that she will have to go into hospital for a little while when the baby comes. It will also help if the child knows what a new baby looks like and that he cannot expect a playmate.

Before the new baby comes, a mother should tell her child that when the baby arrives, it will need to be fed on milk, will cry sometimes, and will need to be looked after very carefully. The child can help her to collect all the things the baby will need. The mother should try to make sure that he knows and likes the people who will look after him while she is away.

Fears

Fear is a natural response to danger, or to the thought of danger. Therefore it is quite normal for children to become frightened from time to time.

Young babies show fear by crying when there is a sudden noise or when they feel they are falling. At nine months they may cry when strangers take notice of them. Between the age of two and three years they develop particular fears, such as fear of the dark, thunder, dogs, spiders, 'nasty men', noisy machines, or even the hole in the bath. These fears are very real to them. They come about because the child's imagination is developing and he is not yet old enough to understand. The natural fears of childhood can be increased when other people:

- **talk carelessly** in front of children — about fires, burglars;
- **make threats** — 'I will lock you in the cupboard', 'I will run away and leave you';
- **let the child know that they themselves are afraid** — of the dark, thunder, or spiders.

Nightmares (night terrors)

Some children have nightmares quite often, others rarely do. They may occur when an infection is just beginning, when the children have been particularly tired, or following a heavy meal just before going to bed. The frightening dreams either wake them up or they appear to be terrified while still asleep and they cry out with fear. An adult needs to go promptly to the frightened child to comfort, reassure him and give him security.

Nightmares are no cause for worry unless they happen nearly every night. Then they are likely to be due to unhappiness or insecurity at home or school. The cause should be looked for and removed.

Child study

Have you noticed the child behaving in any of the ways in List A? How did you, or the parents, react to the behaviour? Does the child have nightmares?

Questions

1. a What might an insecure child be trying to obtain by bad behaviour?
b List some of the ways in which insecurity may show in a child's behaviour.
c Suggest reasons why a child may feel insecure.

2. a What is a sibling?
b (i) When may sibling rivalry be a problem in the family?
(ii) When will the older child's jealousy disappear? (iii) How can parents help to reduce this form of jealousy?

3. a Why is it normal for children to have fears?
b Suggest a reason for the development of fears in a two-year-old.
c Suggest three ways in which other people may increase a young child's fears.

4. a (i) What is regression? (ii) Give an example.
b (i) What can parents do to help a child return to his normal behaviour? (ii) What reaction (by the parents) is likely to be unhelpful?

To do

1. How many types of behaviour in List A have you noticed in children? Choose four from the list. For each:
a Name the behaviour.
b Describe how the child behaved.
c In your opinion might the reason have been any of the suggestions in List B? If not, make your own suggestion.

2. How would you prepare a child for the arrival of a new baby in the family?

12 Discipline

Discipline (or the lack of it) will affect the ways in which children behave and their social and emotional development.

The need for discipline

Children need sufficient discipline to control them and to make them pleasant people to live with. They require discipline from their parents throughout childhood so that, by the time they have become adults, they have learnt to control their own behaviour by self-discipline. A child will show that he has self-discipline when he behaves well because he knows he should, and not because he has been told or forced to do so.

Parents do not always find it easy to get children to co-operate with them. Children often resent being told what to do. Parents must either try to give their children sufficient discipline to make family life happier for all, **or** they must put up with their badly behaved children.

Good discipline

Discipline which is **firm, kind, reasonable** and **consistent** benefits children because it:
- **makes them feel secure** since they know what is expected of them;
- **helps them to behave in a way acceptable to others**, who will like them better for it;
- **teaches them what is safe and unsafe**;
- **helps them to develop self-discipline**.

Lack of discipline is often harmful. It results in a 'spoilt' child who is likely to be:
insecure — because no limits are placed on his behaviour;
greedy — he expects to get everything he wants;
disobedient and **unco-operative** — he never wants to do as he is told;
rude — he does not consider other people's feelings;
selfish — he always expects to get his own way;
accident-prone — he is not taught to be aware of dangers.

Excessive discipline is also harmful because, although it may stop a child from some types of poor behaviour, it leads to others. Excessive discipline:

- **gives rise to continuous nagging** by the parent — 'Don't do this', 'Don't do that', 'Do as you are told';
- **demands too much of a child** — too much obedience, tidiness, good table manners;
- **makes a child miserable** — there are so many things he seems not to do right even when he tries.

Excessive discipline makes it difficult for a close and loving relationship to develop between child and parent.

The perfect child?

No child is perfect. Parents' efforts to try to make a child perfect are likely to lead to two types of behaviour. Either the child becomes timid and withdrawn; or the child rebels, in which case he will behave very badly by displaying one or other forms of antisocial behaviour, for example, temper tantrums, biting, stealing, aggression.

NO CHILD IS PERFECT

When should discipline begin?

There is no point in trying to discipline children until they are mentally old enough to understand what is wanted of them. Discipline can only be applied gradually as their understanding develops and they come to realise that their parents are pleased by some things and not by others.

Young babies simply do not understand instructions. By one year old, most children have begun to understand the meaning of 'NO'. However, it will be quite a while before they understand what is meant by words like 'hurry', 'wait', 'tidiness' or 'quiet'. By two years of age they have more understanding of what they are being asked to do. By three years, they should have quite a good understanding of what they are expected to do and not to do, but there will still be times when they do not appreciate what is required of them.

How to discipline?

It is the parents' responsibility to discipline their young children. They may sometimes find it a difficult job. To make this task easier, parents should try to:

Set a good example   Children learn a great deal by imitating their parents and copy both good **and** bad behaviour.

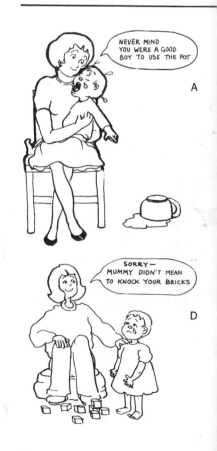

NEVER MIND
YOU WERE A GOOD
BOY TO USE THE POT

A

SORRY —
MUMMY DIDN'T MEAN
TO KNOCK YOUR BRICKS

D

Praise rather than punish   Rewarding good behaviour by a hug, a smile, or by showing interest in what the child does, is more effective than punishment for bad behaviour.

Be reasonable in what they expect   A child needs time to learn, and if parents expect too much too soon it will only make them all unhappy.

Be consistent   When a rule is made, every effort should be made to keep to it. The child will then know whether he is doing right or wrong.

Mean what they say   A child will learn the rules more quickly when 'NO' means 'NO'. If parents do not mean what they say, then the child will be confused about the limits he is allowed. This can make him feel insecure.

Avoid battles they cannot win   A child cannot be forced to eat or sleep or use the toilet, no matter how much parents shout, threaten or slap.

Say sorry when they have behaved badly   All parents are at times short-tempered and unreasonable. If the parents can say sorry afterwards, it helps the child to learn to say sorry.

Questions

1.(i) What type of discipline benefits children? (ii) Give four ways in which children benefit.

2. How may lack of discipline show in a child?

3. a Give three harmful effects of excessive discipline.
b Give four examples of antisocial behaviour which may result from parents' efforts to make their child perfect.

4. a Why is there no point in trying to discipline a young baby?
b (i) Name one word which a one-year-old will have begun to understand. (ii) Name four words which he will not yet know the meaning of.

5. a Whose responsibility is it to discipline young children?
b Give seven suggestions which make it easier to discipline.

To do

1. The drawings A to E show different aspects of the section 'How to discipline?'. Say which one you think each illustrates the best, giving your reasons.

2. *Discuss* 'Some parents consider discipline is harmful because it limits a child's freedom to develop in his own way.'
a What is your opinion of this attitude?
b Give other reasons why children may not be disciplined.

Child study

Give examples of occasions when the child is disciplined. How does the child react to discipline?

13 The training of children

Praise and punishment both have a part to play in the training of children.

Praise

As mentioned in the previous topic, praise and encouragement are likely to be more effective than punishment. For example, a baby who gets praised when he feeds himself learns faster than one who is punished for making a mess. A toddler who is praised when he uses the potty will learn to be clean and dry more quickly than if he is smacked for soiling his pants.

Distraction works wonders

Punishment

Although praise is more important than punishment in their training, children need occasional punishment in order to learn that: antisocial behaviour results in unpleasantness;
parents mean what they say.

At what age should punishment start?   A child should not be punished until he is old enough to understand why he is being punished. Otherwise he will learn nothing, and only become confused and insecure and more difficult to deal with.

   For this reason, babies under the age of one year should not be punished. When a baby is doing something that his parents do not like, then it is up to them to stop him. They can do this either by turning his attention to something else (distraction), or by removing the cause of the trouble (e.g. if the food is removed, he cannot throw it on the floor).

   During his second year, the child will begin to understand when he has done something wrong, although this stage is unlikely to be reached until at least the age of 18 months. If the right sort of punishment is given now, it will help the child to be obedient. By the age of three, he should be well aware of whether he is being 'good' or 'naughty'.

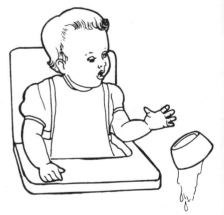

Displeasure   Often all that is necessary is for parents to show that they are not pleased by what the child is doing. If he has been given plenty of praise and encouragement when behaving well, then he will soon notice when his parents are not pleased with him.

46

Punishment should be immediate   If it is necessary to punish a young child, then it should be done immediately so that he knows what he is being punished for. A young child will not remember what all the fuss is about if he has to 'Wait until Daddy comes home'.

Link punishment with misbehaviour where possible, for example:
- if a child scribbles on the wall then the crayons should be taken away;
- if the child deliberately hurts another child, he should be sent away to be on his own in a corner or another room for a short while;
- if he will not leave his play to come for his dinner then it should be cleared away. The child will not starve, but he will be ready for the next meal.

Physical punishment   It is rarely necessary to smack or hit a young child in order to train him. Other ways of punishing will be more effective. Most parents probably smack their children at one time or another. Sometimes they hit out when they lose their temper or self-control and are letting off steam. Smacking for this reason does not usually benefit the child, and could cause harm or injury.

Threats of punishment should not be made unless the parent actually intends to carry them out. Empty threats will not teach a child to be obedient. Such a situation is shown on the right.

I TELL HER EVERY DAY TO TIDY HER TOYS OR SHE WON'T GET AN ICE CREAM

How often to punish and how severe?

The less often punishment is given, the less severe it needs to be in order to have an effect. The opposite is also true — the more often punishment is given, the more severe it has to be to have any effect.

Frequent punishment disturbs a child and can lead to troublesome behaviour — temper tantrums, bed-wetting, disobedience and so on. When parents are frequently punishing the child, they should **ask** themselves why.
1. Are they asking too much of the child before he is ready to understand?
2. Is the child being frequently punished because he is copying the parents' behaviour? Do the parents frequently lose their temper, shout, argue, hit each other, damage things?
3. Is the child behaving badly because of any of the factors in List A?
4. Are the parents punishing frequently because of any of the factors in List B?

List A
Children behave badly more often when they are
   hungry
   worried
   tired
   unwell
   bored

List B
Parents tend to punish more often when they are
   cross and upset with
     each other
   worried
   tired
   unwell
   lonely

1. Is praise or punishment likely to be more effective in training a child
a to feed himself,
b not to wet his nappy?
Explain each answer.

2. a (i) Why should babies under one year old not be punished? (ii) Name two ways by which parents can stop the baby from behaving in a way they object to.
b (i) By what age should children be well aware of being 'good' or 'naughty'? (ii) Give two reasons why children need occasional punishment.
c Why should punishment be immediate for young children?

3. a Describe two ways of punishing a child other than by smacking.
b Suggest a reason why parents may smack a child.

4. a What effect is frequent punishment likely to have on the child?
b What questions should parents ask when they find they are punishing their child often?
c Compare List A and B on p. 47.

1. Compare your answers to Question 4, Topic 12, with the answers to Question 2 in this topic. How do they link together? Put them in one list in order of age of the child.

2. a From your own experience, describe some occasions when punishment has been administered to a child (perhaps punishment to yourself as a child).
b For each, do you consider that any of the factors in (i) List A, (ii)

What punishment is the child given, and what are their effects?

List B, had any connection with the punishment? You may consider that other factors were involved, in which case name them.

3. *Discuss* 'Do you agree or disagree that:
a 'Encouragement and praise are more effective than punishment in the training of children.'
b 'Children need love most when they are behaving badly.'
c 'Smacking is never necessary.'

14 *Mental development*

Mental development is the development of the mind. The **mind** is the thinking part of the brain — the part which is used for recognising, reasoning, knowing and understanding.

A child's mind is active from the time he is born. Day by day, as the child grows, the mind develops as he:

- learns about people;
- learns about things;
- learns new skills;
- learns to communicate;
- acquires more memories;
- gains more experience.

Development of intelligence   As his mind develops, a child becomes more intelligent. How intelligent the child becomes will depend, as in any other field of development, on two factors:

1 Genes   They control the amount of natural intelligence he has.

2 Environment   The use the child makes of his intelligence will be very much influenced by the environment in which he grows up.

Throughout childhood, the genes and environment continuously interact to produce people whose minds develop in a great variety of ways. For example, children vary in their ability to remember, their artistic or musical talents, skill at languages or mathematics, academic ability (ability to study), cleverness with the hands, and whether they have a good understanding of people and their problems.

How to encourage mental development

In the first year development of the mind is helped when parents:

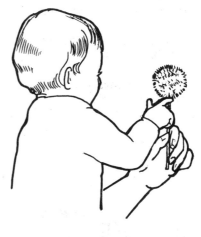

- talk to the baby;
- play with him;
- place him in a position where he can see what is going on around him;
- provide toys and objects which he can handle and investigate;
- allow him to practise new skills as soon as he is ready — chewing, feeding himself and so on;
- at the end of the first year, start to read to him, tell him stories and show him pictures.

After the first year development of the mind is helped when the child is encouraged to:

- talk;
- practise new skills — dressing himself, drawing, playing games;
- be curious and ask questions;
- explore new places;
- play with other children;
- play with toys which stimulate his imagination;
- be creative and make things;
- read.

Conditions which hinder development of the mind

The following conditions can slow down the rate of development of a child's mind. If these adverse conditions persist for too long, they may prevent full development of the child's natural intelligence:

- lack of enough opportunities for talking and playing;
- nothing of interest for the child to do;
- constant nagging or bullying from older people;
- deafness;
- poor eyesight;
- frequent illness;
- frequent absence from school.

How a child learns about the world around him

WHO CAN BUILD BRICKS?

WHAT IS HIS NAME?

Young babies are far more aware of their surroundings than was once thought. From their earliest days, they are aware of stimuli from the environment in the form of light, sound, touch and smell, and they learn as they **look, listen, feel** and **smell**. Babies take most interest in what is new or different. They are more likely to be kept alert and happy by changing patterns of stimulation, whereas the repetition of sounds and movements will often send them to sleep.

From the age of three months onwards, they want to **touch** objects and to **handle** them and put them in the mouth. They come to recognise an object by its shape, what it feels like, how it looks and behaves when turned in all directions, and how it sounds when it is moved or banged. They are gaining information all the while, and new objects interest them more than familiar ones.

When children are able to move around, they approach objects or places to **explore** them. Places which they find interesting will encourage exploration and will increase their information about the environment.

When children are able to talk, they start to **ask questions**. At 2½ years they ask 'What?'and 'Who?'. At 3 years they ask 'Where?'. At 4 years they want to know 'Why?', 'When?' and 'How?'. Their questions are continuous and demanding as they try to make sense of their world. Children who have their questions answered find out a great deal of information. They are now at an age when they can begin to understand about places and people they have never seen, and about events which have happened in the past or will happen in the future.

When adults encourage children to use books, they are helping to increase the children's knowledge and awareness. **Looking at pictures** with an adult helps in understanding the pictures. **Hearing stories** helps in learning to listen and to concentrate. When children can **read**, they have the means of exploring a vast store of knowledge.

Learning by imitation (by copying)

Children learn a great deal by imitating the behaviour of others. For example, they learn to:

- speak by copying sounds;
- write by copying letters and words;
- help in the house and garden by copying adults;
- know the difference between right and wrong (as long as the people around them tell the truth);
- show kindness and consideration for others (from adults who behave in this way).

1. a The intelligence of a child depends on two main factors. Name them.
b How does each of these factors affect a child's intelligence?

2. Suggest seven conditions which can hinder the development of a child's mind.

3. How does a baby come to recognise an object such as a rattle?

4. Suggest ten things parents can encourage their children to do which help them to learn about their environment.

5. Give some examples of what children learn by copying other people.

To do

1. Can you find pictures to illustrate both lists under the heading 'How to encourage mental development'?

2. Obtain some books intended for young children. List each title and
a say what age group it is suitable for.
b state briefly your opinion of the book.
c give ways in which you think it would help a child's mind to develop, e.g. in imagination, general education, improving reading ability.

Child study

1. Describe aspects of the child's behaviour he has learnt by copying other people.

2. What has the child recently discovered about the world around him? Give some examples.

51

15 Bladder and Bowel control

The body produces waste matter which is stored in the bladder and bowels before being discharged. The bladder stores liquid waste called **urine**. The solid waste which comes from the bowel has the technical name of **faeces**. Faeces are often called **stools** or **the motion**. At intervals the outlet from the bladder or bowel opens and waste matter is released.

Babies

Bowel movements   When in the womb, the baby's intestines contain a sticky, greenish-black substance called **meconium**. The baby gets rid of this during the first few days of life by passing greenish-black stools. The stools gradually change to a yellow colour as milk is taken and the baby's digestive system gets into working order.

It is common for babies to go red, grunt and strain when passing a stool, even a soft one. The stools of a baby fed entirely on breast milk are always soft. Bottle-fed babies have stools which are firmer, browner and more smelly.

Young babies are not able to control the outlet of either the bladder or the bowel, and the bladder in particular opens many times a day.

Some mothers try to teach their child to use a potty when the baby is a few months old. Usually they do not have any success because a baby of this age is still far too young to learn. However, an occasional baby will perform regularly on the potty. This is not because the baby has learnt what to do; the reason will be either that the cold rim of the potty triggers the outlet of bladder or bowel to open, or the baby has regular bowel or bladder movements at particular times of the day.

Older babies   Babies who use the potty in the early months may refuse to do so at 9–12 months old. A mother who then tries to force her baby to sit on the potty runs a real risk of starting a 'battle'. A baby of this age is not yet old enough to have any voluntary control over the bowel or bladder outlets. The mother needs to wait for a few months and then try again.

When should training begin?

There are no hard and fast rules. Some parents want their child to be toilet trained as soon as possible, others don't mind how long the nappy stage continues (within reason).

There is nothing wrong in putting a baby on a potty at any age, and if successful it saves a wet or dirty nappy. Problems will only result if the baby is forced to sit on the potty against his will. This is the commonest cause of later difficulties.

Toilet training can only start properly when the child begins to learn how to control the muscles which open the bladder and bowel. This rarely happens before the age of 15–18 months and is sometimes later, there being great variation in the speed at which normal children develop. Even children of the same family become clean and dry at quite different ages. When a child begins to be aware of passing urine or stools, he needs to know how to use a potty.

Who is likely to become potty trained first?

Development of control

Bladder control   The usual stages of development of bladder control are as follows:

1. It begins when the child is aware of passing urine, and he tells his mother he **has** a wet nappy: see **A** below.
2. He tells her when he **is** wetting his nappy: **B**.
3. Next, he tells her when he is **about to** do so: **C**.
4. Shortly after this stage is reached, he is able to tell her **in time** to be put on the potty or lavatory (toilet, loo, or whatever it is called): **D**.
5. He becomes dry **during the day**. Most children are dry during the day by the time they are 2½ years, but some may not be so until 4–5 years or older. Girls tend to acquire control earlier than boys.
6. He becomes **dry during the night** as well.

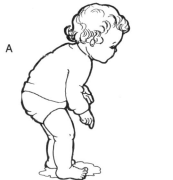

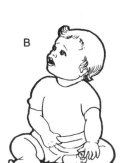

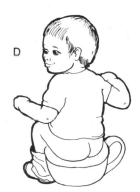

Bowel control is likely to be learnt before bladder control, and is acquired in the same way.

Relapse of control (regression)

It is quite common for a child who has learnt to control his bladder and bowels, to stop doing so for a while, and to return to wetting and soiling his pants. The cause may be teething, illness, change of surroundings, arrival of a new baby, or there may be no obvious reason.

The relapse is likely to be short if the child is given praise and encouragement on the occasions when he is clean and dry. But it will usually last for a much longer time if he is smacked or punished and made to feel unloved and insecure.

Forcing a child to sit on the potty

Children who have been forced to sit on the potty against their will are those who in later months refuse to use it. They may:

- deliberately soil or wet their pants as soon as they get off;
- withhold the motion and become seriously constipated as a result;
- become bed-wetters.

These problems are not likely to arise if the child is taken off the potty as soon as he wants to get off, whether he has passed anything or not. A child who comes to associate the potty with smacking and scolding will not want to use it.

Bed-wetting

Some children take much longer than others to learn control of the bladder. By the age of five years, one in ten children still wets the bed occasionally. They will eventually grow out of it. Bed-wetting rarely persists into adult life.

How parents can help

Parents should remain calm, patient and hopeful so that the child does not feel worried or under stress about bed-wetting. It helps if parents do not offer the child a drink at bed-time, and lift the child during the night. If the problem persists, a doctor may advise:

- using a device involving a pad under the sheet which triggers an alarm as soon as any urine touches the sheet. The bell wakes the child, who can then use the potty.
- medicines which will help.

1. a What is the liquid waste from the body called?
b Give three names for solid waste.

2. a (i) Do babies have any voluntary control over the bladder and bowel? (ii) Give reasons which may explain why a baby may perform regularly on the potty.
b At about what age do most children begin to learn to control the muscles which open the bladder and bowels?
c By what age are most children dry during the day?
d Is bowel or bladder control likely to be learnt first?

3. a List six stages through which children usually pass as they learn to control the bladder.
b Give four reasons for relapse of control.
c What type of treatment of the child is likely to increase the length of time of the relapse?

4. Name three possible conditions which may arise in children when they are forced to sit on the potty against their will.

5. When a child wets the bed,
a what attitude are parents advised to take and why?
b what advice may be given by a doctor?

1. Read 'The great pot battle' in the book 'Pyjamas Don't Matter' and/or the sections on 'Potty training' in other books (see p. 273). Note any suggestions which you consider might be helpful.

2. *Discuss* 'Problems which can arise in the training of children to be clean and dry, and how to deal with them'.

What stage has the child reached in bowel and bladder control? Describe the child's progress in 'potty training'.

Exercises

1 a Give the approximate age at which children usually become able to:

(i) smile at their mother.
(ii) know when they have done something wrong.
(iii) start asking questions.

b Give two reasons why it is sometimes more difficult for an only child to mix with other children.
c What is meant by parallel play? At about what age might children play like this?
d Study the drawing [opposite]

(i) It is a mistake to interpret children's drawings too much but suggest two things about this drawing which tell you about the child's awareness.
(ii) Describe two ways parents can help a child's drawing without actually making the child copy. (*SWEB*)

2 Describe fully any two aspects of development of a child of whom you have made a special study. Your description should cover a span of approximately six months. (*EAEB*)

3 A child may become frightened for many reasons. Suggest one reason for a child's fear in each of the following situations and, in each case, describe how the child could be helped to overcome its fear.
a A child is having recurring nightmares every Tuesday evening.
b A toddler sees a spider and screams.
c A 3-year-old girl cries every time great-uncle George visits the family.
d A 2-year-old is very upset when he has to go to bed on winter evenings. (*EAEB*)

4 In one study on the effect of the home environment on the development of young children it was found that:

In the homes of children who were developing well	In the homes of poorly developing children
The mother spoke continuously to the children.	Children were kept out of the way of the mother.
If play-pens were used, the children were only confined to them for brief periods.	Play-pens were extensively used and for long periods of time.
The children were encouraged to explore and there was a high degree of tolerance to infant clutter and disorder.	Children were subjected to ready-made experiences in the form of television.

Discuss reasons why the points made in the first column have helped children to develop well, and the points in the second column hindered development.

5 The graph on p. 272 shows the average height of boys and girls from birth to 7 years.
a Use information from the graph to complete Tables 3 and 4.
b On graph paper, copy the graph to show the average height of boys from birth to 7 years (do *not* put in the graph for girls). Add to this graph, two more graphs to show the growth in height of Ben and Terry, using a different colour for each boy:

	Height in cm at:							
	(Birth)	1 yr	2 yrs	3 yrs	4 yrs	5 yrs	6 yrs	7 yrs
Ben	56	79	84	88	103	113	118	125
Terry	43	68	82	91	100	109	112	117

c Study the three graphs you have drawn and answer the following questions:
    (i) Terry was born 6 weeks prematurely. At what age did his height reach the average height for boys?
    (ii) Ben was unfortunate in being severely ill for about a year. How old do you think he was when this happened? Was it followed by a time of 'catch-up' growth?

6 Language encourages intellectual development.
a State four reasons why a child needs to communicate by using language.
b Describe three stages in the development of language and explain how the adult can help at each stage.
c Suggest how three different activities at playgroup could encourage language development.
d Describe with examples three ways language helps intellectual development.
e In what ways does a good vocabulary help a child to be independent when he starts school? (*SWEB*)

Section 3

Caring for babies

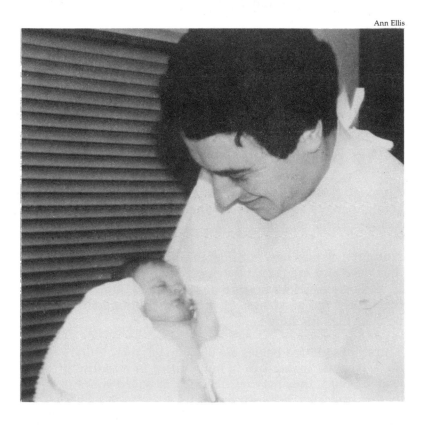

Ann Ellis

16 Crying

All babies cry — it is the only way they have of telling other people that they are hungry, lonely, bored, uncomfortable or in pain. A short cry does not harm a baby, but crying for a longer time is distressing to the baby and may worry the parents.

Babies vary in the amount they cry. Placid ones are often content to wait for quite a long time before crying for attention, whereas others scream the moment they wake up. During the first three months, some babies have a regular time of the day at which they cry. Usually this is in the evenings.

It is impossible to teach a young baby to be patient by letting him cry for a long while before attending to him. At this stage he is too young to learn, and only becomes more distressed. During the first three months, parents need not worry about 'spoiling' their baby by picking him up when he cries. After that, he begins to cry to get his own way, and an older baby can be 'spoilt' by always getting what he wants the moment he cries for it.

Tears are not usually shed until the baby is 3–4 weeks old. Sometimes older babies cry without producing tears and when this happens the baby is really shouting for his mother.

Why babies cry

Although it is not always possible to tell why a baby is crying, parents soon learn that there are a number of reasons. These include:

Hunger Babies vary considerably in the amount of food they need and how often they get hungry. A rigid time-table of feeding every four hours may be right for some babies. For others, it is not good enough, and they cry frequently because they are hungry.

Thirst Bottle-fed babies are likely to get more thirsty than those who are breast-fed. In hot weather or a centrally-heated house, they may need a drink of boiled water or diluted fruit juice between feeds.

Loneliness   A common cause of crying in babies is loneliness. They want to be picked up and cuddled and to feel close to another person. In many Asian and African countries, babies are carried in a sling on the back of their mother or elder sister. These babies cry much less than babies who spend a long time on their own in a cot or pram. A baby carrier or baby sling, shown below right, is becoming increasingly popular in other countries.

Discomfort   Babies cry when they are uncomfortable, perhaps because of a wet or soiled nappy, or if they are too hot or too cold, when a bright light is shining in their eyes, or when they have wind (Topic 19) or are teething (Topic 39).

Pain   A baby in pain will cry — maybe loudly or just a continuous whimper. When a baby cries for no apparent reason **and** behaves in an unusual way, then a doctor should be consulted.

Tiredness   A tired baby becomes cross and irritable (like an adult) and, in addition, shows his feelings by crying. It may be possible to soothe the baby and rock him to sleep. If left on his own to cry, the baby will continue to do so until he falls asleep through exhaustion.

Colic (abdominal pain). This is a common cause of crying in the first three months and it occurs mainly in the evenings. The baby appears to be in pain and screams for 2–20 minutes with his legs drawn up. He then stops and is just about to go off to sleep when another attack occurs.

Many suggestions have been put forward as to the cause of 'evening colic' but no reason has as yet been discovered. Fortunately, the colic does not seem to do the baby much harm. These crying sessions have usually stopped by the time the baby is three months old — to the great relief of the parents.

Dislike of the dark   Some babies cry when they are put in a room to sleep and the light is turned out. It may help to leave a small night light on.

Boredom   A baby will cry with boredom if he is put in his pram or cot to sleep when he would much rather be watching what is going on in the world about him, or playing with a toy. The extent to which a baby is liable to suffer from boredom depends on his personality. An alert and interested baby will want to be propped up in his pram or carried round by his mother more than a placid and contented baby.

Noise   A sudden noise may make a baby cry.

The babies are comforted by closeness to their mother and can watch what is going on around them

Soothing a baby

When a mother tries to stop her baby from crying, she rocks him up and down and makes soothing noises in a low tone of voice. Low noises have a more soothing effect than high-pitched sounds. A rhythm of sounds similar to that of the adult heartbeat (about 60 times per minute) have a particularly soothing effect. The repetitive sounds and movements will help to send the baby to sleep.

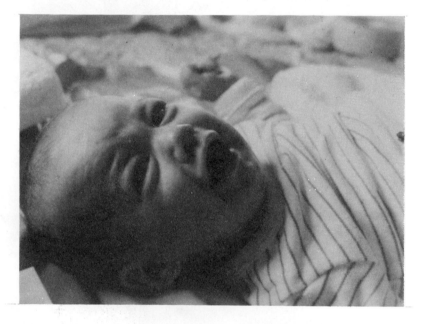

Questions

1. **a** Look at the photograph of baby John crying. Why is he crying? Make a list of at least ten suggestions.
b (i) Will leaving him to cry teach him to be patient? (ii) Why?
c (i) Will it spoil John to pick him up every time he cries? (ii) Might it spoil him when he gets older?

2. **a** Can you see any tears?
b Was John able to produce tears at birth?
c When he gets older and cries without producing tears, what will this tell his mother?

3. Perhaps John is crying because he is lonely.

a If so, what will stop the crying?
b Name two advantages which result from carrying a baby in a sling.

4. Perhaps John is crying because he has colic.
a What is colic?
b Describe how babies with colic behave.
c By what age is it usual for 'evening colic' to stop being a problem?

5. **a** Suggest what John's mother can do to try to soothe her baby and stop the crying.
b What helps to send the baby off to sleep?

To do

1. When you get the opportunity, listen to the crying of babies and young children and, if possible, tape record them. Can you tell the cry of a new-born baby? Do babies have different cries for different reasons?

2. Find out the possible effects on a mother if her baby cries a great deal. If the mother asked for advice, what suggestions would you consider sensible?

Child study

How often does the child cry? What are the reasons for crying? What will stop the crying?

Sucking comes naturally to babies. If put to the breast immediately after birth, they will start to suck. At this stage there will be no milk but a yellowish liquid called **colostrum**. Besides containing water, colostrum is rich in protein. It also contains **antibodies** to protect the baby against disease. Colostrum continues to be produced in small quantities until it is replaced by milk. See next topic.

A baby who is to be bottle-fed, may at first be given water to drink — water which has been boiled and then cooled.

Milk

Milk contains all the necessary food ingredients that a new baby needs. It is about 90 % water and 10 % food substances — sugar, fat, protein, vitamins and minerals (including salt). The sugar in milk is a type called **lactose** (milk sugar). Lactose is much less sweet than the ordinary type of sugar (**sucrose** — from sugar cane or sugar beet).

Breast milk

Breast milk is the natural milk for babies.

1 It contains the right amounts of all the necessary food substances.   As the baby grows, the amounts of the various ingredients alter to meet the changing needs of the baby. This helps the baby to grow at the right pace.

2 It contains antibodies to help protect the baby against infections.

3 The milk is at the right temperature — not too hot to burn the baby's mouth, nor too cold to make the baby cold.

4 It is easy for the baby to digest and absorb.

5 It is clean and safe   Fully breast-fed babies almost never get gastro-enteritis (sickness and diarrhoea). See Topic 19.

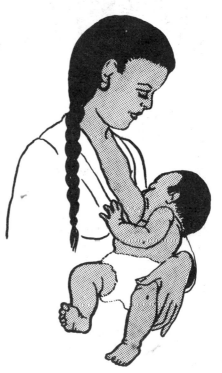

A mother breast-feeding her baby gives him comfort as well as food

Cow's milk

Cow's milk is the natural milk for calves. It differs from human milk in having:

different types of fat and protein;
more protein;
more salt and other minerals;
less sugar;
antibodies which help to protect a calf against disease but are no use to babies.

Cow's milk is more difficult for babies to digest.   Besides having more protein, it also has a much higher amount of a particular protein called **casein**. Casein forms curds in the baby's stomach and is difficult to digest. Little white lumps (curds) of undigested protein may be seen in the baby's stools.

Fat is present in milk in the form of droplets. Although the fat content of both cow's milk and breast milk is about the same, the fat droplets in cow's milk are larger and more difficult to digest.

A baby held while being bottle-fed also receives comfort

Cow's milk has a higher salt content.   The amount of salt in the body needs to be kept at a more or less constant level and this is normally done by the kidneys. However, the kidneys of a young baby are unable to remove excess salt, so if he is given too much salt he will become very ill. This can happen if the baby is fed on undiluted cow's milk or given strong feeds, see Topic 19. (Salt is a compound of two elements — sodium and chlorine. It is the **sodium** which is so dangerous to young babies in large amounts.)

Modified baby milk

Nearly all bottle-fed babies are given 'Baby Milk'. This type of dried milk is made from cow's milk which has been altered (modified) to make it more like human milk. In Britain, milk which is sold specially for babies must meet the standards recommended by the Department of Health.

Questions mothers ask

Is the baby getting enough food?   If the baby is gaining weight satisfactorily, then he is getting enough to eat. See p. 15.

Are extra vitamins required?   The doctor or health visitor may recommend that babies over one month old be given vitamins in the form of vitamin drops or fruit juices.

Vitamin drops contain vitamins A,C and D. They may be recommended for breast-fed babies. Bottle-fed babies normally obtain enough of these vitamins in baby milk.

Fruit juice contains vitamin C. Unsweetened orange juice, blackcurrant juice and rose-hip syrup are suitable fruit juices for babies.

Are extra minerals required? Milk contains all the minerals a baby needs for the first few months of life. Although milk is low in iron, a baby is born with several months' supply stored in the liver.

Is extra water needed? Breast milk contains all the water a baby needs. Unless the weather is extremely hot, and provided the baby is allowed to feed as often as he wants, there should be no need to give extra water between the feeds. Giving water between feeds may cause the baby to suck less well on the breast and therefore to receive less food.

In the case of bottle-fed babies, the baby can be given water between feeds if he wants it. Topics 18 and 19 deal with the feeding of babies in more detail.

Questions

1. a Name the main substance in milk. **b** Name five other substances.

2. Comparison of Breast Milk and Cow's Milk (grams per 100 ml)

	Sugar	Fat	Protein	Minerals	Water
Breast milk	7	4	1.2	0.4	90
Cow's milk	4.7	4	3.3	0.75	88

a (i) Which type of milk is sweeter? (ii) How does milk sugar differ in taste from ordinary sugar?
b (i) Is the fat content the same for both milks? (ii) Why is the fat in cow's milk less easy for a baby to digest?
c (i) Which type of milk has the most protein? (ii) Why is the protein in cow's milk less suitable for babies?
d (i) Which type of milk has a higher mineral content? (ii) Which particular mineral can be dangerous for young babies in large amounts?
e What type of milk is 'Baby Milk'?

3. Give five reasons why breast milk is right for babies.

4. a How does a mother know if her baby is getting enough food?
b Should babies be given water between feeds if they are (i) breast-fed, (ii) bottle-fed?
c Milk has a low iron content; does a baby need to be given iron or other minerals?
d Which vitamins are contained in vitamin drops?

5. When a baby is held close while being fed, what else is being provided besides food?

To do

1. Add to your notes, pictures of babies being breast-fed and bottle-fed.

2. What extra problems are involved in feeding twins? How may these problems be overcome? Is it possible for a mother to breast-feed both babies?

18 *Breast-feeding*

Breast-feeding is the natural way to feed a baby. Early on in pregnancy, the breasts enlarge and start to prepare for the job of supplying the baby with milk. In the last twelve weeks or so of pregnancy they secrete colostrum. When colostrum is first secreted it is clear and colourless; later on it becomes a yellow colour.

The baby's birth is the signal for the breasts to begin producing milk and two or three days later it starts to flow. This is the right time for the baby as the appetite develops slowly. Very little food is needed in the first few days and this is supplied by colostrum. Breast milk tends to look watery and bluish at the beginning of a feed and creamy towards the end.

How many feeds a day?

Babies should be put to the breast regularly in the first few days. They will not get much food, but they will enjoy sucking.

Between the third and sixth day, babies become much more hungry and may want to be fed ten or twelve times a day (a day being 24 hours). This may be inconvenient for the mother, but it helps to establish a good supply of milk — because the more the baby sucks, the more the breasts are stimulated to produce milk.

After that, the baby soon settles down to a pattern of wanting to be fed about six times a day, with the intervals varying between three and five hours. Gradually, the interval between feeds in the night gets longer so that by the age of three months, the night feed is usually given up altogether.

Structure of the breasts

Each breast contains about twenty sections (lobes) in which milk is produced from milk glands. Each section has a duct which opens on the surface of the nipple; the milk therefore comes from about twenty tiny openings. The dark area around the nipple is called the **areola**.

The size of the breasts before pregnancy depends on the amount of fat tissue and not the number of milk-producing glands. So women with naturally small breasts will be able to breast-feed just as well as those with larger breasts.

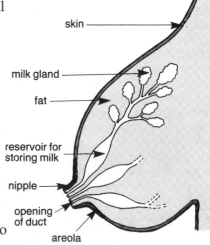

skin

milk gland

fat

reservoir for storing milk

nipple

opening of duct

areola

Advantages of breast-feeding

1. It is **safe**.
2. It is **easy** — there are no bottles to sterilise, or feeds to mix and get to the right temperature.
3. Breast milk **never causes indigestion** (unless the mother has been eating unwisely, e.g. eating an excessive amount of fruit or taking certain laxatives).
4. Breast milk **contains antibodies**.
5. The baby is **less likely to become overweight.**
6. The baby is **less likely to develop nappy rash.**
7. The baby is **less likely to develop eczema**.
8. It is **cheaper**.
9. Breast-feeding gives time for a **bond of affection** to develop between mother and baby. A mother who breast-feeds spends a long time each day in very close contact with her baby. This gives the opportunity for a close and loving relationship to develop between them which is very important for the future well-being of the child.

Breast-feeding is safer for the baby   In the first few months of life, and especially when new-born, babies do not have very much resistance to infections such as coughs, colds and diarrhoea. They are likely to become more ill at this age than when older, and complications are more likely to follow.

Compared with bottle-fed babies, breast-fed babies get fewer infections, are less prone to severe infections, and almost never get gastro-enteritis.

Benefits for the mother   Besides giving the child a good start in life, breast-feeding also benefits the mother. Her womb will shrink back to size more quickly. Her periods will take longer to return, so she is more relaxed and contented for not being bothered by the irritable feelings often linked with menstruation. A mother who enjoys breast-feeding feels especially close to her baby.

How long should breast-feeding continue?

Many doctors advise mothers to try to breast-feed at least for the first two weeks, and ideally for 4–6 months. In the latter case, the babies are then at the right age to be weaned gradually from breast milk to a mixture of other foods. As the amount of nourishment from other foods increases, the need for breast milk decreases. Breast-feeds become fewer and smaller until either the supply of milk fails or the baby refuses to feed from the breast any more.

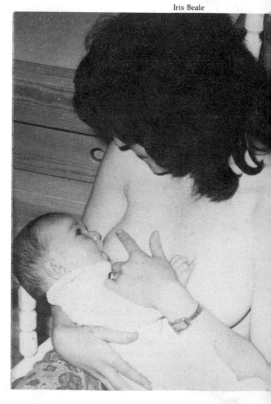

Iris Beale

Some mothers continue to breast-feed for a year or longer, although with older babies, perhaps for only one feed a day. A baby who is fed entirely on milk beyond the age of about six months may find it difficult to take to new foods. If weaning has not started before 9–10 months, there is a danger of anaemia due to the shortage of iron in breast milk.

Reasons for not breast-feeding

A few mothers do not have enough milk to breast-feed and a few more are unable to breast-feed for medical reasons. But although nine out of ten mothers are able to breast-feed their babies, many choose to bottle-feed. Those who could breast-feed, but decide not to do so, give reasons which include:

'Breast-feeding will spoil their figure'   The mothers fear that their breasts will enlarge and they will not regain their former figure.
- Breast-feeding does not alter the shape of the breasts permanently and they should return to normal size about six months after breast-feeding has ceased.

'The mother is anxious that her baby may not get enough milk'
- Regular weighing of the baby will show if this is so.

'The mother feels embarrassed about feeding her baby on the breast'
- It may help to overcome the embarrassment to realise that breast feeding is nature's way to feed a baby.

'It is impossible to breast-feed if it is necessary to leave the baby for long intervals in order to go out to work'
- A compromise here would be for the mother to breast-feed for the first few weeks, then change to bottle-feeding when she needs more freedom. Some mothers overcome the problem by using a breast pump to express their milk into bottles. A baby-minder can then give the breast milk to the baby whilst the mother is at work.

To do

1. What reasons do mothers give for deciding not to breast-feed? Suggest a solution in each case.

2. Ask some mothers for their opinions on the feeding of young babies.

3. Carry out a survey of young children to find out what proportion were breast-fed.

Questions

1. It is usual for a mother to start breast-feeding her baby within a few hours of birth. At this stage there is no milk but a yellowish liquid.
a Name this liquid.
b Name three substances which the liquid contains (see previous topic).
c When do the breasts begin to produce milk?
d What helps to establish a good supply of milk?
e Between 3 and 6 days old, how often may a baby want to be fed?
f About how many times a day will the baby want to be fed when he settles down into a pattern?
g By what age have most babies given up the night feed?

2. a Draw a diagram to show the structure of the breast.
b Whereabouts in the breast is the milk produced?
c Does milk leave the breast from one opening or many?
d Before pregnancy, what does the size of the breasts depend on?

3. Give nine advantages of breast-feeding.

4. a Name three ways in which a mother can benefit from breast-feeding.
b What is considered to be an ideal length of time for a baby to be breast-fed?
c Name two possible effects of breast-feeding for a longer time.

Child study

Find out if the child is/was breast-fed or bottle-fed. If the mother had any problems with feeding, how did she overcome them?

19 Bottle-feeding (artificial feeding)

Not all mothers wish to breast-feed their babies and in a few cases they are unable to do so no matter how hard they try. The babies will then be bottle-fed. If properly bottle-fed, there is no reason why the babies should not thrive, grow and develop in the same way as breast-fed babies.

Four essential rules of bottle-feeding are:
1. Use the right type of milk for a young baby, see Topic 17.
2. Keep every piece of equipment scrupulously clean.
3. Follow the instructions on the container for making up the feed.
4. Give the baby similar cuddling and attention to that which it would receive in breast-feeding.

Advantages of bottle-feeding

Bottle-feeding has some advantages over breast-feeding.
1. The mother knows how much milk the baby is taking.
2. The baby can be fed anywhere. This is an advantage to mothers who would be embarrassed to breast-feed in public.
3. Other people are able to feed the baby besides the mother. When the father takes a turn in giving the feed, it provides him with an opportunity to cuddle and get to know his baby.
4. When the mother does not have to be present at feeding times, it means that she can return to work before the baby has been weaned.

Equipment for bottle-feeding

Feeding bottle   A suitable feeding bottle is one which:
- is easy to sterilise;
- has a wide neck for easy cleaning;
- is made of clear material — to check that it is clean inside;
- has graduated measurements on the side — in millilitres or fluid ounces;
- has a cap to keep the teat clean;
- has been designed so that the teat can be placed upside down in the bottle for storage or travelling.

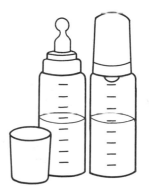

Teat   The most important thing about the teat is the size of the hole. A hole of the right size allows the milk to drip out rapidly without having to shake or squeeze the bottle. The hole readily becomes blocked by dried milk and should be tested before every feed.

When the hole is too large, it may cause the baby to choke as he tries to swallow the milk. When the hole is too small, the baby will suck so hard and for so long that a great deal of air will be swallowed. The baby will then have trouble with wind. The hole in the teat can be made larger by using a red-hot needle.

Jug with a lid   The jug needs to be sufficiently large for all the feeds for one day to be made up at the same time. The milk can then be stored until needed either in the jug with its lid on, or in individual bottles. The milk should be stored in a refrigerator or other place which is equally cold. Remember, germs only grow and multiply and become a danger when warm. For more information about germs see Topic 38, p. 146, and Supplement, p. 265.

Cleaning and sterilising

Equipment used for bottle-feeding must be sterile to prevent germs getting into the milk or mouth. It can be sterilised in two ways — either by boiling, or by placing in a sterilising solution, but first of all it must be made clean.

1. Wash your hands thoroughly.
2. Clean the teat by rubbing both the inside and outside with a little salt. This removes stale milk which collects inside the small pores. Rinse off all traces of salt.
3. Clean the bottle by using hot water, detergent and a bottle brush. Rinse off the detergent. Bottles are easier to clean if they have been rinsed out with cold water immediately after use.
4. Sterilise the equipment:
   a by placing in a sterilising solution and leaving for at least three hours. Make sure that everything is completely covered by the solution and that there are no air bubbles. Metal spoons or other metal objects should not be put in the sterilising solution because they will dissolve. The solution needs to be made up fresh every day. Or
   b by boiling for 10 minutes. This is not recommended as regular treatment for plastic bottles. They soon become rough and cloudy and may crack.
5. Wash your hands again. Remove the bottle and teat from the sterilising solution. Drain off excess liquid but do not dry. Put milk in the bottle, put the teat on, and protect with the cap.

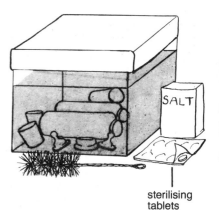

sterilising tablets

Preparing feeds

Follow the instructions on the container   The tins or packets of baby milk carry detailed instructions on how to mix the feeds — and they should be followed precisely. The amount of milk powder and water has been carefully worked out to make the feed just right for the baby. Even if the milk seems tasteless to you, do not add extra sugar and **never** add salt.

It is important to measure the necessary amount of boiled water into the jug or bottle before adding the milk powder, not to put the powder in first.

Scoop   The scoop provided with the milk powder is an accurate measure when used correctly. To obtain the exact quantity, fill the scoop, then gently level off the powder with the back of a plastic knife. Do not pack the powder down, or heap it up.

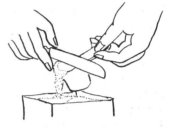

Water   The water used for making the feeds must be boiled and then cooled to the temperature recommended in the instructions. Too much water will make a poor feed. Too little water will make the feed too strong.

Harmful effects of making the feed too strong

When using milk powder there is a tendency to think that it is 'good for the baby' to add more powder than the instructions say. This results in a strong feed which contains too much protein and salt. A baby who is given a strong feed is likely to become thirsty and cry. He may then be given another feed instead of boiled water because the mother thinks he is still hungry. If this happens often, the baby may become too fat. A worse danger is that the extra salt in strong feeds may make the baby very ill, possibly causing convulsions, coma and permanent brain damage.

Giving a bottle

When giving a bottle feed:
1. Make sure that the milk is at a suitable temperature for the baby. If the milk has come out of the fridge, it will need to be warmed up before being given to the baby. This can be done by placing the bottle in a jug of water or in a special bottle heater. To check that the milk is not too hot, sprinkle a few drops onto the wrist.
2. Check that the hole in the teat is not blocked.

3. Hold the baby in a comfortable position. Tilt the bottle so that the teat is kept full of milk, otherwise the baby will suck in air as well as milk.

4. From time to time, remove the teat from the baby's mouth to let air get into the bottle, otherwise a vacuum is created. When this happens the teat goes flat and no milk can pass through. If the baby continues to suck on a flattened teat he will take in air — and this will result in wind.

5. After a feed, help the baby to bring up any wind.

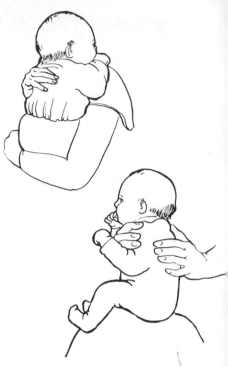

Giving the baby plenty of cuddling and attention

When a mother holds her baby close to her and talks and smiles at him as she feeds him from the bottle, she can feel just as loving towards her baby as the mother who breast-feeds.

Care needs to be taken to give bottle-fed babies the same amount of time to develop a bond of affection with the mother as when breast-feeding. This will not happen if a variety of people hold the baby when he is being fed, or if the bottle is propped up so that the baby feeds himself.

The mother will feel more comfortable if she chooses a chair which supports her back and arms. If she also takes the opportunity to relax as she feeds, she will enjoy the contact with her baby as much as the baby enjoys being held close and fed.

Leaving the baby to feed himself When the baby is left to feed himself:
- there is a danger he might choke;
- he is deprived of the comfort of being held close and of feeling loved and wanted;
- there is no one to notice that he is taking in air by sucking on a flattened teat or when the bottle is empty;
- there will be no one to help bring up his wind.

Wind

'Wind' is air which has been swallowed. All babies suck in air when feeding. An air bubble which forms in the stomach may cause the baby to cry with discomfort until it has been brought up.

When a baby takes too long on a feed, he will swallow air instead of milk. If a baby is bottle-fed, he may take in air because the hole in the teat is too small, or if breast-fed, because there is too little milk present.

Bringing up wind (burping the baby)   When breast- or bottle-feeding, it is usual to give the baby the chance to bring up wind. Whether this is done once or twice during the feed, or at the end, depends on what seems to suit the baby. There is no good reason for interrupting the baby's meal while he continues to feed happily. Babies do not 'burp' with every meal — it just depends on how much air they swallow.

The wind can escape more easily when the baby is held against the shoulder (a cloth on the shoulder helps to catch any milk which comes up with the wind). Gently patting the baby's back may help. Some mothers prefer to use one hand to hold the baby in a sitting position and leaning slightly forwards; the other hand gently rubs the baby's back, see p. 70.

Normally wind, if any, is brought up without much trouble. If the baby cries a great deal after a meal, it is likely to be due to reasons other than discomfort from wind, for example, for any of the reasons mentioned in Topic 16.

Gastro-enteritis

Gastro-enteritis is inflammation of the stomach and intestines. Illness of this type is rare in breast-fed babies but far too common in those who are bottle-fed. Each year in Britain about 100,000 babies suffer badly from this infection. Much of the illness could be prevented with better hygiene, particularly when preparing bottles or dealing with nappies.

Germs which cause gastro-enteritis live in the bowel and also thrive in warm, moist food. These germs can be given accidentally to the baby when:

- the equipment used for bottle-feeding is not sterilised properly;
- the water used to mix with the milk powder is unboiled;
- the feed is stored in a warm place before being given to the baby;
- dirty hands contaminate the teat or milk.

The symptoms of gastro-enteritis are vomiting, diarrhoea and abdominal pain, and their effect is that the baby loses too much water from the body too quickly. The body cannot function properly when it is **dehydrated**, i.e. short of water.

1. a Suggest four advantages of bottle-feeding over breast-feeding.
b When deciding to bottle-feed, give four essential rules to follow.

2. a Describe a type of feeding bottle which would be considered 'suitable'.
b Why does the hole in the teat need to be the right size?
c What test can be made to find out if the hole in the teat is the right size?
d Describe how to sterilise feeding bottles.

3. a How should the scoop be used to obtain the correct amount of milk powder?
b Name two substances which should never be added to a milk feed.
c Why is a strong feed likely to make a baby thirsty?
d What should a thirsty baby be given?
e What is the danger of giving a baby too much salt?

4. Describe how to give a bottle-feed.

5. a Name four disadvantages of leaving a baby to feed himself from a bottle.
b Give one reason why a baby might swallow air instead of milk while (i) breast-feeding (ii) bottle-feeding.

6. a What are the symptoms of gastro-enteritis?
b Why is this a dangerous illness in babies?
c About how many babies suffer from gastro-enteritis in Britain each year?
d Are these babies likely to be breast- or bottle-fed?
e Name four ways in which gastro-enteritis germs can be given to a baby.

1. Find pictures to illustrate
a sterilising bottles,
b making a feed.

2. Copy out the instructions for using sterilising tablets or liquid (they will be on the container).

3. Describe in words or pictures, two ways to 'wind' a baby.

4. *Discuss* 'Should a mother who does not breast-feed her baby feel guilty?'

20 Keeping the baby clean

It is almost impossible to keep a baby spotlessly clean all the time, nor indeed is it necessary. After a meal, babies often bring up a little milk (a posset). They frequently wet and soil their nappies. When they start to feed themselves they make a great deal of mess. This is all part of babyhood, and the mother would be far too busy if she changed her baby's clothes every time they were a little soiled. The mother's aim should be to keep the baby's skin, clothes, bedding and other equipment sufficiently clean so that they do not become a breeding ground for germs, or harm the baby in other ways.

Some of the germs which can harm a baby live in the bowel and are present in the stools. Other types of germs grow and multiply in urine. They can also thrive in milk and other foods.

Protection by cleanliness

A mother can protect her baby against germs by:
1. keeping her hands and nails clean. She should always wash her hands after visiting the toilet, changing a nappy, and before giving a feed;
2. washing nappies thoroughly;
3. regular washing of clothes and bedding;
4. regular cleaning of nursery equipment and toys;
5. not giving the baby stale food, or food which has been kept in a warm place for several hours.

Changing the nappy

The nappy will need to be changed several times a day.
Points to note are:
1. The job can be done more quickly when the equipment needed is collected together first.
2. The job is easier when the baby is placed on a flat surface rather than the lap. Both hands are then free for nappy changing.
3. Placing the baby on a changing mat or plastic sheet helps to prevent dirtying objects underneath.
4. There is no need to wash the baby's bottom every time a nappy is removed.

5. When the nappy has been soiled, any solid matter on the baby's skin should be gently removed with cotton wool or tissues. (When the baby gets older, a corner of the nappy can be used.) The skin can then be cleaned with cotton wool and warm water. Alternatively, the skin can be wiped with tissues. These may be bought ready moistened with a special solution which neutralises ammonia and therefore helps to prevent nappy rash.

6. Make sure the skin is dry. A little cream can then be smoothed over the skin before the clean nappy is put on. The cream may be zinc and castor oil cream, silicone barrier cream, or other type of cream, lotion or oil made for the purpose. It helps to prevent nappy rash by forming a protective layer over the surface of the skin. Cream does not need to be used at every nappy change.

This type of changing mat prevents the baby from rolling off the bed or table on which the mat has been placed

Nappy care

Washable nappies need to be kept both clean and free from germs. This can be done either by washing in very hot water with soap or detergent, or by soaking them for several hours in a special solution which cleans and sterilises. This solution is made by mixing a steriliser with water (see p. 74).

Washing nappies with soap or detergent   When a nappy is removed from the baby:
1. **Remove any solid matter**. One way of doing this is to hold the nappy under the flushing water in the lavatory. This may be unnecessary if a nappy liner has been used. Remove the nappy liner and flush it away.
2. **Store in a covered nappy pail**. The cover on the pail keeps the smell in. The nappies will be easier to wash if the pail contains water.
3. **Wash in hot water with soap or mild detergent**. The water should be at least 60°C. Boiling helps whiten nappies as well as sterilising them, but it is not considered necessary every time the nappies are washed.
4. **Rinse thoroughly**. All traces of soap or detergent should be removed by rinsing in several changes of clean water. A 'nappy softener' can be added to the last rinsing water. It is unnecessary unless the nappies have become stiff, as it may cause irritation to the baby's skin.
5. **Dry**. Drying outside in the open air helps to keep nappies soft. Sunlight whitens them and also helps to destroy germs. Drying nappies on radiators or hot pipes makes them stiff. Tumble driers are useful for drying nappies on wet days.

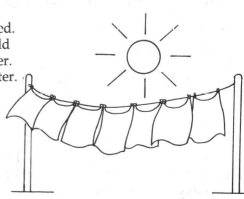

Washing nappies in sterilising solution Sterilising solution needs to be made up fresh each day and stored in a plastic bucket. One bucket or two can be used. When there are two buckets, one is used for nappies that are only wet, the other is used for soiled nappies.

1. Make up the sterilising solution according to the instructions on the container.
2. When nappies are removed from the baby, those that are only wet can be placed straight into the sterilising solution. Soiled nappies should first have the solid matter flushed off into the lavatory.
3. Leave the nappies to soak overnight. Next day, remove from the bucket, rubbing well any nappies which are stained.
4. Rinse thoroughly and dry as described above.

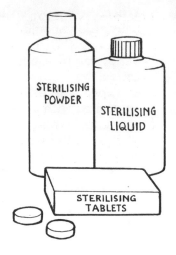

Nappy rash (ammonia dermatitis)

The first sign of nappy rash is when the skin becomes red and sore in the nappy area. If the rash is not promptly treated, the skin becomes rough and wrinkled. Septic spots may also appear.

Nappy rash is caused by ammonia and a strong smell of ammonia may be noticed when the nappy is changed. The ammonia is made from urine when the urine comes into contact with germs in the stools. The same type of germs may also be present in a nappy which has not been properly washed. The longer the baby lies in a wet, dirty nappy the more time there will be for the germs to produce ammonia. The ammonia irritates the skin and a rash appears.

Breast-fed babies are less likely to suffer from nappy rash because their stools are more acidic. This is because the acid discourages the activity of the germs which produce ammonia.

Prevention of nappy rash Nearly all babies get nappy rash at one time or another, but much can be done to prevent it. The rules to observe are:

1. Wash towelling nappies thoroughly every time they are removed from the baby.
2. Use one-way liners.
3. Do not let a wet, dirty nappy remain on the baby for longer than is necessary.
4. Apply a protective layer of a suitable cream or lotion to the baby's bottom.
5. Leave off the nappy whenever possible.
6. Do not use tightly fitting plastic pants more than is necessary. They keep warmth and moisture in and encourage nappy rash.

Treatment of nappy rash   When a baby develops nappy rash, the bottom needs to be kept as clean and dry as possible to allow the skin to recover. It is best to leave the nappy off altogether, but this is not always practical. Alternatively:

- leave the nappy off as often as possible;
- use only sterilised nappies;
- change the nappy as soon as it becomes wet or soiled during the day time;
- change the nappy at least once during the night;
- use nappy liners;
- do not use plastic pants;
- apply cream every time the nappy is changed;
- seek medical advice if the rash becomes wet and oozing.

Other causes of soreness

A baby's skin is very delicate and it is quite common for the bottom to become sore, however well the baby is cared for. There are a number of causes besides nappy rash. For example, a rash similar to nappy rash can develop if the soap, detergent or sterilising solution is not removed from the nappies by thorough rinsing. Nappy softener has also been known to be the cause of such a rash.

Soreness around the anus is caused by the skin being in contact with the wet stools. It is common in very young babies and at times of diarrhoea when older. The chances of it happening are increased by failure to change the nappy frequently. For treatment — follow the guidelines for nappy rash.

The nose

It is necessary to wipe a baby's nose to prevent soreness or blockage of the nostrils. By the age of two years, children should be able to do this for themselves. It is often very difficult to get them to blow the nose, but it is a useful skill for them to learn before starting school.

The feet

To keep the feet healthy:
1. Dry thoroughly between the toes after washing;
2. Use baby powder if there is much sweating;
3. Wear clean socks every day;
4. Cut toenails regularly. Cut them straight across, but not too short nor down into the corners;
5. When shoes are necessary, it is essential that they should fit well (see Topic 27).

(see Topic 27)

Questions

1. Name five ways in which cleanliness by the mother helps to protect her baby.

2. Give one reason for doing each of the following when changing a baby's nappy:
a collecting the equipment needed first,
b placing him on a flat surface,
c using a changing mat,
d using zinc and castor oil cream.

3. Describe two different ways of washing nappies.

4. a What is ammonia dermatitis?
b Where does the ammonia come from?
c Name two places where germs which cause nappy rash may be found.
d Describe what nappy rash looks like.
e Give six rules that help to prevent nappy rash.
f Give eight suggestions for the treatment of nappy rash.

5. Name two other causes of a sore bottom apart from nappy rash. What treatment would you recommend in each case?

6. a Give two reasons for wiping a baby's nose.
b By what age should children be able to wipe their own noses?
c How can feet be kept healthy?

To do

1. Find pictures of equipment mentioned in this topic.

2. How many different ways are there of folding a nappy? Describe, giving the advantage of each way.

3. Compare the information given with different brands of nappy steriliser.

21 Bath-time

When babies get used to the idea, they enjoy being bathed and this makes bath-time fun. Some mothers prefer to give an evening bath as they find the activities of bath-time help the baby to sleep more soundly. Others find it more convenient to bath the baby in the morning. It does not matter which.

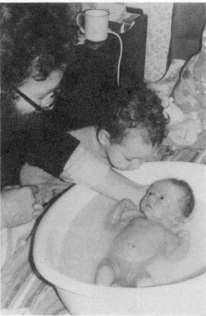

National Childbirth Trust

Preparations for bath-time

A warm room Young babies lose body heat very quickly and easily become chilled. Therefore it is important that the room in which the baby is to be bathed is draught-free and warm — at least 20°C (68°F).

Warm water The bath water should be warm but not hot — about body temperature, 37°C (100°F). It is usual to test the temperature of the bath water with the elbow. Another thing to remember is always to put the cold water in the bath before the hot water, because if hot water goes in first, the bottom of the bath may burn the baby.

Equipment Collect everything needed for washing, drying and dressing the baby.

Bath-time routine

The following routine, or one very similar, is often recommended for bathing young babies.
1. After washing your hands, undress the baby apart from the nappy and wrap in a warm towel: **A**.
2. Test the temperature of the bath water to check that it is right for the baby: **B**, p. 77.
3. Gently wash the face with wet cotton wool: **C**. Soap should not be used. The eyes should only be cleaned if infected or sticky. Wipe each eye from the inside corner outwards, using a clean piece of damp cotton wool for each eye.

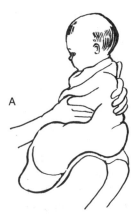

A

4. Wash the scalp with water. Soap or shampoo only needs to be used once or twice a week. The hair must then be well rinsed, using a jug of clean, warm water for the final rinse.

5. Take off the nappy and clean the bottom with wet cotton wool and soap: **D**. Do not try to force back (retract) the foreskin of little boys. This action is likely to tear the foreskin and make it bleed. The foreskin will gradually become able to retract, usually completely so by the age of three years.

6. Soap the baby all over (apart from the face). When turning the baby over to soap his back, the safest way to turn him is towards, rather than away from, the mother. An alternative and easier method is to add liquid soap to the bath water.

7. Place the baby in the bath to rinse off the soap. The baby needs to be held securely; note how one of the mother's hands holds the baby's shoulder, while his head rests on her arm: **E**.

8. Lift the baby out on to a towel: **F**. Dry by patting gently, **G** — not by rubbing. Pay particular attention to the creases of the neck, armpits, groin, back of the knees and back of the ears. If the creases are not dried, they easily become sore.

9. Apply zinc and castor oil cream (or other type of baby cream) to the bottom and put a little talcum powder into the creases to help keep them dry.

Cleaning the ears

Wax can be cleaned away from the end of the ear canal (ear hole), but the inside of the canal should never be cleaned. The wax is there for protection. Cotton wool buds can be useful for cleaning outside and behind the ears, but should never be poked inside. Anything which is poked into the ear canal may damage the ear drum.

Cradle cap

Cradle cap is the name given to the greasy scales or crusts which form on the scalp of many young babies. It first appears around four weeks of age and clears up by itself after about six months. It is harmless. If it is considered to be unsightly, it can be removed by the use of a special ointment made for the purpose.

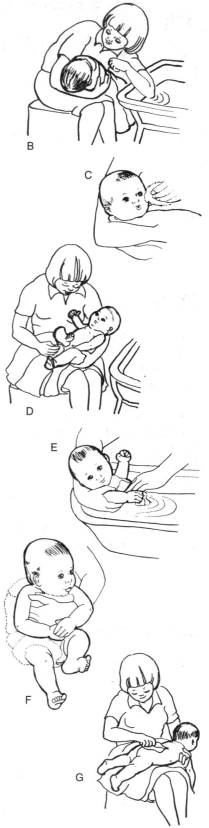

B

C

D

E

F

G

Cutting the nails

The finger nails of very young babies grow quickly and need to be cut every few days. This is best done while the baby is asleep. If the nails are left to grow too long, the baby will scratch himself. With an older baby, the nails can be cut immediately after a bath.

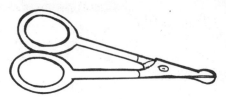

Topping and tailing

It is not necessary to bath the baby every day as long as the face, hands and bottom are kept clean by 'topping and tailing'. To do this:
1. Clean the face and hands with warm water and cotton wool, and then dry.
2. Clean the bottom using warm water, soap and more cotton wool. Dry and then apply a zinc and castor oil cream.

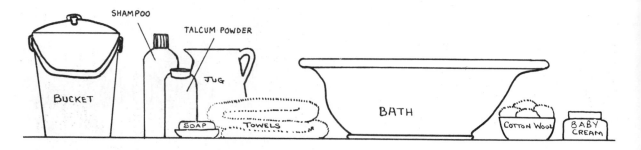

Questions

1. a (i) What is a suitable room temperature for bathing a baby?
(ii) Why does the room need to be at this temperature?
b (i) What is a suitable temperature for the bath-water?
(ii) Give one method of testing the temperature.
c Why should cold water be put into the bath before hot water?

2. List the items in the drawing above which have been collected together in preparation for bath-time.

3. When bathing the baby:
a (i) Do the eyes need to be cleaned? (ii) If so how?
b Should soap be put on the face?

c How often does shampoo need to be used on the scalp?
d Why should the foreskin not be forced back?
e When a baby on the mother's knee is turned over, in which direction is it safest to turn him?
f How should a baby be held when in the bath?
g (i) Why should the creases in the skin be thoroughly dried? (ii) What can be applied to help keep them dry?

4. a Why is it dangerous to poke anything into the ear canal?
b What is cradle cap and how can it be removed?
c Is it necessary to bath a baby every day?
d Describe how to 'top and tail' a baby.

To do

1. Describe the bath-time routine using pictures and/or words.

2. Use a life-size doll to practise bathing a baby.

3. Accompany your answer to question 2 with pictures of bath-time equipment.

Child study

Help the mother to bath the child. Describe the bath-time routine and the child's behaviour when being bathed.

22 *The layette*

The **layette** is the baby's first set of clothes. A new baby does not need many clothes, just enough to keep him warm. Baby's clothes get dirty in various ways so it is, in general, best to have three of each item of clothing, one to wear, one for washing and one ready for use.

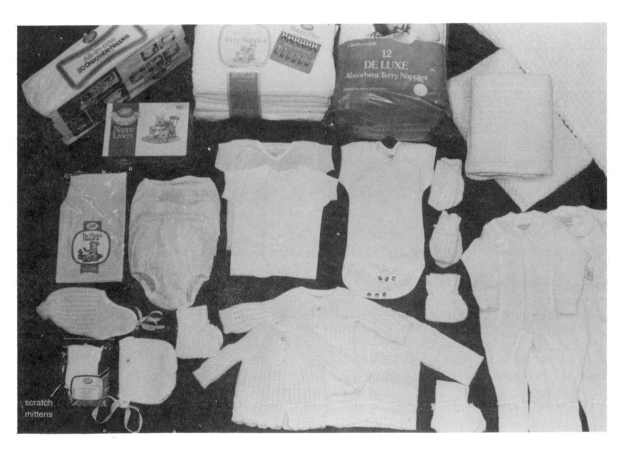

scratch
mittens

Choosing the layette

Expectant mothers often enjoy collecting items for the layette. They may be tempted by pretty or attractive clothing. This may give the mothers pleasure, but it is not of importance to their babies. The requirements of the babies are rather different.

Requirements for baby clothes   Baby clothes should be:
- loose and comfortable;
- easy to put on and take off;
- easy to wash and dry;
- lightweight, soft and warm;
- non-irritant (will not scratch or otherwise irritate the skin);
- porous (so that moisture can escape);
- flame-resistant (will not easily catch fire).

Points to remember
1. Clothing should not be tight, especially round the neck and feet. When young toes are cramped for a long while they can become deformed.
2. Babies grow quickly and stretch suits will not stretch indefinitely.
3. Several layers of lightweight clothing are warmer than one thick, bulky layer.
4. The amount of clothing a baby needs to wear depends on the temperature. There are cold days in summer and it is very warm in an over-heated house in winter. In hot conditions, the minimum of clothes is required, and when very hot, a nappy is all that is necessary.
5. Most mothers have a limited amount of money to spend. Therefore it is sensible to buy only the essential items required for the layette. The money can be saved until later when the baby needs more clothes:
    - in larger and more expensive sizes;
    - for day-time and night-time;
    - because he will get dirty more easily and more often.

Materials used for baby clothes

Both natural and synthetic (man-made) materials are used for baby clothes.

Natural materials
- wool — warm to wear and therefore more suitable for cold weather.
- cotton — absorbent and therefore more comfortable to wear next to the skin when the body is hot, as it can absorb sweat.

Synthetic materials are easier to wash and dry than natural materials. In general, they are cold to wear in winter because they do not retain body heat, and hot and clammy in summer because they do not absorb sweat. There are exceptions; acrylic gives warmth and viscose is absorbent. Synthetic materials include:
- **nylon** — very strong and does not shrink;
- **viscose** (e.g. rayon) — absorbent, retains whiteness, pleasant to handle but lacks strength;

- **polyester** (e.g. Terylene) — crease-resistant and does not catch fire easily, therefore suitable for nightdresses;
- **acrylic** (e.g. Acrilan) — a bulky fabric which is soft and warm to the touch, light-weight, crease-resistant and non-irritating to the skin.

Many baby clothes are made of mixtures of different types of material. In this way, the advantages of different materials can be combined.

Washing baby clothes

Woollen garments   Wool is a very useful fabric for children's clothes when warmth is required, but it needs careful washing. If the water is too hot the garments shrink. They can easily be pulled out of shape when being dried. When washing wool:

- use lukewarm water (30°C);
- use good quality soap flakes or liquid detergent;
- squeeze gently to remove the dirt — do not rub;
- rinse at least twice in clear, lukewarm water;
- gently wring out the water or spin briefly;
- lie flat and place into shape for drying.

Cotton garments   Cotton can be washed in hot water, although colour may fade from coloured garments. The advantage of white cotton is that it has no colour to lose and it can be boiled when necessary to remove stains and to whiten.

Synthetic materials and mixtures   Follow the instructions that accompany the garments.

Washing of nappies   See Topic 20.

ESSENTIAL ITEMS FOR THE LAYETTE

Nappies

There are different kinds of nappy:

1 Terry towelling (turkish towelling)   This is the traditional material used for nappies. Nappies of this type are popular because they are the most absorbent and the most comfortable — being flexible, they fit better around the baby's shape. They are also hard-wearing.

2 Muslin squares   Because they are not as bulky as terry towelling, muslin squares may be used as nappies for very small babies. They may also be used to line towelling nappies for babies with sensitive skins.

3 Disposable nappies save time and effort in washing. They can be very useful when washing or drying is a problem, or when travelling with the baby. But as they are less absorbent, they need to be changed more often. Disposable nappies work out more expensive than towelling nappies, even when allowing for the cost of washing.

Disposable nappies can be flushed away down the lavatory (which in many houses may block the drains!) or may be placed in the rubbish bin — this could mean storing them for a week or longer. One type of disposable nappy is a pad of absorbent material which is usually worn with separate plastic pants. Another type has the pad and plastic pants all in one, and all is thrown away after use.

Nappy liners   A nappy liner placed inside a towelling nappy helps to prevent soreness by acting as a barrier between the baby's skin and a wet nappy. Liners are made of material which allows moisture to pass through but does not absorb it. So, when a liner is placed inside a towelling nappy, the urine passes through to be absorbed by the towelling whilst the lining itself keeps dry.

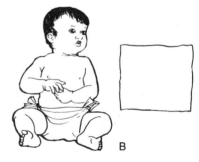

A

Nappy pins are large, curved and have a safety catch which is removed in order to open the pin. When putting the pin in a nappy, keep one hand under the nappy to prevent the baby from being pierced by the pin.

B

Plastic pants

These are worn over the nappy to keep the clothes and bedding dry, and by doing so, reduce the amount of washing. But because the urine remains inside the pants, the baby's skin is kept damp and this encourages nappy rash (Topic 20).

Plastic pants may have elastic at the waist and legs, as **A** above. Those which are tied in place, **B**, may be preferred since they do not cut into the legs, they adjust to the shape of the child, and they are easier to wash and dry. The disadvantage is that they are more difficult to put on to the baby. A third type of plastic pants which are kept in place by press fasteners ('poppers') is shown in **C**.

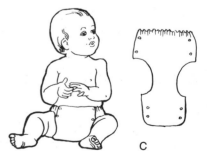

C

Vests

As vests are worn next to the skin, they need to be made of material which is soft and non-irritating. Those made of a mixture of wool and synthetic material (for winter) and cotton and synthetic material (for summer) wash well and keep their shape.

Vests which wrap over and tie in the front, **A**, are the easiest type to put on as they do not have to go over the head. The disadvantages are that they tend to gape and to come undone. Vests with an 'envelope' neck, **B**, make it easier to put this type of vest over the head. All-in-one vest and pants are worn over the nappy and the press fastening at the crutch holds the vest in position as well as making for easy nappy changing, **C**.

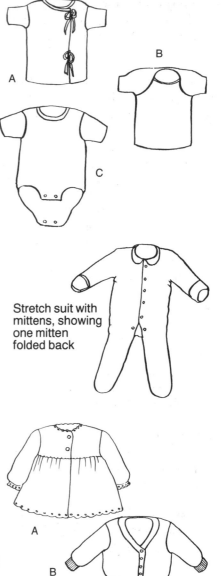

Stretch suits

Stretch suits have largely replaced the gowns that babies used to wear. They cover the baby well, are easy to wash, and need no ironing. As the feet are covered, there is no need for bootees except in cold conditions. Mittens are sometimes attached to the suit. These are useful both to keep the hands warm and to prevent the baby from scratching his face.

Stretch suit with mittens, showing one mitten folded back

Matinée jackets and cardigans

A matinée jacket, **A**, buttons or ties at the back. A cardigan, **B**, fastens lower down. A jacket or cardigan is worn when an extra layer is required for warmth.

Bonnets

These are necessary in cool or cold weather. If the baby is out in hot sun then a cotton sun hat is necessary.

Shawl

A shawl needs to be lightweight and warm. A cellular blanket also makes a good shawl. The holes in a blanket of this type make it lightweight, and air trapped in the holes will hold the heat from the baby's body and help to keep him warm in cold weather.

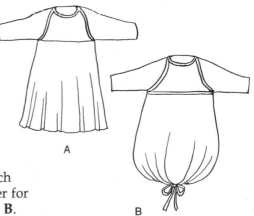

Extra items for the layette

Gowns allow for growth, so they can be used for a much longer time than stretch suits. They can be made warmer for a young baby by having a draw-string at the bottom, as **B**.

Bootees are useful in cold weather, especially when the baby wears a gown. When used with a stretch suit, they can be placed inside **if** there is plenty of room.

Mittens   Warm mittens are essential when the baby is outside in cold weather. **Scratch mittens** are thin mittens which are sometimes put on a baby's hands to prevent him from scratching himself. They are unnecessary if he is wearing a stretch suit with mittens attached.

Pram suit   A warm pram suit is useful for an older baby who has the strength to kick off the blankets in his pram, or who is old enough to sit up in the pram.

Bibs   Paper tissues or paper towels may be used as bibs and thrown away afterwards. Bibs made of terry towelling are absorbent but need frequent washing if they are to remain hygienic. Bibs made of soft plastic or plastic backed material must be securely tied around the waist as well as the neck. This will prevent the plastic from flapping over the face and causing suffocation. For the same reason, any bib should always be removed before the baby is put in his cot or pram. Bibs made of stiff plastic with a 'catch-all' pocket are for older babies.

Questions

1. List each of the items in the layette shown in the photograph on p. 79.

2. a What are the requirements for baby clothes?
b What points are useful to remember when choosing the layette?

3. Of materials used for baby clothes:
a Name two natural materials.
b Name four synthetic materials.
c Name two types of material suitable for wear in cold weather.
d Name two absorbent materials suitable for wear in hot weather.
e Why is polyester a suitable material for children's nightdresses?
f Why are baby clothes often made of a mixture of different materials?

4. a How should woollen garments be washed? Give six instructions.
b When cotton is used for baby clothes, what is the advantage of white cotton?

5. a How is a nappy liner able to act as a barrier between the baby's skin and a wet nappy?
b Describe a nappy pin and how to use it.
c Why does the use of plastic pants help to encourage nappy rash?
d Why may plastic pants which are tied in place be preferred to those which have elastic?

6. a Name three types of vest, giving one advantage of each.
b Give four reasons why stretch suits have largely replaced gowns.
c What are scratch mittens?

d When is a pram suit useful?
e Give an advantage and a disadvantage of using a towelling bib.
f How should a soft plastic bib be secured on a baby?
g When should a bib always be removed?

To do

1. Make drawings or collect pictures of the items you consider to be essential for a layette.

2. Find out the up-to-date prices of the items in the layette and work out the total cost.

3. Compare the advantages and disadvantages of towelling and disposable nappies. Find out the cost of the different types of nappies on sale, and compare.

23 Nursery equipment

Besides needing clothing, a baby also needs somewhere to sleep, to be bathed, to sit and to play. It is also helpful to have some means of keeping the baby safe when necessary and for taking the baby out for a walk to the shops or park. Some of the equipment designed for these purposes is discussed in this topic.

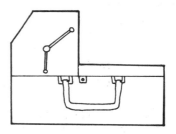

FOR SLEEPING

Carry-cot

A carry-cot makes a suitable first bed. It is useful for the first six months or longer until the baby becomes too big and active to be left in it safely. The sides and hood keep out draughts and it can be carried from room to room, or put in the back of a car, or taken on a bus when travelling. If made of weatherproof material and fitted with hood, apron and wheels, a carry-cot has the added advantage of being a pram as well as a bed.

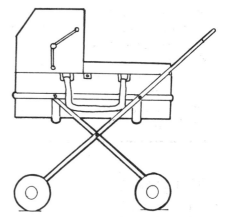

Cradle

A cradle or crib can be used as a bed for a young baby. The advantage of having such a bed with bars or latticed sides is that the baby can see out. The disadvantage is that it will not be draught-proof. If draughts are a problem, the cradle can be lined, and made to look very pretty. Cradles and cribs are sometimes made to rock. Moses baskets are sometimes used for young babies.

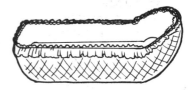

Cot

A cot of the type shown on p. 86 is suitable for all babies, even when new-born. If protection is needed from draughts, a blanket can be pinned firmly around one side.

A young baby who has been using a carry-cot as a bed, will need the space and safety of a cot of this type after the age of about six months. Another advantage is that the slatted sides will allow him to see out.

The safety features to check for in a cot are:

1. The bars should not be more than 7 cm ($2\frac{3}{4}$ in) apart to prevent the baby's head from being caught between them.

2. The mattress should fit so that there is just enough room for the bed-clothes to be tucked in. There should be no dangerous gap in which the baby's head, arms or legs can become stuck.

3. Cots usually have one side which drops down, and with a catch to hold the drop-side in the upper position. The catch needs to be too difficult to be undone by the baby or a young brother or sister. When the baby can climb out of the cot it is time for a bed.

Cot bumpers   These are foam padded screens which fit around the sides of the cot. They protect the baby from draught, and from knocking his head on the sides.

Mattresses are needed for the carry-cot, cot and pram. The baby will spend much time lying on a mattress, so it should be comfortable. A firm mattress is safer than a soft one because the baby cannot bury his head in it and suffocate. A waterproof covering on the mattress allows it to be sponged down and kept clean and unsmelly.

Blankets and sheets   It is better for these to be made of materials which are easy to wash and dry. Babies often dribble milk on them, or are sick, and they can also become very damp and smelly with urine after a night's sleep.

   Sheets are needed to cover the mattress of both cot and pram. A minimum supply of three is required, although six will be more useful as they need to be washed regularly. The material which is usually recommended when warmth is required is flannelette.

   Acrylic blankets, particularly the cellular ones, are lightweight, reasonably warm, and easily washable. Woollen blankets are warmer, but they do not wash so well and take much longer to dry.

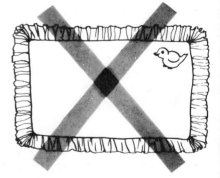

Pillow   A baby does not need a pillow for sleeping. He will be safer without one because of the danger of suffocation. When a pillow is used to prop up the baby in a chair or pram, it should be firm and not soft.

FOR GOING OUT

Pram

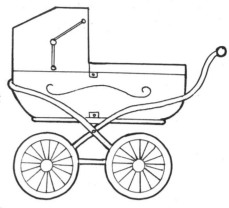

A pram can be a carry-cot on wheels or a specially made baby carriage. Some of the lighter prams have a body which can be lifted off and a base which folds for easier storage. The baby will not mind what type of pram it is or whether it is new or secondhand. A suitable pram should:

- have efficient brakes;
- be stable — should not tip over easily;
- be easy to steer;
- have anchor points for a safety harness;
- have a basket which fits underneath. This is the safest place for a basket as heavy parcels will not cause the pram to overbalance;
- be the right height for the mother to be able to push easily without stooping and yet still be able to see where she is going.

There are short mothers and tall mothers

Safety harness It is necessary to use a harness in the pram, pushchair and chair as soon as the baby is able to turn himself around without help. The harness should fasten over the shoulders as well as round the waist, and be adjusted so that the baby cannot kneel or stand up. When the baby can walk, the harness can be made into walking reins.

Cat net If there are cats around, a cat net over the pram will prevent one from snuggling against the baby's face for warmth and comfort.

Push-chair

Push-chairs (baby buggies) are for babies who are old enough to sit up. Being smaller than prams, push-chairs are often more convenient for shopping and travelling. But as they are not so well sprung, they give the baby a more jerky ride, and do not give such good protection against the weather. Nevertheless, a push-chair is a very useful piece of equipment which is likely to be in use until the child has passed through the toddler stage.

Baby nest

This looks like a tiny sleeping bag with or without handles. It is designed to keep the baby warm while being carried. The baby will only be safe when on his back; if he lies on his side or front, his face may become buried in the soft surface and he will suffocate. For this reason, a baby should never be left alone when in a baby nest, nor should the nest be used like a carry-cot for sleeping.

FOR SITTING

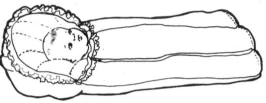

Bouncing cradle

The baby can be propped up in a chair from the age of a month or two, or be put in a 'bouncing cradle' or 'safe sitter' which is specially designed for this purpose. This makes a change for the baby from lying on his back in the cot or pram and he will enjoy looking around. When a bouncing cradle is used, it will be safer placed on the floor rather than the table. Babies can wriggle quite a lot and may cause it to move and fall off the table.

Baby chair

High chair or low chair?　Parents have to make the decision whether to use a high chair or a low chair for their baby. High chairs have the advantage in that the baby is at table level and can be part of the family at meal-times. Low chairs are safer because, being less top-heavy, they do not topple over so easily.

Whichever type of chair is used, it needs to have a broad base and to be very firm so that it will not easily topple over. Besides a harness, the chair should have a central bar between the baby's legs so that he cannot slip through.

Baby chairs have trays in front which can be used at meal-times or for toys. The best type of tray is large and with rounded corners which are easy to clean.

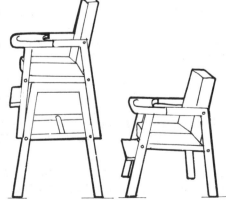

FOR BATHING

Baby bath

A baby bath is is not an essential item of equipment because a young baby can be bathed in the wash basin. Care must then be taken to ensure that he does not knock himself on the taps. There is also the danger that he could receive burns from touching the hot tap. Some parents therefore prefer to buy a baby bath.

After a few months, the baby will reach the stage when he loves to splash the water. The best place for him then is the ordinary adult bath. A rubber mat in the bottom of the bath will help to stop the baby from slipping.

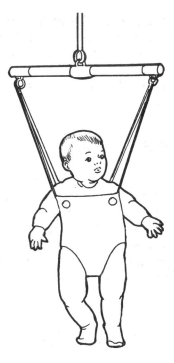

FOR PLAYING

Baby bouncer

Although not an essential item of equipment, baby bouncers are popular with babies from three months onwards. The harness supports the back, so the baby can be put in a bouncer for a short while as soon as he can hold his head steady. Babies like bouncing gently up and down and it gives them the freedom to move their legs and arms. It is also good exercise and helps to strengthen the legs.

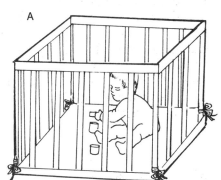

A

Play-pen

A play-pen is useful when the baby begins to move around. It will keep the baby safe while the mother is busy or out of the room for a short while. Most babies play happily in a play-pen until they object to their freedom being restricted. This stage can take one week or several months to reach. A baby in a play-pen will learn to pull himself into a standing position and to walk while holding onto the edge for support.

It is an advantage if the play-pen folds up easily for storage and both the types shown here do this. A square play-pen fits more easily into a corner. The plastic mat, which is tied in position in **A**, protects the floor and makes it more difficult for the child to push the play-pen around or escape underneath. The raised floor of play-pen **B** keeps the baby off the ground.

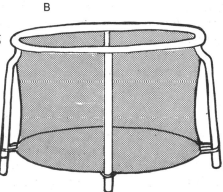

B

1. a Name four advantages of using a carry-cot as a bed for a young baby.
b Give three advantages of a cot when the baby reaches the age of about six months.
c Name three safety features to check when choosing a cot.
d Why is a firm mattress safer than a soft one?
e (i) Does a baby need a pillow for sleeping? (ii) Give a reason.

2. a Give six points to check when choosing a pram.
b At what stage does the baby require a safety harness?
c Describe how a safety harness should be used.
d What is a cat net for?
e Comparing a pram with a push-chair, give (i) two advantages of a push-chair, (ii) three advantages of a pram.

3. a Describe a baby nest.
b For what purpose is a baby nest designed?
c Why should a baby never be left alone to sleep when in a baby nest?

4. a Name four safety features desirable in a baby chair.
b Name one advantage of a high chair and one advantage of a low chair.
c Why should a bouncing cradle not be placed on a table when in use?

5. a When may a play-pen be useful?
b Why do babies like baby bouncers?
c (i) What can be used instead of a baby bath? (ii) What care has to be taken?
d What helps to stop a baby from slipping when in the bath?

1. Draw or find photographs of the pieces of equipment mentioned in this topic to accompany your notes.

2. What other equipment can be bought for babies? For each item, say what age group it is designed for, and whether you consider it to be useful or unnecessary.

Discuss with the mother the items of nursery equipment mentioned in this topic. For those which she has used, did she find them useful, well made, or a waste of money?

Exercises

1 a What is the usual cause of nappy rash?
b State two safety checks which should be made before buying a second-hand pushchair.
c How can a mother recognise 3-month colic? Suggest one way of treating this condition.
d (i) What is a suitable room temperature for a young baby's bedroom?
  (ii) Why is it important to maintain this temperature?
e List four fabrics which are suitable for baby clothes and in each case give a reason for your choice. (*LREB*)
f Give two important points to remember in preparing for baby's bath-time.
g Which two of the items below are *not essential* for a baby. Give a reason for *each* of the items you choose.
Pram; towelling napkins; nappy liners; soap; baby bath; carrycot. (*SWEB*)

2 Preparing a feed Add the following words to complete the instructions for preparing a bottle feed:
  boiled; cap; wipe; dissolve; hot; knife; milk powder; scoop; sterilising; teat; wash; wrist.
  (i) . . . . . your hands.
  (ii) Remove the bottle from the . . . . . solution. Shake off excess liquid but do not . . . . . .
  (iii) Measure the required amount of warm, previously . . . . . water into the bottle.
  (iv) Add the required amount of . . . . to the bottle, levelling off each . . . . . of powder with a clean, dry . . . . . .
  (v) Place the . . . . . on the bottle and shake well to . . . . . the powder.
  (vi) Place the . . . . . on the bottle.
  (vii) Before feeding, shake a few drops of milk on to the inside of your . . . . . to make sure that the milk is not too . . . . . for the baby.

3 a List six nutrients present in milk and give reasons why each is important in the diet of an expectant mother.
b Describe fully why breast-feeding is generally regarded as best for babies. (*EAEB*)

4 a List all the equipment that is necessary if the baby is to be bottle-fed.
b Describe and explain how and why the feeding equipment should be sterilised.
c Discuss possible reasons why some mothers prefer to bottle-feed rather than breast-feed their babies. (*EAEB*)

5 What factors should affect the choice of each of the following:
a a pram,   **c** a play-pen,
b a baby-chair,   **d** a drop-side cot? (*EAEB*)

6 a Which type of nappy would you buy for your baby?
b Give clear instructions for changing a baby's nappy.
c Explain how you would deal with the soiled nappy. (*WJEC*)

7 Carol has a 3-week-old baby, Kim, who weighed 6½ pounds at birth. Breast-fed, she has been gaining weight steadily for the past ten days. Carol's biggest problem has been to keep the baby warm, for the small flat has no central heating and the weather is cold for April. Suddenly Carol falls ill, and has to go to hospital with an infectious illness. Her sister comes to stay in the flat and look after the baby. Describe how she should care for the baby, using the following headings:
  (i) food,   (iv) hygiene,
  (ii) warmth,   (v) sleep.
  (iii) love and security,   (*SEREB*)

Section  4

Childhood

Mike Wells/Save the Children

24 The importance of play

Children play because it gives them pleasure. Play is also an essential part of their education because whilst they are playing they are learning.

Children need opportunities both to play with other children and to play on their own. When two or more children are together, many different games are possible. Whatever the game, the children will be learning how others behave and how to mix easily with them. At other times, children need to play on their own and without interference in order to learn how to amuse themselves. If adults spend too much time playing with a child, the child will feel bored and miserable when left on his own. Then, instead of playing happily, he will spend his time trying to demand attention.

A

Benefits of play

1 Play enables children to find out about themselves and the world. It allows them to:

a discover
b experiment
c create
d concentrate
e express ideas
f develop speech
g develop muscles
h invent
i learn new skills
j learn how other people behave
k role-play (pretend to be someone else)
l share possessions
m use the imagination
n co-operate with others
o show off (children like to let others know what they can do)
p act protectively towards someone less powerful than themselves

2 Play helps towards happiness A child who is absorbed in play is likely to be a happy child as play produces feelings of satisfaction and achievement.

3 Play helps prevent boredom Preventing a child from being bored is very important as boredom quickly leads to bad temper, irritability and destructiveness.

B

4 Play can help reduce stress The acting out of stressful situations can help them to seem more familiar and therefore less frightening. For example, by playing 'schools', a child becomes familiar with the idea of going to school. This will help to reduce any nervousness about school which the child might have. In the same way, playing 'doctors and nurses' can help prepare a child for a stay in hospital.

94

5 Play can help divert aggressive instincts Using a hammer to nail pieces of wood together to make a 'boat' is preferable to using the hammer to hurt someone or destroy property.

Different types of play

Children like variety and during the day will change from one type of play to another. Sometimes they use the same toy. More often they use different toys because changes stimulate different types of play. Six types of play can be recognised and each forms part of a child's total development.

1   Discovery play enables a child to find out about things: what they are like — their size, shape, texture, colour; how they are made; what he can do with them. The child will also discover that they can be broken, and this can help to teach him to take care of his possessions.

2   Physical play takes place when a child is actively moving around — running, jumping, climbing, crawling, balancing, swinging, throwing a ball and so on.

3   Creative play is when a child expresses his own ideas and feelings to make something which is original, for example, a picture or story, model in plasticine, a 'Lego' house, and so on. A young child is able to express feelings and ideas more easily by painting and drawing than by using words. As the child becomes more skilled with words, he may then be able to write a story, poem or play.

4 Imaginative play is pretend or fantasy play. The child imagines that he is someone else or an animal such as a rabbit or dog. Children imitate the ways of adults when they play at 'Mothers and Fathers', 'Cowboys and Indians' or 'Shopping'. Attempting to behave like someone else helps the child to understand more clearly the ways other people behave.

F

5 Manipulative play involves skilful use of the hands. During manipulative play the hands, eyes and brain are being trained to co-ordinate, that is, to work smoothly together.

Babies become increasingly skilful with their hands as they play with rattles, soft toys and other objects. Later on, they benefit from playing with such things as water, sand and play-dough.

6 Social play takes place when children play together. It teaches them to co-operate, to share, and to be honest. It also teaches them that anti-social behaviour like cheating, leads to isolation and loss of friendship. Children often quarrel and in doing so, learn about each other's reactions.

At any one time, a child may be involved in more than one type of play. For example, when a baby plays with a rattle, he discovers what it is like as he learns to use his hands — this is both discovery and manipulative play. When a group of children play with bricks it could involve all types of play.

To do

Study the six pictures **A** to **F** in this Topic.

1 Each of the six pictures is intended to represent a different type of play. Decide which type of play each picture best represents. Give a reason why you consider it represents that type of play.

2 Take each picture in turn and say which of the items in the list **a–p** are involved in that particular play situation.

3 (i) Most of the toys used by the children in the pictures are objects which have been found around the house and garden. Make a list of the objects which are being used as toys. (ii) Suggest other objects which could be used as toys.

Child study

Watch the child at play for a few hours or, if possible, throughout the day. Keep a record of what the child does and the approximate time spent on each activity. Could you recognise each of the six types of play mentioned in this topic? What did the child discover about himself and the world? Repeat this study on several occasions either with the same child or a different child and compare the results.

Questions

1. a Why is play considered to be an essential part of education?
b Give a reason why children need to play (i) with other children, (ii) on their own.
c List briefly five benefits of play.

2. What does play allow children to find out about themselves and the world? Give at least ten suggestions.

3 Play can be classified into six different types. Name and describe each type.

25 Toys

As we saw in the previous topic, children play happily with many different objects which they find around the house and garden. They use these objects as toys. Nevertheless, toys which are specially made for children will also give them much pleasure and help to increase the variety and interest of their games.

Choosing a toy for a child

Toys come in many forms. Those which give pleasure will be used. Because they are used, they will give the opportunity to learn. Toys sold as 'Educational Toys' will only be played with if the child finds them either fun or interesting.

A successful toy is one which a child both likes and uses often. Such a toy:

1. **is right for the age of the child** — the child is old enough to enjoy it, but not too old for the toy to seem babyish;

2. **is strong enough for the child to use**;

3. **provides more than temporary interest** — it will either
   - give scope for the imagination,
   - give scope for learning new skills,
   - make the child think,
   - or have special appeal for the child;

4. **is safe to play with** — for example, the eyes of soft toys are firmly fixed and cannot be pulled out; there are no sharp edges or points; toy cars and tricycles are stable and will not easily tip over. Toys sold in Britain are controlled by Safety Regulations.

Toys for children of all ages

Many toys are used only during a particular stage of development. However, a few seem to appeal to children of all ages and are used over a long period of childhood. These include bricks, climbing frames, dolls and soft toys.

Bricks

Bricks probably have the longest life of any toy and both boys and girls enjoy playing with them. Building with bricks encourages children to concentrate, be patient, to invent and to be skilful with the hands.

When a baby first plays with bricks, he has difficulty in placing one brick on top of another. He has to learn:

- **to use hands and eyes together**;
- **to develop fine control** over the muscles which move the fingers;
- **to concentrate** as both time and effort are needed to achieve a satisfactory result;
- **to persist** and keep on practising until the bricks can be placed where they are wanted.

As the child gets older, more use is made of the imagination to arrange the bricks in different ways. There are a large number of games in which bricks can be used. For example, bricks can be made into walls, towers, steps, houses, roads, tunnels and patterns. They can keep one child amused or occupy a group of children playing together.

Enough bricks   For bricks to be a really useful toy, there needs to be enough of them. A few bricks are not much use except to a baby. Older children need many more, probably over 100. Hundreds of bricks require quite a lot of space, both for storage and when they are being played with. Parents must be prepared to have half-finished games left over a large part of the table or floor.

Interlocking bricks   'Lego' and other small bricks of this type keep children happily occupied for many hours throughout the years of childhood. Children can start to play with them as soon as they have the skill to lock them together **and** when they have grown out of the stage of wanting to put small things in the mouth. If a collection of bricks is begun when the child is young, then added to from time to time, it can be made to keep pace with the developing skills and imagination.

A climbing frame

This large and expensive toy takes up a great deal of space and, once put up, has to be left in place. The advantages of a climbing frame are that it can be used throughout childhood both for physical play and for many other activities. It can be erected wherever there is enough space, either inside or outside.

This toy is particularly useful for children who do not have a large garden or nearby adventure playground in which to

play. It gives opportunity for children to use their muscles, gain control over their movements, test their skills and use up energy. A young child using a climbing frame has to decide where to put his hands and feet, how far to climb and how to hold the body to stay in balance. As experience is gained in moving around, the child will become more confident and adventurous. Adding objects to the climbing frame such as a rope, plank, hammock or blanket increases the interest and provides ideas for many imaginative games.

Dolls and soft toys

The favourite doll or teddy or cuddly animal becomes a 'sort of person' to whom the child can turn for companionship or comfort. Unlike people, they are always ready for play, do not make demands, can be talked to in confidence and then left alone until wanted again. Sometimes children prefer to share their grief, anger or pleasure with dolly or teddy rather than with people. Many children rely on them for comfort throughout childhood.

Dolls come in many shapes and sizes. Some are elaborately dressed and seem to appeal to grown-ups. However, children usually seem to prefer a simple doll or soft toy as there is more scope for the imagination and less to go wrong.

Toys in the first year

Babies begin to play at three months or earlier. They love having objects to handle and to look at. They find new objects more interesting than familiar ones. Most mothers do not give their child too many toys to play with at once. They change them around for variety. The child will then show renewed interest in a toy which has not been played with for a few days.

In general, babies prefer toys which are brightly coloured and make a noise. Toys for this age group should be attractive, manageable, fun, unlikely to break, washable and safe. **Safe** means that the toy can be handled and put in the mouth without causing harm. It must have no sharp edges, or points, or small pieces which could be swallowed. Also it should be splinter-proof. Stuffing should be clean and paint should not contain lead.

3 months   The baby's first toy is likely to be a rattle. The rattle has to be placed in the baby's hand and he cannot pick it up if he drops it. The rattle should be light and with a handle which is the right size for a baby to grasp.

4 months   The baby will get pleasure from waving the rattle about. He will also enjoy beads on his pram and a mobile above his cot.

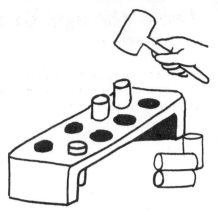

5 months   Now that the baby is able to pick up objects, a wide variety of toys will give him pleasure — in the pram, on the tray of his chair, on the floor, in the bath and in the garden.

10 months   Children of this age enjoy putting things into containers (bags, boxes, tins, etc.) and taking them out again.

1 year   Children now take an interest in books. Those made of firm cardboard are suitable for this stage.

Toys for children aged 1–2 years

Most of the toys for children under one year old will still be used at this age. In addition, the children can now put discs on to a peg, and will like picture books with simple stories or nursery rhymes. Push and pull toys are very popular with children who can walk. Towards the age of two, they are able to thread large beads, play with a ball, enjoy a paddling pool, and like 'helping' with the cleaning and cooking.

Toys for children aged 2–3 years

They now have sufficient skill with their hands to play with barrels of different sizes which unscrew. Children of this age can also manage large interlocking bricks, the 'posting box', peg boards with pegs of different shape, peg boards with pegs to hammer, blackboard and chalks, coloured pencils and poster paints, plasticine, doll's pram, doll's house and doll's clothes. They also like books with pictures that they can look at or books in which they can draw and colour.

   Towards the end of the third year, they are able to use scissors to cut out pictures, and to match pictures or colour them. Playing with a doll's tea set is also popular.

Toys for children aged 3–5 years

Children of this age group appreciate toys for imaginative play — drawing and painting materials, coloured gummed paper to make patterns, and dressing-up clothes. They enjoy being active and outdoors with toys like balls, 'space hoppers', climbing frames and tricycles. They will be beginning to show interest in books which help in learning to read.

From the age of five years onwards

Children are now becoming ready for jigsaws, card games, board games like 'snakes and ladders', sewing kits, and books which they are able to read for themselves.

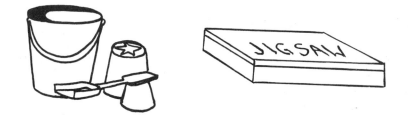

To do

1. Sort out the toys shown in this topic into three groups according to whether you consider them to be particularly suitable for children (i) under the age of 1 year, (ii) aged 1–3 years, (iii) aged 3–5 years. Make a collection of pictures of suitable toys to accompany your answers.

2. Balls are popular with children of all ages. Draw or collect pictures of (i) different types of balls, (ii) balls being used in play. Suggest ways in which children can use the different types of ball.

3. Watch a child play with bricks or try to remember playing with them yourself. Then read the section on bricks in this topic. Comment on how the points mentioned in the topic relate to what you saw or what you remembered.

4. Watch children playing on a climbing frame — many parks and schools have them. Describe how the climbing frame was being used and note the approximate age of the children.

Child study

1. The child will almost certainly have a favourite doll or soft toy. Describe it, and observe when and how the child plays with it.

2. Play with the child. Describe the way he, or she, plays with different toys. Which are the favourite toys and which are never used? Where are the toys kept? Who puts them away when the child has finished playing with them?

Questions

1. a Give four points which make a toy successful.
b Give four reasons why a toy might be of more than temporary interest.

2. a Name three types of toy which are used over a long period of childhood.
b What is a young child learning when he plays with bricks? Give four suggestions.
c Suggest four reasons why at times, children prefer the favourite doll or teddy to people.

3. a (i) For which children is a climbing frame particularly useful? (ii) Name four opportunities it gives to such children.
b When parents are thinking about buying a climbing frame (i) name two advantages of such a toy, (ii) name three points which may be considered as disadvantages.
c Name four objects which can be added to a climbing frame to make it more interesting.

4. a At what age do children start to play?
b When choosing a rattle for a baby, name seven safety factors to be considered.

5. What is the average age at which children become able to
a enjoy beads on the pram,
b pick up toys,
c put toys in containers and take them out again,
d take an interest in books,
e walk along pushing a toy,
f unscrew the pieces of a toy.
g use scissors,
h enjoy dressing up,
i enjoy card games?

26 Learning to draw

From an early age, a child begins to form pictures (images) in the mind. These pictures involve himself and the world about him, and also include other people and the way he sees them.

By two years of age, the imagination has developed enough for the child to be able to use signs and symbols to represent things. For example:

- dolls represent people;
- small toy cars represent real cars;
- words are used for objects and actions;
- drawings describe events and express feelings.

At times, it is very hard for young children to separate the real world from their imaginary world.

Drawing

Drawing is important as it helps a child to express his feelings and imagination and to record his experiences.

Children love to draw. They are ready to do so as soon as they can hold a pencil or crayon, which is between the age of 12 and 18 months. The first drawings are scribbles. This is followed by 'big head' figures. The drawings gradually become more realistic as the child develops more control over the pencil, and as he comes to notice and understand more about the world.

Learning to draw

Children pass through most or all of the following stages as they learn to draw. These stages often overlap, so when looking at a drawing made by a child, it may be difficult to place it in any one particular stage.

Stage 1 The child's hand moves backwards and forwards to produce a scribble.

Stage 2 The child becomes able to lift the pencil from the paper and move it in different directions.

Stage 3 He begins to scribble in circles.

Stage 4 He becomes able to draw round and round in circles.

Stage 5 He now starts to draw people and uses a circle to represent a face. Marks are put inside for eyes, nose, mouth.

Stage 6 Lines are added all round the circle as well.

Stage 7 The lines are arranged in bunches to represent hair, arms, legs.

Stage 1

Stage 2

Stage 3

Stage 4

Stage 5

Stage 6

Stage 7

Montessori 3 to 5,
Wimbledon

Stage 8 The arms come straight out at the sides of the face. The legs come from a smaller circle which is drawn below for the body.

Stage 9 The body becomes much more important and the legs have feet.

Stage 10 Clothes are added. The drawings also have trees, houses, animals, cars and other objects in the child's world.

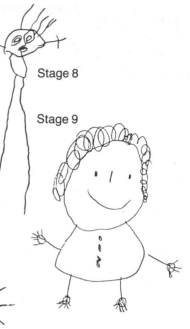

Stage 8

Stage 9

When a drawing is finished

Children generally like to have their drawings admired and perhaps even pinned on the wall for everyone to see. However, sometimes after completing a drawing, they scribble or paint over it so that it can no longer be seen. This often seems to give them pleasure similar to that which they get from knocking over a pile of bricks or a sand-castle.

Stage 10

David Winter

Questions

1. Name four ways in which children use signs and symbols.

2. a When are children ready to start drawing?
b What are the first drawings like?
c What type of drawings follow next?
d When do the drawings become more realistic?

3. Describe the ten stages which children pass through as they learn to draw. Accompany each stage with a simple drawing.

To do

Above right are shown three stamps which were drawn by children — Samantha Brown, aged 5; Lucinda Blackmore, aged 6; Sophie Sharpe, aged 8. Which girl do you think drew which picture? Give your reasons.

The Post Office

Child study

If the child is old enough, encourage him to draw a picture, but without telling him either what to draw or how to do it. When the picture is finished, ask the child to tell you about it. Have you learnt anything about the child's imagination or feelings? Repeat this exercise every few weeks. Make a collection of the drawings and compare.

27 *Children's clothes*

Clothes for young babies were discussed in Topic 22. Once the babies begin to move about, different types and a greater variety of clothes become desirable.

A list of requirements for baby clothes is given on p. 80. The same list applies to clothes for children of all ages, together with additional requirements.

Additional requirements for children's clothes

1. Children's clothes should be: loose enough for movement but not so big as to get in the way; hard-wearing; easy for a child to put on; easy for the child to take off for toilet needs.
2. Shoes are required from the toddler stage onwards.
3. Different types of clothes are needed for daytime, night-time, to wear outside in cold, hot and wet weather.

Different types of clothes

The following are some examples of different types of clothes for children.

A Sleeping suit   This keeps the child warm even when not covered by blankets. When running around the house, he does not need a dressing-gown or slippers. The soles of the sleeping suit are made of material which can be easily wiped.

B Pyjamas   Unlike a sleeping suit, these have the tendency to part in the middle, thus giving a bare midriff, but they are easier to remove for the toilet.

C Night-dress   A night-dress does not keep a child as warm as a sleeping suit or pyjamas. This can be an advantage in hot weather and for toilet needs. All ready-made night-dresses for children must be made of flame-resistant material.

D Rompers   Rompers help to stop nappies from falling down and ensure that there is no gap between jersey and trousers. Rompers of the type shown here have the added advantage in that they keep the feet warm.

E Clothes for toddlers   These 'easy-to-wash' clothes are suitable for warm weather.

F One-piece weatherproof suit   This is a useful garment for wet or cold, windy weather. It needs to be loose enough to go over other clothing and still give freedom of movement.

G Anorak and jeans   These are hard-wearing garments for active children. They are often in deep colours which do not show the dirt so easily.

Learning to dress

When children are very young, they do not mind what they wear. By the time they reach the age of three years, they take an interest in their clothes, and often make a great fuss about what they want, or do not want, to wear. They are also starting to dress themselves. At this stage, dressing is a slow job, and the clothes are often put on inside out and back to front. Adults know they can do the job easily and quickly and will be tempted to do so. However, the children are likely to get very cross if adults interfere as they want to do it themselves. Battles can rage between mother and child when it is time for dressing!

Making it easier   Mothers can make it easier for children to dress unaided by providing clothes that are simple to put on. This gives children the satisfaction of being independent at an earlier age. Dressing dolly or teddy gives practice in using the fingers to do up buttons, zips, hooks and eyes, press fasteners, laces, toggles and bows.

Dressing for play

It is natural for children to get dirty. They easily spill food or drink, and they love playing with water, or in a muddy garden, or with paints. A mother will be happier if she accepts that it is natural for children to get dirty. Children will be happier if they are dressed in hard-wearing clothes which can be easily washed.

Children who are nagged too much about keeping clean, are likely to react by worrying. The worry will result in them getting far less enjoyment out of their play.

Shoes

Shoes and other types of footwear are a very important part of clothing and need particular attention. Although we shall be talking mainly about shoes, much of what is said applies to other types of footwear such as those shown on p. 109.

Children do not need shoes until they are walking. They then only need them when it is necessary to protect the feet against damage, or to keep them warm. Going barefoot as much as possible allows the bones and muscles to develop in the natural way to produce strong, healthy feet.

The need for well-fitting shoes

Childrens' shoes need to be the right shape and size to allow the bones and muscles of the feet to develop properly. The bones in a young child's foot are very soft and rather like rubber. These bones can be easily bent by badly fitting shoes. The bones harden as the child grows. If the foot is kept in perfect shape, the bones will harden in a perfect shape. If the feet are crushed into shoes which are too small, the bones harden into an imperfect shape, and the muscles will be poorly developed. The child rarely feels any pain when wearing tight shoes and therefore will not complain. Pain may come later, because many of the foot and back troubles which develop in later life are caused by ill-fitting footwear in childhood.

Room for growth

The photograph below shows how the toes and toenails may be damaged by the pressure of ill-fitting shoes. Corns, callosities and hardening and thickening of the skin are also caused by pressure. All these problems are avoided by wearing shoes that fit properly.

Startrite Shoes Ltd

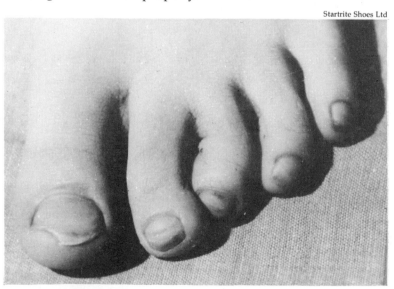

106

Rate of growth of feet

Feet grow about 2–2½ sizes each year until the age of four years. As a result, young children usually outgrow their shoes every three months. New shoes should be fitted to leave 12–18 mm (½–¾ in) growing space between the end of the longest toe and the end of the shoes. The shoes also need to be wide enough to allow the toes to move.

The most suitable shoes for children are those which are made in whole and half sizes, and in several different widths to suit thin feet, fat feet and those in between.

One type of shoe in four different widths

Choosing shoes for a child

Measuring the feet   When buying shoes for children, it is best that their feet are measured by a trained fitter in a shoe shop. Children should always stand upright when having their feet measured and shoes fitted, as feet alter a little in shape when the full body weight is placed on them.

Uppers   The upper part of a shoe may be made of plastic or leather. Leather is hard-wearing and stretches to take the shape of the foot. It also allows moisture to pass through. This means that sweat from the feet can escape and the shoes will be more comfortable to wear for a longer time. Shoes with plastic uppers are often cheaper and need less cleaning, but they do not stretch in the same way as leather or allow moisture to escape.

Soles   Soles which are light and flexible bend with the foot. This encourages a natural springy step which makes for easier walking. Soles which are anti-slip are safer. They also give greater confidence to a child who is learning to walk.

How to use the chart shown below

2 3 4 5 6 7 8 9 10 11 12

Mothercare Ltd

Chart for measuring feet

Points to check   Shoes for children should:
- give support and protection to the feet;
- be smooth inside and with no hard seams;
- be wide enough to allow the toes to move;
- have room for growth;
- have an adjustable fastening;
- have flexible uppers which bend as the foot bends;
- have soles which are light and flexible;
- have a firm fitting heel;
- have a low heel so that the foot does not slide forwards.

The illustration shows a type of shoe considered to be suitable for children.

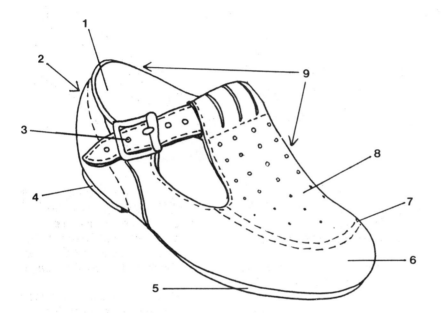

Other types of footwear

Pram shoes are not meant for walking. They are sometimes worn when the baby is dressed for special occasions.

Sandals are useful for wearing in hot weather as they allow air to get to the feet which reduces the unpleasant effects of sweating.

Plimsolls are lightweight canvas shoes with rubber soles which are useful for energetic games because they bend easily. As plimsolls are not usually made in half sizes or a variety of widths they are not usually a good fit.

Wellington boots are made of rubber or plastic to keep water out. Water from sweat is also kept inside. When the boots are worn in hot weather, the feet quickly become hot and sweat. This makes the feet uncomfortable if the boots are worn for a long period of time. When the boots are worn in cold weather, the feet quickly become cold unless warm socks are worn inside. The size of the boots should allow for this.

Socks should be big enough to give a loose, easy fit at the toes. Tight socks cause foot troubles in the same way as tight shoes. On the other hand, over-large socks can be very uncomfortable to wear.

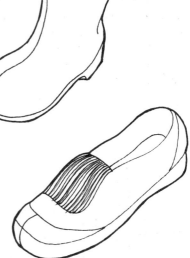

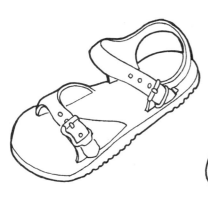

Questions

1. What are the requirements for children's clothes in addition to those required for the layette?

2. List the different types of clothing worn by the children in the drawings on pp. 103-4, giving one reason why each would be a useful garment.

3. a By what age do children take an interest in what they wear?
b How can mothers make it easier for children to dress themselves?
c (i) Name four situations when children are likely to get dirty. (ii) What clothes are most practical for children?

4. a Give two reasons for wearing shoes.
b Why is it important that shoes are the right shape and size?
c Why are the bones in a child's foot easily bent?

d Why do children usually not complain when their shoes are tight?
e What caused the twisted toes in the photograph on p. 106?

5. a How much growing space needs to be left at the end of new shoes?
b What is the advantage of having a choice of shoes in a variety of widths?
c Give two advantages of having the uppers made of (i) leather, (ii) plastic.
d Why are light and flexible soles considered to be an advantage?

6. a Name the types of footwear shown above, and say when each would be of use.
b Give reasons why socks should not be (i) tightly fitting, (ii) over-large?

To do

1. Copy the drawing of the shoe opposite and match each of the numbers with one of the 'Points to check' at the top of the page.

2. Make a collection of pictures of different types of children's clothing, including shoes. Give your opinion of the usefulness of each garment.

3. *Discuss* 'The advantages and disadvantages of dressing identical twins in the same clothes'.

Child study

1. Use the chart on p. 107 to measure the child's feet. Are they both the same size?

2. Discuss children's clothes with the mother. What are her views on the way children should be dressed? Has the child any views on the clothes which he, or she, wears?

109

28 Behaviour in early childhood

All children behave 'badly' or are 'difficult' from time to time. This is a normal part of growing up. At one time or another they are all likely to show the types of behaviour discussed in this topic — the negative phase, attention-seeking, temper tantrums, telling lies, hitting, biting and stealing. The extent to which children behave in these ways depends both on the child's own nature and the way in which the parents deal with the behaviour.

The point at which such behaviour will cause the parents concern varies from family to family. What seems very bad behaviour in one family may be regarded as normal in another. The types of behaviour mentioned above only become real problems when carried to excess. Children then need to be helped to grow out of them or they may continue into adolescence or adult life.

The negative ('No!') phase

It is normal for children between the ages of nine months and three years, and especially at 1½–2½ years of age, to go through a stage of saying 'NO' to anything they are told to do. They then want to do the opposite. Being tired, hungry or unwell tends to make them worse. Active, determined children are likely to be more trouble in this respect than placid ones.

Children can be very difficult to manage at this stage. It helps parents to be more patient and tolerant when they realise that this negative phase is a normal part of a child's development and not just naughtiness, and that it will pass. Although there will be good days and bad days, the bad days get fewer as the child gets older. On the other hand, if the parents are determined always to make the child 'do as he is told', then long-term behaviour problems are very likely to develop. For example, frequent temper tantrums or persistent bed-wetting.

Attention-seeking

It is normal for a child to want to be the centre of attention, especially between the age of 1 and 3–4 years. Youngsters of this age group feel important when they are noticed. As a result, they will do many things to show off and attract other people's attention, including:

- making lots of noise;
- coughing;
- spitting;
- refusing to eat;
- eating earth;
- holding their breath until blue in the face;
- refusing to sit on the potty;
- passing urine in the wrong place at the wrong time;
- having temper tantrums.

All these tricks are aimed at making the child the centre of attention. If they succeed, they are likely to be done repeatedly and to become habits.

Reasons for attracting attention   Often it is just the normal desire for attention that every child has. If this is the reason, then ignoring the habit (if possible) is the best way to stop it. Sometimes, when the habit persists, it indicates that the child's basic needs are not being met — he is not being taken enough notice of, or being loved and praised enough. So the child finds that the only way to get attention is to do something naughty.

Temper tantrums

A temper tantrum is a period of uncontrolled rage. The most common age for tantrums is between 18 months and three years. This is at the stage at which a child wants to do things his way, and loves to say 'NO'. Tantrums are more likely to happen in determined children with abundant energy, and not to be a problem in those who are placid and easy-going.

When in a tantrum, the child screams and kicks and may deliberately throw things in order to damage them. He pays no attention when told to stop, and will not listen to reason. The natural reaction of parents is to smack the child, but this rarely helps and is much more likely to make matters worse.

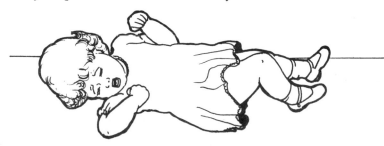

The child is punished by no-one appearing to take any interest in the outburst, although it may be necessary to prevent the child from hurting himself, or others, or from damaging property.

Possible causes   A temper tantrum once in a while can be considered normal behaviour. But when a child has frequent temper tantrums the cause may be:

1. **Frustration** at being unable to do what he wants or tell other people what he wants or feels. Often a child's feelings develop faster than the ability to use words to express these feelings.
2. **Imitation** of older children or adults. He sees them lose their temper and does the same.
3. **Emotional starvation.** The tantrum draws attention to the child's need for love and stimulation.
4. **Blackmail** to get his own way. If a child finds that he can get what he wants by having a tantrum, he will certainly go on having them.

Trying to understand why a child has temper tantrums will help in knowing how to deal with them.

Telling lies

It is natural for young children to use their imagination to play pretend games and to make up 'tall stories'. It takes time for them to understand the difference between what is real and what is make-believe. Therefore, truthfulness can only develop slowly. A child's greatest help in learning to be truthful is having parents who set a good example.

By the age of five years, most children understand that unless they speak the truth, people will never know when to believe them. One danger of punishing young children too severely for untruthfulness is that they may continue to tell lies in order to escape punishment.

I HAVE <u>NOT</u> GOT TEDDY

Stealing

Young children have a natural desire to take what they want and they have to learn that they cannot take things which belong to other people without asking first. A simple way of teaching this lesson is to allow children to have their own possessions and somewhere to keep them. A child will then know what it feels like if they are borrowed without permission. The good example of the parents is also very important in teaching children not to steal.

Stealing is not usually a problem during the first five years. It occurs more amongst school-age children.

Hitting and biting

The occasional hitting and biting of others is normal behaviour in young children. It must be expected when they are at the stage of learning to play together and do not yet fully understand the consequences of their actions.

Aggressive behaviour   A child who is often extremely quarrelsome and frequently attacks others by hitting, biting, kicking or shouting, is said to be **aggressive**. The cause of this aggressive behaviour needs to be sought. It can then be dealt with in a way which will be of most help to the child in overcoming the problem. Causes for the aggression may include jealousy, a means of attracting attention, or imitation — if a parent frequently hits a child it will be natural for the child to hit others, especially someone smaller.

Questions

1. a List the types of behaviour discussed in this topic and say at which age each is most likely to occur.
b Name two factors that influence the extent to which children behave in these ways.

2. a What is meant by the 'negative phase'?
b What may help parents to be more patient in dealing with a child who is passing through such a phase?

3. a Name some ways in which children attract attention to themselves.
b When may these ways become habits?
c Give two reasons why a child may want to attract attention.

4. a Describe a temper tantrum.
b Name four possible causes of frequent temper tantrums.

5. a Why does truthfulness in a young child only develop slowly?
b (i) What does a young child have to learn about other people's belongings?
(ii) Describe one way of teaching this lesson.

6. a Why can occasional hitting and biting be considered normal behaviour in young children?
b When is such behaviour said to be aggressive?
c Name three possible causes of aggression.

To do

Discuss 'Children need to be helped to grow out of behaviour problems or the problems may continue into adolescence or adult life'.

Child study

Take each of the types of behaviour mentioned in this topic in turn and describe an occasion when you have noticed such behaviour either in the child you are studying or others. Say
a what may have caused the behaviour;
b how adults dealt with the behaviour;
c what was the child's reaction.

113

29 *Habits in early childhood*

Habits are regular actions which are carried out without any, or very little, thought. Examples of habits commonplace in children include the sucking of a thumb or dummy, nail biting, and the need for a comforter. Habits of this kind are used by children to comfort themselves when they are tired or unhappy. They are sometimes called 'comfort habits'.

As children grow older, these habits often fade away. In other cases, a great deal of will-power is required to break the habit. Occasionally, the habits persist into adult life.

Thumb and finger sucking

All babies suck their thumbs or fingers, sometimes even before they are born. Some babies suck their thumbs or fingers more than others. Many will stroke a doll, blanket or other material at the same time, or twiddle a piece of hair. They may do it when they are feeling sleepy, shy, bored, in trouble or when a tooth is coming through. The skin on the thumb or finger may thicken or become sore or blistered by the sucking.

Thumb sucking is a harmless habit in a young child, and as it is harmless, no attempt need be made to stop it. If it is ignored, the child will be very likely to grow out of the habit naturally by the age of four years. On the other hand, if the parents try to stop the habit, the child will object strongly when his thumb is removed from his mouth. If they make a great deal of fuss, the child will do it all the more.

When thumb sucking continues after the age of five, it may prevent the front teeth growing properly into place when the permanent teeth come through. Thumb sucking may need to be stopped for this reason, and by now the child should be old enough to understand.

Sucking a dummy

Mothers often have strong opinions about dummies. Some say that a dummy stops a baby crying because it soothes and keeps him contented. Others think that a dummy is a poor substitute for the love and attention that should be given when the baby cries. Another point of view is that dummies should not be used because they are difficult to keep clean and can pass on germs to the baby.

It is generally thought that dummies do not do much harm — unless they contain sweet substances for the baby to suck, which will encourage the front teeth to decay. Most children give up their dummy between 1–2 years of age — if the mother does not continue to encourage its use.

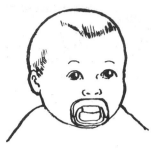

The need for a comforter

Most children have one favourite cuddly toy or piece of material which gives comfort and security, especially at bedtimes. The child loves it however scruffy it gets, and will be very upset if it is lost. A child may even be very upset if it smells different after it has been washed. Some children need their comforters for several years.

Nail biting

So many children over three years old bite their nails that it can be considered a normal thing to do. These children bite their nails without realising what they are doing. It often happens when they are nervous or tense or deep in thought. The only harm it does is to make the nails look unsightly. Probably the only thing the parents can do is to ignore it. Nagging or punishing the child does not usually stop the habit because the child seldom realises when he is doing it. Some children just seem to grow out of the habit of biting their nails. For others it is an effort to stop, and a few still continue to bite their nails as adults.

Head banging, head rolling and body rocking

Some babies have the following rhythmical habits:
1. Repeatedly banging the head against something hard, perhaps the end of the cot. This may make a lot of noise but it does not seem to hurt the child. Padding the end of the cot, or using cot bumpers, helps both to reduce the noise and the possibility of bruising.
2. Rolling the head from side to side. The hair on the back of the head becomes rubbed off in the process.
3. Rocking their bodies to and fro. When a young child in a cot does this, the rocking action usually moves the cot across the room and it then bangs repeatedly against the wall. The cot may need to be fixed in some way to stop it from moving.

Babies are at least six months old before these habits appear. If ignored, the habits rarely continue after the age of three years. Efforts to stop them are likely to make the habits continue for a longer time.

Some parents are worried by these habits. If seriously worried, they should discuss the matter with their doctor, health visitor or clinic.

Handling the genitals

Babies discover their genitals in the same way as they discover their toes, and they will touch and explore in the same way. Because handling the genitals is a natural thing for young children to do, there is no reason why they should be made to feel naughty or guilty. After all, the mother also touches these areas when she washes them.

A child is likely to play with the genitals less often if the parents ignore it or gently divert the child's attention to something else. Gradually, children come to understand that parents disapprove. From the age of six until puberty, children become less interested in sexual matters anyway.

Masturbation (handling the genitals for pleasure) only becomes a problem when done to excess. This may happen when a child masturbates for comfort because he is deeply unhappy, bored, lonely, worried or afraid. Telling children that it is naughty or wrong to do it only makes them more unhappy — and guilty as well.

To do

1. Choose one of the habits mentioned in this topic. Carry out a survey to find out how common the habit is in different age groups. If the habit has been discontinued, at what age did it stop?

2. *Discuss* 'Should parents try to stop comfort habits and if so, how?'

Child study

Describe any comfort habits the child may have.

Questions

1. a What is meant by a 'habit'?
b What habits are shown by the illustrations in this topic?
c Why are habits of this type called 'comfort habits'?
d As a child grows older, what may happen to these habits?

2. a Why is there no need to stop a young child from sucking his thumbs?
b If parents do try to stop the habit, what may be the result?
c When a 6-year-old still sucks his thumb, give one reason for trying to stop the habit.

3. a Give one reason for and one against the use of a dummy.
b When does the use of a dummy encourage tooth decay?
c (i) By what age will most children give up their dummy?
(ii) What may encourage its use after that?
d Give one reason why a child may be upset when his comforter is washed.

4. a Why may nail biting be considered a normal thing to do?
b When are children more likely to bite their nails?

c Is nail biting a harmful habit?
d Why does nagging or punishing the child rarely stop the habit?

5. a Name three rhythmical habits of young children.
b What is the usual age at which these habits occur?

6. a Are young children being 'naughty' when they touch their genitals?
b (i) What is masturbation? (ii) When may it be a problem?
c Give five possible causes for the problem.

30 Looking after other people's children

Parents sometimes make arrangements for their children to be looked after by other people. They may do this because:
- both parents have jobs outside the home;
- both parents may want to go out in the evening, or during the day;
- one parent is ill and the other is working;
- it is a one-parent family, and the parent has to go out to work, or for other reasons.

Who will care for the children?

Parents may use one or more of the following for the care of their children:
1. Relatives;
2. Child-minders: **a** registered, **b** unregistered;
3. Day nurseries;
4. Crèches;
5. Baby-sitters.

Relatives

A child who is looked after by a relative will usually be in the care of a person the child knows well. As a result, there are no problems of getting used to strangers and to different surroundings and ways of doing things.

Nowadays, grannies, aunts or other relatives are often not able to help. They may be very busy people with jobs, or else live too far away. So the parents have to find someone else to look after their child.

Child-minders

A **child-minder** is a person who looks after other people's children, under the age of five years, in her own home.

Choosing a child-minder   Any person who looks after a child has an influence on the way that child develops, so it is important for parents to choose child-minders carefully. They should:
- go to see several before making up their minds;
- always choose registered child-minders.

Parents should not expect the child-minder to look after a child who is ill. This is the time when the mother is needed. Also it is not fair on any other children in the child-minder's home, because a sick child needs a lot of extra attention and may be infectious.

Registered child-minders   Child-minders are required by law to register if they receive payment for looking after one or more children who are not related to them, for more than two hours a day.

A registered child-minder will have a **certificate** to show that the Social Services Department consider her to be a suitable person to look after children. She is expected to:

1. like children and give them the love and care that all young children need;
2. be healthy;
3. have a clean home;
4. have a safe, warm place for children to play;
5. have adequate toilet and kitchen facilities;
6. look after not more than three or four young children, including any under-fives of her own;
7. take them outside regularly, or have a garden in which they can play.

People who enjoy child-minding find that it gives them:
- the satisfaction of doing important work;
- the pleasure and interest of working with children;
- the chance to meet other families;
- the opportunity to earn a little money.

Day nurseries

Nurseries provide all-day care for children whose mothers have to go out to work or who are otherwise unable to care for the children themselves. These nurseries take in children whose ages range from a few weeks to five years. They are open every day from about 7.30 a.m. to 6 p.m., and are run by the Social Services Department with trained staff. The parents pay according to their means. There are only a limited number of places, so those who attend are mainly from families in real need of help with their children, for example, children of single-parent families, or those of mothers who have to go into hospital.

Some day nurseries are run by private organisations and these have their own rules, but they must be registered by the Social Services Department.

Crèches

A crèche is a place where children are cared for while their parents are occupied. It may provide all-day or part-day care. Large factories, hospitals, colleges and offices sometimes run a crèche for the children of their employees. A crèche can also be a place where mothers can leave their children while they are temporarily away, for example, shopping, attending a meeting or a religious service.

Baby-sitters

Baby-sitters are people who look after children in the children's own homes while the parents are out.

Although called baby-sitters, they may be required to look after children of any age. The sitters can be male or female; it does not matter which, as long as they are suitable people to be trusted with children.

The parents are usually only happy to leave their child or children when they feel that the baby-sitter can cope with any situation which may arise. A sitter for a young baby needs to be able to comfort a crying child, change a nappy and give a bottle. Whereas, for an older child, it is better if the sitter is someone the child knows and likes, who understands the behaviour of his age-group, and is agile enough to cope.

Baby-sitters provide a useful service. They allow parents to have a break from their children for a short while. This helps to remind them that they are husband and wife as well as parents. They are able to do things together and to go to places where children would not be welcome. Having a break from their children now and again, often helps parents to enjoy their children all the more. The children can also benefit from meeting new people, especially when they enjoy the baby-sitter's company.

Instructions for the baby-sitter

Bedtime routine   Most baby-sitting is done in the evenings, so the baby-sitter will need to know the bedtime routine:
- the time for bed;
- whether the light is to be left on or off;
- whether the bedroom door is to be left open or shut;
- the need for a favourite cuddly toy, or a drink, or biscuit, or cleaning the teeth, or a bedtime story.

Daytime baby-sitting   During the daytime, the baby-sitter needs to know about meals, the rules about watching television, where the children are and are not allowed to play, bath-time, and so on.

It helps baby-sitters to look after children if they are given information which includes:
- the child's usual routine (e.g. what time is bedtime);
- the words the child uses when asking for a drink, or special toy, or to go to the toilet;
- where to find the First-Aid kit;
- what to do in an emergency — how to contact the parents or neighbours, or the telephone number of the doctor;
- where to find refreshments such as milk, biscuits, coffee;
- how to use the television etc;
- the approximate time the parents are expected back.

To do

1. A mother is looking for a child-minder for her daughter Jane. Below is a list of questions the mother will ask herself.
- Is the child-minder a warm, welcoming person?
- Does she have a stable routine so that Jane will quickly get used to new surroundings?
- Will she give Jane nourishing food?
- Will the discipline be firm but kind?
- Are there toys to play with?
- Is the place clean?
- Is the child-minder registered?

In your opinion how many of the answers to these questions need to be 'Yes' for the mother to be able to leave Jane here with confidence? Give your reasons in each case.

2. What is a Baby-sitting Bank or Baby-sitting Circle? How do they operate?

3. Describe any baby-sitting that you have done. Say why you were needed to baby-sit. What information were you given? What problems did you have and how did you deal with them?

31 *Pre-school groups*

Pre-school groups include playgroups, nursery schools, nursery classes and mother and toddler groups. Attendance is voluntary, so the parents can decide whether their child goes to a pre-school group or not.

A pre-school group

A pre-school group does not take the place of home, it adds to it by providing a wider circle of adults and children to mix with and a wider range of activities. A good pre-school group provides for young children:
- **the opportunity to learn how to mix** with other children and adults and to enjoy their company;
- **facilities** which include space to run around, apparatus to climb, and toys, paints, paper, clay, etc.;
- **activities** such as stories, music, dancing, singing and games.

Children who benefit most   A pre-school playgroup is useful for almost all children, but it is particularly valuable for those who:
- are the only child in the family;
- have little chance to play with others of their own age group;
- live in a small flat;
- live in a high-rise block;
- have mothers who find them difficult to manage;
- have few toys at home;
- are from extremely poor homes;
- are from over-crowded homes;
- are neglected children — those whose parents do not bother to talk or read or play with them.

It has been noticed that children in the last four groups in the list are the least likely to attend a pre-school group.

When to start   A fairly independent two-year-old may settle into a pre-school group without any trouble. However at this age, many are still too dependent on their mother and timid with other adults and children.

By three years of age, most children benefit from mixing with others of about the same age. This is a good time for a child to start attending a playgroup or nursery school. Many children will want their mothers to stay with them for the first week or two, until they become used to being in a strange place and with a large group of people. If a child continues to be miserable and spends most of the time crying or thumb-sucking, then he is probably not yet ready to be left without his mother. Therefore he is not yet ready for playgroup or nursery school.

Playgroups

A **playgroup** is a group of young children who play together regularly under supervision. Many different play activities are provided for the children so that they can learn through play and at their own speed.

Playgroups take place in hired halls or private houses. They are run by parents who act as playgroup leaders or helpers, with one adult to every eight children. Playgroup leaders do not need to have any qualifications, but often they are people who have been trained to look after children, for example, teachers, nursery nurses, or mothers (and sometimes fathers) who have attended playgroup training courses.

Playgroups usually take place in the mornings for 2–3 hours, sometimes not every morning, and sometimes in the afternoon. The children attend on a regular basis, perhaps once or twice a week, perhaps every day. All playgroups must be registered with the Social Services Department. It is

Bob Bray/Preschool Playgroups Assoc.

Playgroup

also necessary for them to charge fees to cover the cost of hiring a room, paying the helpers and buying equipment. Sometimes the Social Services Department pays the fees for children in need.

Many playgroups belong to the Pre-School Playgroups Association (PPA). This voluntary organisation links together playgroups and mother and toddler groups. In England and Wales, this involves about half a million children and their families.

Mother and toddler groups

These are often held in the same halls as playgroups. They usually take place in the afternoons for about a couple of hours. The age range of the children is greater than that of playgroups — from young babies to those nearing school age (the 'rising-fives'). Unlike playgroups, the mothers (or fathers) must remain with their children. A small fee is charged to cover the cost of hiring the hall and for the equipment and refreshments.

Bob Bray/Preschool Playgroups Assoc.

Mother and toddler group

A mother and toddler group is an ideal situation for mothers to meet and chat while their children play. The youngsters can have fun exploring a world which is wider than home, and with different toys. At the same time, they have the opportunity to get used to playing with other children gradually. As the children get older and become happy to play without their mothers, they may reach the right stage to attend a playgroup.

Nursery schools

These are schools for children aged 2½–4 years, and the staff are trained nursery teachers or nursery nurses. Nursery schools are open on the same days as other schools and keep to the same term times. Although the school day is from about 9.30 a.m. to 3.30 p.m., most children attend for only half the day, either in the mornings or the afternoons. There are not enough nursery schools for all children and some of the schools have long waiting lists.

Nursery schools provide the same kind of activities as playgroups. Staff do not deliberately teach the children to read and count.

Nursery classes

A nursery class is a class for 3–4-year-olds in an ordinary school. It gives children the opportunity to begin school before the compulsory age of five. The teacher in charge may not always be trained for nursery teaching as in nursery schools.

To do

1. **a** Describe what the children are doing in the photographs shown on pp. 122 and 123.
b List other activities that are likely to be available to the children.
c Describe the activities of the adults.

2. Find out the whereabouts of pre-school groups in your district. If possible, arrange to visit one or more of the groups.

3. Find out more about the Pre-School Playgroups Association. Information can be obtained from a local playgroup or mother and toddler group, or from the headquarters (see p. 275).

Child study

If the child attends a pre-school group, talk with the child to try to discover what happens there and how the child feels about it.

Questions

1. **a** Give four examples of different types of pre-school group.
b What does a good pre-school group provides for young children?
c Which children are likely to benefit most from attending a playgroup?

2. **a** Why are many 2-year-olds not ready to attend a playgroup?
b What is generally a good age to start?
c What signs indicate that a child is probably not yet ready to be left without his mother?

3. **a** What is a playgroup?
b What do playgroups provide and for what purpose?
c Which other type of pre-school group provides the same kind of activities as playgroups?
d Comparing a nursery school with a nursery class (i) Which is part of an ordinary school? (ii) Which takes younger children? (iii) Which may not have teachers trained for nursery teaching?

4. Give the following information about playgroups and mother and toddler groups:
a To which organisation are these groups likely to be linked?
b Is attendance voluntary?
c Which of the groups has to be registered, and with whom?
d At which of these groups do parents remain with their children?
e Which group has a wider age-range of children?

32 Starting school

Education in Britain is compulsory from the age of five years. Children are legally required to attend school from the beginning of the term after their fifth birthday. Some schools take them earlier, either full-time or part-time.

Changes to the child's life

For a child, starting school is the next stage in becoming independent and building up a separate personality. Youngsters enter a new world alone and soon come to know more about it than their parents. They can decide what to tell them about it and what to keep to themselves. They find themselves in a large building with lots of unknown people. They join classes with other children of about the same age and they all share the attention of one adult. They are expected to keep to a time-table. New friends are made. The playground is shared with larger and older children. Some stay to dinner and must get used to school meals. All must abide by the rules and codes of behaviour necessary for the smooth running of larger organisations. These are great changes to a young child's life, apart from the necessity of being away from home and mother for a large part of the day.

Preparing a child for school

How can parents help?   Parents can help by talking to their children about school, and telling them what to expect, and by making it sound exciting. If the mother is sad at the thought of losing her child's companionship and of being left alone in the house, she should not show it. It may worry the child and make it difficult to settle at school. The child who is happy and secure at home, is least likely to have difficulties at school.

Whatever the size of the class, the teacher will not be able to give continuous attention to one particular child. Therefore, children who have been encouraged by their parents to 'stand on their own feet' are likely to find it easier to adjust to school than those who are used to the continuous attention of their parents.

Attending a pre-school group can help   A child who has been to a playgroup or nursery school will be used to:
- being away from home;
- being separated from his mother;
- mixing with other children;
- sharing the attention of an adult with other children;
- the noise and movement created by a large number of children.

Schools can help   Infant teachers are well aware that all children, to a greater or lesser degree, worry about starting school. They understand the big step the child takes when he moves from the small social world of home to the much larger social world of school. At school, he has to face all sorts of new situations without the support of his parents.

Many schools try to help new children settle into school life easily and happily, and they do this in a variety of ways. For example, they may:
- invite new children to visit the school in the term before starting;
- arrange 'staggered' starts so that only a few new children start on the same day;
- allow half-day schooling in the first few weeks;
- let parents stay in the classroom for a while;
- encourage parents to talk to the teacher about matters which affect the child. It helps the teacher to know about the other members of the child's family and any health or behaviour problems. It is also helpful for the teacher to know if the child is left-handed.

Bernie Brech

Useful skills

When children start school it helps them to fit into the new environment more easily if they have already acquired certain skills. For example, the ability to:
- say their name and address clearly;
- tie shoe laces;
- blow their nose;
- put on clothes;
- do up buttons;
- go to the toilet without help;
- wash their hands;
- eat with a knife, fork, etc.

Children in this age group like to be able to do the same things as others in the class. If they have already acquired the skills listed above by the time they start school, it will help them not to feel inferior or different from the other children. It also gives a degree of independence as they do not continuously have to seek the help of the teacher.

Helping children to do their best

Children do better at school when their parents:
- give them lots of love and security at home;
- are interested in what they do **and** talk to them about it;
- encourage them to enjoy all the activities;
- understand and support them when they have difficulties.

Bernie Brech

Questions

1. a At what age are children in Britain legally required to attend school?
b Name five ways in which children can be helped to settle into school life.

2. Name five ways in which attending a playgroup will help prepare a child for school.

3. Name eight useful skills to have learnt before starting school.

4. In what ways can parents help their children to do their best at school?

To do

1. a Give ten examples of how a child's life will change when he starts school.
b How would you suggest that parents prepare their child for these changes?

2. Compare the photographs on the right and on p. 126 with that on p. 122. How many differences can you notice between school and playgroup?

3. Visit an infant school (first school), if possible as a helper.
a Write an account of your visit.
b Watch the children arrive at school, leave school, and when in the playground. Observe their behaviour and note any interesting points. How did the children react when they were reunited with their parents after school?

Exercises

1 a Give two reasons why play is vital to a child's development.
b Suggest two ways in which parents can encourage their baby to learn to use his hands.
c Suggest three suitable playthings for a 10-month-old baby, and give reasons for your choice.
d Give reasons why water is a good play material.
e What is the value of a sand-pit in the garden to a 3-year-old child?
f Suggest two ways in which a 4-year-old can be encouraged to play with other children.
g The development of play follows a definite pattern starting with solitary play. Suggest, in order, two other stages through which play passes before group play occurs.
h Suggest two hygiene rules to teach toddlers.
i Give two reasons why new shoes for a toddler should be fitted correctly.
j A child is likely to be jealous of a new brother or sister. Suggest three ways of helping the older child to accept the new baby.
k Why should you not scold or make fun of a young child for sucking his thumb? Give two reasons.
l Suggest two ways of encouraging kindness in young children.

2 Describe fully a winter outfit for each of the following:
  (i)   a baby in a pram;
  (ii) a baby in a push-chair or buggy;
  (iii) a toddler in the garden;
  (iv) a five-year-old walking to school.
Give reasons for your choice.   (*WMEB*)

3 In early childhood, play is one of the principal ways of learning. Explain this statement by giving examples of how play activities help to develop:
  (i)   language,
  (ii) physical skills,
  (iii) social behaviour,
  (iv) intellect,
  (v)   imagination.   (*EAEB*)

4 A toy should provide safe, enjoyable play.
a Name five qualities of a good toy and give a reason why each of these qualities is important.
b A month-old baby needs visual stimulus. Suggest three things he/she can look at and explain what the baby will be learning.
c (i) Why does a one-year-old need toys to encourage physical development?
      (ii) Name two suitable toys and show how each will fulfil this need.
d Why might television be classed as a toy for a pre-school child?   (*SWEB*)

5 Playgroups and nursery schools provide opportunities for children to develop their minds, skills and personalities.
a List six advantages to the child of either playgroup or nursery school.
b How might a playgroup or nursery school help
  (i) a withdrawn child?
  (ii) an aggressive child?   (*EAEB*)

6 The following groups are all concerned with the care of the under-fives. Explain as fully as you can how each one is run, how it is paid for, and what are the similarities and differences between
a playgroups,
b nursery classes in infant schools,
c childminders.
Give three ways in which a mother can help her child to benefit from attending any one of these.   (*SEREB*)

7 The first day at school is an important landmark in a child's life. Suggest ways by which parents can help to make it a happy occasion. Use the following headings:
a The child's previous training and experience.
b Organisation on the day.   (*EAEB*)

8 a Describe carefully how a child behaves in a temper tantrum.
b Give reasons why a child is particularly liable to these outbursts at about two years of age.
c How should an adult treat a child in a temper tantrum? Suggest ways of helping the child to outgrow this difficult phase.   (*SEREB*)

9 Imagine that you and your friend are going to take two children of three and six years old out for the day. Remember that to a young child the world about him is full of wonder and delight, unless he is too tired, hungry or uncomfortable to enjoy it. Plan your day carefully, taking into account the following:
a Where will you go and why have you chosen this place?
b How will you make the actual journey enjoyable?
c What activities will the children find there? Will you need to take anything with you?
d What difficulties could arise and how will you plan to avoid them?   (*SEREB*)

Section 5

Food

Fiona Pragoff

33 Food

People take in food to satisfy feelings of hunger and because they enjoy eating and drinking. The body needs this food to provide materials:
1. For growth.
2. To replace worn out or damaged tissues.
3. For the wide range of chemical activities which take place inside it.
4. For energy for physical activities.
5. To give heat to keep the body warm.

Food substances

All foods consist of one or more of the seven types of substances listed below:
1. Proteins
2. Fats
3. Carbohydrates ⎫ these substances are called **nutrients**
4. Minerals
5. Vitamins
6. Fibre
7. Water

A few foods, for example white sugar, contain only one of the substances. The great majority of foods are a mixture of several substances.

A variety of foods needs to be eaten to provide the body with sufficient of each of the substances in order to grow and develop properly, to be active, and to keep healthy.

Protein foods

Animal proteins

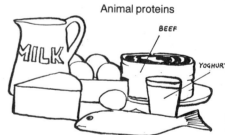

Proteins

Proteins are used to build the body and keep it in good repair. They are particularly important in childhood for building the brain, muscles, skin, blood and other tissues in order to make a strong healthy body. Protein foods can be obtained from both animals and plants.

Plant proteins

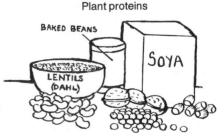

Carbohydrates

Carbohydrates provide energy. Starch and sugar are both carbohydrates. Some of the more common carbohydrate

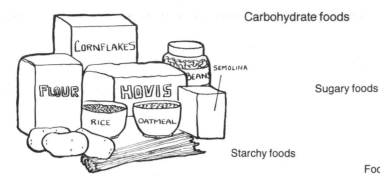

Carbohydrate foods

Starchy foods

Sugary foods

Foods rich in both starch and sugar

foods are shown here. They have been grouped according to whether they contain mainly starch, mainly sugar or are a mixture of both.

When more carbohydrate is eaten than the body can use, the remainder becomes changed into fat and is stored in the body until needed.

Fats

Fats may be in solid form like butter, or in a liquid form like oil, depending on the temperature. Generally, at room temperature animal fats are solid and plant fats are liquid and called oils. Margarine differs because, although made from oils, the oils are processed in such a way as to make a solid fat.

Fats provide energy. They have a much higher energy value than carbohydrates. That means, weight for weight, they contain more calories (see p. 269). Some foods consist almost entirely of fats and many popular foods contain large amounts of fat.

The body needs a certain amount of fat but when more is eaten than is used, the extra becomes stored as body fat.

Fats and oils

Minerals

Minerals are substances like calcium and iron which occur naturally in the earth. Fifteen minerals are known to be essential for various chemical activities which take place in the body. Some of these minerals are also used to build and repair certain tissues. The minerals are obtained in the following ways:
1. From foods derived from plants which absorb minerals from the soil.
2. From foods derived from animals which have eaten plants.
3. Because they are dissolved in drinking water.

Nearly all foods contain one or several minerals so they are rarely in short supply. The only minerals which are sometimes in short supply are calcium, iron and fluoride.

Calcium is essential for strong bones and teeth. Chief sources include milk, cheese, white bread, yoghurt, ice-cream, green vegetables.

Iron is essential for the formation of red blood cells. Chief sources are red meat, eggs, green vegetables, wholemeal bread.

Fluoride helps to produce strong, healthy teeth. If it is not present in the water supply, it can be given to children in tablet form and in toothpaste (see also Topic 39).

Other essential minerals include potassium, magnesium, phosphorus, sodium and chlorine.

Vitamins

Vitamins are complex chemical substances made by plants and animals. Generally, the human body cannot manufacture vitamins so they have to be obtained from food. They are needed for various chemical activities. Only very small quantities of each vitamin is required for the body to keep healthy and active. Vitamins so far discovered include:

Vitamin A is found mainly in foods containing fat, for example, milk, butter, margarine, fish liver oils. Carrots and green vegetables also provide vitamin A. Vitamin A is essential for being able to see in the dark and for a healthy skin.

The B vitamins   Vitamin B is now known to be not just one vitamin but a number of vitamins including **thiamin** (B_1), **riboflavin** (B_2) and **niacin** (also called **nicotinic acid** — nothing to do with nicotine). These vitamins occur in foods like wholemeal bread, oats, milk, butter, cheese, and liver. An exception is B_{12} which occurs only in animal products and never in food from plants. Generally, the B vitamins enable the body to obtain energy from food.

Vitamin C is found in fresh fruits and vegetables. Small amounts occur in milk, particularly breast milk. This vitamin easily disappears when fruit and vegetables are kept for a long time or when they are cooked. Vitamin C keeps gums healthy and helps wounds to heal.

Foods which contain vitamin C

Vitamin D can be obtained mainly from foods containing fat such as margarine, butter, herrings, eggs. It can also be made in the skin, when the skin is exposed to sunlight. Vitamin D is essential for healthy bones and teeth.

Fibre (roughage)

Fibre consists of plant material which cannot be digested. It is present in vegetables, fruit, wholemeal bread, pulses (peas, beans, lentils [dahl]) and breakfast cereals (oats, wheat, bran).

Fibre is an important part of the diet because by increasing bulk it encourages the movement of food through the intestine which helps to prevent constipation.

Water

Water is the main substance in the body and accounts for about two-thirds of its weight. It forms part of all the body tissues and is the liquid in which the chemical activities in the body take place.

Water is continuously being lost from the body in sweat, breath and urine. The water that is lost needs to be replaced. It enters the body as part of solid food as well as in drinks.

Questions

1. a Give five ways in which the body uses food.
b Name seven substances found in food.

2. What are proteins used for?
b (i) Name some foods which contain animal proteins. (ii) Name some which contain plant proteins.

3. a What type of substance are starch and sugar?
b (i) Name another type of food besides carbohydrate which supplies energy. (ii) Which of these substances has a higher energy value? (iii) What happens to these substances when more is eaten than is used?

4. Of these eight foods — olive oil, pastry, sweet biscuits, sweets, rice, butter, bacon, beans — which is mainly or completely (i) liquid fat, (ii) fat and protein, (iii) fat and carbohydrate, (iv) solid fat, (v) starch, (vi) carbohydrate and protein, (vii) sugar, (viii) sugar, starch and fat?

5. a Name eight minerals.
b Briefly, what is the difference between minerals and vitamins?
c (i) Name two minerals which are sometimes in short supply in the diet. (ii) Why is each essential? (iii) From what foods can each be obtained?

6. a Which two vitamins are found mainly in foods containing fat?
b Which vitamin is only found in animal products?
c Which vitamin can be made in the skin?
d (i) Which vitamin is found in fresh fruit and vegetables? (ii) Why do they have to be fresh?

To do

1. Draw or find pictures to add to your note-book of two or more examples of foods containing:
a protein,
b fat,
c starch,
d sugar,
e calcium,
f iron,
g vitamin A,
h the B vitamins,
i vitamin C,
j vitamin D.

2. Read the information on margarine containers, breakfast cereals packets, etc. to find out what ingredients they contain. Add the labels to your notes or copy them.

34 *Diet*

Parents who care about their children will want to feed them well to give them a good start in life.

Sensible feeding begins during pregnancy when the expectant mother eats sufficient protein, fresh fruit and vegetables, to supply enough nourishment for herself and the developing baby. After the birth, the baby is fed entirely on milk for the first few months, then is weaned on to other foods. The child will then get nourishment from a variety of foods containing different types and amounts of nutrients. A child who is to grow into a healthy adult needs a balanced diet.

A balanced diet

The word 'diet' means the usual type of food that is eaten. For example, a young baby has a diet of milk, whereas the diet of an older child is a mixture of foods. 'Going on a diet' is rather different. When someone 'goes on a diet', that person is restricted to eating certain foods, perhaps because of an illness such as diabetes, or in order to lose or gain weight.

A **balanced diet** is one which contains enough of all the necessary food substances. This does not mean that every meal has to be 'balanced', or that the right amounts of each of the seven substances listed on p. 130 have to be eaten each day. It means that over the course of several days, the body needs to take in enough of the right kinds of food substances to grow and to stay healthy. Children who eat a balanced diet are more likely to:

- develop a strong, well-formed body;
- have energy to enjoy life and to keep warm;
- keep healthy;
- grow to their full potential height (the height which their genes will allow).

A rough guide to a balanced diet   Parents do not need to worry too much about giving their child a balanced diet. If they offer a variety of food during the day, the child will eat what his body needs.

Generally speaking, a child should have each day:

- at least one pint of milk;
- an egg;
- one helping of meat, poultry, fish, cheese or beans;
- vegetables — raw or cooked;
- fruit;
- bread, wholegrain cereals, potatoes.

Variations — likes and dislikes   The list above is only a rough guide. A good diet can be obtained in a number of ways. For example:

- A child who won't eat meat or fish can get sufficient protein from milk, eggs, cheese, beans, peas and nuts.

- Some children do not like vegetables. They will come to no harm as long as other foods containing minerals, vitamins and fibre are eaten.

- Other children do not like fruit, but they may like fruit juice drinks such as blackcurrant or rose hip.

- Children who do not like drinking milk can be given it in the form of milk puddings, custard, yoghurt, cheese or ice-cream.

The cost of good food   Good feeding does not have to be expensive. Nourishing foods are often less expensive than the high calorie foods mentioned (p. 136). When a mother knows which foods are nourishing (i.e. supply proteins, vitamins and minerals) she is able to serve good meals, which may well cost less than meals of poorer quality.

An unbalanced diet

The diet can be unbalanced because of shortage of food, too much food or lack of essential substances in the food. Children whose health could be improved by more food or better food are suffering from **malnutrition**. Such children fail to thrive, lack energy, and are unable to resist trivial infections. (See also Topic 4.)

Deficiency diseases

When particular items in the diet are absent or in short supply (are deficient), illnesses called **deficiency diseases** develop.

Examples of deficiency diseases

Shortage	Deficiency disease
Iron or Vitamin B_{12}	**Anaemia** The lack of red pigment (haemoglobin) in the blood results in a shortage of oxygen throughout the body and feelings of 'no energy'.
Calcium or Vitamin D	**Rickets** Children's bones do not form properly, are soft and weak and bend under pressure.
Vitamin C	**Scurvy** The gums become soft and bleed. Teeth become loose, and wounds fail to heal properly.
Vitamin A	**Night blindness** (not being able to see in the dark). There is also reduced resistance to diseases, especially those affecting the skin.
Protein	**Kwashiorkor** This is a disease of malnutrition. The starving children have pot-bellies which are swollen with water.

High calorie foods

There are some foods which are high in calories but have very little other nutritional value. They contain a great deal of sugar, starch or fat and include sweets, chocolate, cakes, biscuits and pastry. Children often love them because they are sweet and easy to eat. There is no reason why they should not be part of the diet in small amounts.

When this type of food is eaten in large amounts, a child has less appetite for more nourishing foods. Too much high calorie food may also cause a child to put on too much weight.

Obesity (fatness)

Fat babies and children are often not healthy. They take less exercise and are more likely to pick up infections such as bronchitis. Being overweight is caused by eating more food than the body needs.

Overeating is a habit which, once acquired, is difficult to break. Children (like adults) vary in the amount of food they can eat before getting fat and some seem to put on weight very easily. The tendency to be overweight often seems to run in families. So also does the tendency to give children lots of high calorie foods.

Questions

1. a What is the difference between 'diet', a 'balanced diet' and 'going on a diet'?

b Give four reasons for having a balanced diet.

2 a Suggest a rough guide for a balanced diet.

b If a child does not like drinking milk, in what other forms can milk be given?

c A child in a vegetarian household would not be given meat or fish. What other foods could supply the child with sufficient protein?

d What can children who do not like fruit be given instead?

3. a Give three ways in which a diet may be unbalanced.

b What causes a deficiency disease?

c What items in the diet are in short supply when the following deficiency diseases develop (i) anaemia, (ii) rickets, (iii) scurvy, (iv) night blindness, (v) kwashiorkor?

4 a Name five high calorie foods.

b Name two disadvantages of giving a child large amounts of high calorie food.

c Name two possible effects of obesity on health.

To do

1 Complete the chart below to show the types of food substances present in the eight meals shown above. Information about the foods can be obtained from Topic 33. Place a tick in the appropriate column if the food substance is present.

2 Find out more about kwashiorkor and the effects of starvation on children.

Child study

Describe the child's diet. What types of food does the child like and dislike?

Description of meal	protein	carbo-hydrate	fat	calcium	iron	vitamin A	B vitamins	vitamin C	vitamin D	fibre
1 Cheese sandwiches, ice cream										
2										

35 *Weaning*

Weaning is the gradual change-over from a diet of milk to a variety of foods. Most of the foods are solid rather than liquid.

Milk is the perfect food for the first few months of life. As babies get older, they begin to need foods containing starch and fibre. They also need more vitamins and minerals, particularly iron, than are present in milk alone in order to continue growing and developing properly.

When to start weaning

It takes several months for a baby's digestive system to develop fully. For example, starch cannot be readily digested until the infant is a few months old. There is no point in weaning a baby until he is able to make proper use of the food. The danger of weaning too early is that the baby may become too fat, develop allergies to food, or suffer from indigestion.

The time to begin weaning is when the baby is 3 to 4 months old and still seems hungry and restless after a good milk feed or wakes early for his next feed and starts to suck his fists.

Weaning should not be a battle

New foods should be introduced one at a time. Even at this young age, babies make it clear whether they enjoy the taste or not. Babies are like adults in preferring some foods to others. If they are forced to eat a particular food it can easily lead to a feeding problem (see Topic 37). When a baby appears not to like a food, it is wise to wait for a week or two before offering it again. By this time there might be a change of mind.

Stages in weaning

Starting to wean   Young babies cannot yet chew. They also have difficulty in swallowing and digesting lumps. So solid food such as cereals, fruit, vegetables and meat needs to be ground up finely to remove the lumps. It is then mixed with milk or other suitable liquid to make a thickened liquid which can be given to the baby on a spoon.

Ways of removing lumps from food

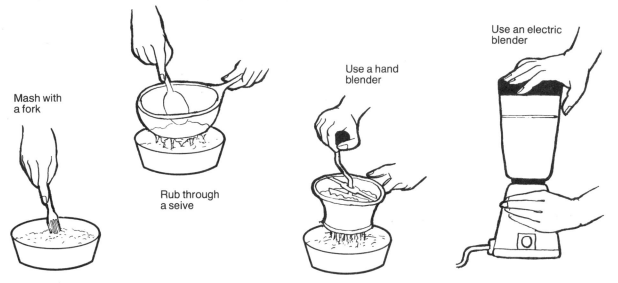

Mash with a fork

Rub through a seive

Use a hand blender

Use an electric blender

A small amount of such food once a day is enough to start with. Soon the baby comes to expect a little with each milk feed and the amount gradually increases. Different sorts of food should be given so that the baby gets used to a variety of flavours. Examples are 'baby' rice mixed with milk, mashed potato with gravy, mashed banana, vegetables which have been made into a purée, meat stew which has been put through a blender.

Giving solid foods   Most babies learn to chew at about six months, whether they have teeth or not. It is then important for them to be given hard foods such as crusts and rusks on which to chew. A baby who is not encouraged to chew at this age may refuse to do so a few months later.

A baby who is able to chew can be given solid foods such as sandwiches, toast, chocolate, cheese, whole banana, boiled egg and a wide variety of other foods. There is no need to wait until the baby has a mouthful of teeth before giving such foods. However, the tougher foods such as meat should be cut into small pieces first.

Reducing the amount of milk   As the amount of solid food increases, the need for milk decreases. Usually, by the age of nine months to one year, a baby has given up the breast or bottle and is fully weaned on to a diet of mainly solid foods. He can then be eating food that is not very much different from the rest of the family. A pint of milk is still needed each day, but it can be given in different forms such as milk puddings, etc.

Drinking from a cup   A 6-month-old baby can be given cow's milk. It need not be boiled as long as it is pasteurised and fresh. Although breast- or bottle-feeding may continue until the baby is 9–10 months or older, the number of feeds becomes less and eventually stops. Cup-feeding usually begins about 5–6 months of age. Milk from a cup gradually replaces that from the breast or bottle.

It is quite common for babies suddenly to refuse to take any more milk from breast or bottle. Other babies are reluctant to give up the bottle. They drink readily from a cup during the day, but still like a bottle before going to bed. After the age of one year, the older the baby gets, the more difficult it becomes for him to give up his bottle.

Weaning foods

Tins, jars and packets of baby foods can be very useful for weaning. They are quick and easy to prepare, convenient when only small quantities are required, and very useful when travelling. These commercially prepared foods provide good nourishment and come in an increasingly wide variety.

Commercially prepared foods should not replace fresh foods and home-prepared foods altogether. Babies can try most foods served to the rest of the family. This provides a greater range of tastes and textures than is found in the commercially prepared foods and makes eating more interesting. More important, the baby gets used to eating the same food as other members of the family.

Gluten is a type of protein found in wheat and rye. A few babies are unable to digest gluten and this only becomes apparent when they are being weaned. These children have a very rare condition called **coeliac disease**. They need to have a gluten-free diet, and cannot eat foods containing wheat and rye flour.

Questions

1. a What is meant by 'weaning'?
b When is the right time to begin weaning, and what signs does the baby give?
c Name two food substances that babies need as they get older.
d Name one mineral that is supplied by foods other than milk.
e Name three possible dangers of weaning too early.

2. a Give two reasons why young babies should not be given lumpy food.
b Describe ways of removing lumps from food.
c (i) What is the advantage of giving babies a variety of foods? (ii) Name some suitable foods.
d (i) When may it be convenient to use the weaning foods in the photograph on p. 141? (ii) Give two reasons why such foods should not replace fresh food altogether.

3. a By what age can most babies chew?
b Name foods that babies may be given when they can chew.
c Do babies need to have teeth before they are given the foods mentioned in **b**?

4. a At what age does cup-feeding usually begin?
b (i) At what age can babies be given cow's milk?
c By what age is it usual for babies to be fully weaned?

To do

1. The Do's and Don'ts listed in the table on the right are included in the Health Education Council's pamphlet entitled 'Starting Your Baby on Solid Food'. Take each item in the lists in turn and give reasons why it can be considered sensible advice.

2. Collect some advertisements or labels from jars, tins and packets of weaning foods to show the variety of such foods on sale. Read the information on the containers and comment on any points of interest. Taste some of the foods and give your opinion of the taste, saltiness and sweetness.

Do	Don't
Give your baby a variety of foods for a variety of tastes.	Don't add salt or sugar to feeds.
Mash or sieve all your baby's food at first.	Don't give cereal at more than one meal a day.
Feed at your baby's pace rather than yours.	Don't give your baby food that's too hot.
Give extra water, especially in hot weather. There's no need to sweeten it.	Don't give sweet foods or drinks between meals.
	Don't leave your baby when eating.

Weaning foods

36 Mealtimes

Mealtimes are more than just times when food is eaten. They should be social occasions as well.

Food and emotions

A young baby is unhappy when hungry and happy when fed. A mother feeding her baby is providing happiness and love. So the baby comes to link food with happiness and love. These feelings help towards the development of a bond of affection between mother and child.

Gradually, during weaning, babies want to feed themselves and to decide what they eat. Children who are allowed to feed themselves and to eat as much or as little as they want, will continue to enjoy mealtimes and to link them with love and affection. However, if every mealtime is a battle over what is eaten or how it is eaten, then food will become linked with bad-temper, wilfulness and fussiness. This can create a problem which may last throughout childhood and even longer.

Happy mealtimes   When mealtimes are happy occasions:
- the child eats the food without a fuss;
- the parents and child will enjoy being together at this time;
- they will have the opportunity to talk **and** listen to each other.

A mother can do much to encourage her young child to enjoy meal times by:
- serving food attractively;
- varying the food;
- serving small portions, with more to follow if wanted;
- avoiding foods with very strong flavours;
- setting a good example by eating proper meals herself;
- making mealtimes happy social occasions by sitting down at the table with her child and other members of the family.

'Fussy about food'   Encouraging a child to eat a variety of foods and not be fussy has three advantages:
1. he is likely to have a balanced diet;
2. he will find it much easier to eat the food provided when away from home;
3. mealtimes will be happier occasions.

No one, apart from his mother, will have much sympathy for a child who is fussy about food and difficult to feed. He will be regarded as a nuisance and be considered 'difficult'.

Table manners

When babies start to feed themselves, they have no understanding of table manners. At this stage, hands are used as well as spoons to get the food to the mouth. Food is also regarded as something to play with. Babies will undoubtedly make a mess.

During their second year, they learn how to use spoons and cups without spilling the contents. At this stage, they also come to understand that mothers do not approve when they get food all over the place. They are now old enough to learn how to behave at the table. They will begin to copy the table manners of those around them, chiefly the manners of their parents. These are the manners they will have throughout childhood and often for the rest of their lives.

Some hints about feeding

Babies like to be with the family at mealtimes. They enjoy company and they also learn how to behave with food.
Babies like to feed themselves. It is messy, but much more interesting for the baby.
When everything is washable, there is no need to worry about the mess. The chair, harness and tray should be easy to wipe and, if necessary, a plastic covering should be placed on the floor.
A catch-all bib saves a great deal of mess.
Babies know when they have had enough to eat, so never try to persuade or force the baby to eat more.
Babies need to eat at their own pace. This might be very slow and the mother needs a great deal of patience!

Questions

1. How can the mother encourage the child to enjoy mealtimes?

2. Give six hints about feeding.

3. Name three advantages of encouraging a child *not* to be fussy about food.

4. a Why do babies make a mess when feeding?
b When children become old enough to learn table manners, who do they copy?

To do

1. Make a list of as many different table manners as you can think of. For each, decide whether you consider it to be 'good manners', 'bad manners' or whether it 'does not matter', and why.

2. Read the section 'Food and emotions'. Comment on any examples you have come across where you think food and emotions are linked.

3. *Discuss* 'Are mealtimes social occasions or just the time for eating food?'

Child study

Describe the child's behaviour at mealtimes.

37  *Refusal to eat*

The commonest feeding problem in healthy children is **food refusal**. The child refuses to eat as much food as the parents think is needed. Consequently they become very worried about the 'poor appetite'.

Although this is a common problem in Britain, it does not occur in countries where food is scarce. Even in Britain, it is almost never a problem in poor homes where there are lots of children, nor in homes where no fuss about eating is made.

Food refusal

Children with this problem are usually between the age of nine months and four years. It arises from a combination of factors including the following:

1. Children of this age love fuss and attention and have a strong desire to feel important.
2. The baby's rate of growth slows down during the first year and so does the rate of increase of appetite. This is the time of weaning and the mother is probably expecting the child to eat larger and larger quantities of food.
3. Children go through a stage when it is natural for them to refuse to co-operate, and they have learnt to say 'NO'.
4. Children tend to dawdle over their meals and like to play with food. They have no sense of time and will not hurry so that their mother can clear away.
5. Appetites vary. Some children (like some adults) have small appetites. The size of the appetite also depends on whether the child has been very active out of doors, or spent his time quietly indoors.

Do not try to force feed It is unnecessary to try to force a child to eat and attempts will not succeed. No **healthy** children ever starve if left to please themselves how much they eat, but they will enjoy making a great deal of fuss if forced to eat. Typical ways of mistakenly trying to make a child eat include:

- pushing food into the mouth
- coaxing
- nagging
- bribing
- threatening
- smacking

Examples from a doctor's casebook*

Worried parents consulted the doctor about the following feeding problems:

- A ten-month-old baby whose mother, father, aunt and two uncles crept about the room after him with spoonfuls of food, trying to get him to eat something.
- The child who would only eat when his father's car passed the window. As a result, the father had to drive the car backwards and forwards so that each time it passed the window, the mother could put a spoonful of food in the baby's mouth.
- One boy refused to eat unless he was given a toy motor car, and his mother said he had acquired nearly 300 cars in that way.
- A mother who said she never went anywhere without a bag of biscuits in her handbag, so that if her son ever said he would eat something she could give him one.

Advice to parents In **all** the above cases, similar advice was given.
1. There is nothing wrong with the child's appetite. The trouble lies with the parents.
2. When the child is given food, the parents must not appear to show that they care whether it is eaten or not. There should be no anxious looks at the plate, and no remarks about it.
3. A child who refuses to eat at mealtimes should not be given any food in between meals.
4. Healthy children never let themselves starve; they will quickly learn to eat if left alone to decide for themselves.

* These examples are given in the book 'Babies and Young Children', Illingworth and Illingworth, by courtesy of Churchill Livingstone.

Questions

1. **a** In Britain, what is the commonest feeding problem in healthy children?
b What is the usual age of children with this problem?
c In what type of homes is this problem unlikely to exist?

2. Name five factors commonly involved in food refusal.

3. Describe six ways in which parents may try to make a child eat.

4. What advice did the doctor give to worried parents who consulted him about feeding problems?

To do

1. Which of the ways listed under the heading 'Do not try to force feed' is illustrated by each of the pictures opposite and below?

2. Have you come across a food refusal problem in a young child? (Do not confuse 'food refusal' with 'fussy eating'.) Describe the problem. Read the section opposite headed 'Food refusal'. In your opinion, how many of these factors, if any, were involved in the problem you described?

38 *Food hygiene*

Food hygiene is concerned with the care, preparation and storage of food in order to prevent food poisoning. Most food poisoning is due to eating food which has been contaminated by bacteria to such an extent that it upsets the stomach and intestines causing gastro-enteritis. Gastro-enteritis is particularly serious in babies and young children (see Topic 19), and food hygiene is therefore of special importance in Child Care. The two golden rules of food hygiene are:

1. Keep food clean.

2. Keep food cold.

This topic deals only with food poisoning caused by bacteria — often referred to as **food poisoning germs**. Bacteria are too small to be seen with the naked eye and food which contains them often looks, smells and tastes good enough to eat. Several types of bacteria are able to cause food poisoning and three of the commonest types are dealt with in more detail on page 266.

Symptoms of food poisoning

The symptoms of food poisoning are diarrhoea, pains in the abdomen, and sometimes vomiting. Illness usually starts sometime between two hours and two days after eating contaminated food, although it can be almost immediate if the food is badly contaminated. The illness usually lasts for 1–2 days, but sometimes a week or more.

Treatment   The general treatment is to eat nothing but to drink plenty of water to replace the loss of fluid from the body. A special mixture of salts such as 'Dioralyte' can be added to the water. This replaces the salts lost from the body and aids recovery. Kaolin mixture to treat the diarrhoea can be given to older children.

Babies with food poisoning need medical attention. Older children need medical attention if they are not recovering after 24 hours.

How bacteria get into food

Bacteria get into food as a result of contact with:
- dirty hands;
- dirty sinks and draining boards;
- dirty work surfaces;

- dirty dish cloths and sponges;
- dirty towels and drying-up cloths;
- dirty utensils — pots, pans, crockery, cutlery, glassware;
- uncooked meat and poultry;
- coughs and sneezes;
- fingers or spoons which have been licked when preparing food;
- flies;
- septic cuts and sores;
- rats, mice and their droppings.

Bacteria thrive in warm, moist foods particularly those containing protein, for example, both cooked and uncooked meat and poultry, gravy, egg dishes, milk and cream cakes. When such food is kept warm, any bacteria present quickly grow and multiply to become a possible source of food poisoning.

Bacteria multiply by dividing into two and when conditions are right they can do so every twenty minutes. The new bacteria grow quickly and twenty minutes later they are ready to divide again to produce more bacteria. After several hours, very large numbers will have built up in the food.

Prevention of food poisoning

1 Keep food cold   Low temperatures prevent any bacteria which may be present from multiplying.

Refrigeration   The temperature at which refrigerators are usually kept is between 1°C and 4°C, which is too low for food poisoning bacteria to grow. Some other types of microbe are able to grow at temperatures as low as this, but only very slowly. This is why food left in a refrigerator for a long time gradually turns bad.

Cooked food which is to be kept for the next day should be rapidly cooled before placing in a refrigerator. Any bacteria present will not then have a chance to grow and multiply to dangerous levels.

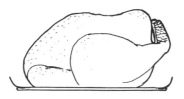

Freezing   When food is frozen, any food poisoning bacteria or other types of germ it contains are unable to grow. However, they are not killed by the cold and when the food warms up they become active again.

2 Keep food covered Food needs to be covered to protect it from dust, dirt and flies. Dust and dirt are quite likely to contain food poisoning bacteria. Flies can carry bacteria in their saliva and droppings as well as on their feet and hairy bodies, especially when they come from rubbish dumps and manure heaps in which they breed.

3 Hands should be washed and then dried on a clean towel before preparing food Particular care to do this thoroughly should be taken after using the lavatory or dealing with nappies because large numbers of bacteria capable of causing food poisoning live in the bowel.

4 Keep the kitchen clean – floors, work surfaces, sinks, cooking utensils, waste-bin, dishcloths, drying-up cloths, etc. Remember, food poisoning bacteria can exist in dirt.

5 Cover any boils or septic cuts with a waterproof dressing. Germs which cause these can also cause food poisoning.

6 Do not sneeze or cough over food Food poisoning bacteria often live harmlessly in the nose and throat.

7 Do not lick the fingers or smoke when handling food This will prevent bacteria from the mouth reaching the food.

148

8 Do not put uncooked meat next to cooked food

Uncooked meat, especially poultry, sometimes contains food poisoning bacteria which could be transferred to the cooked meat.

9 Keep rats and mice away
Remember that food poisoning bacteria live in their intestines and are found in their droppings.

10 Keep away from the kitchen when suffering from diarrhoea or sickness
and do not handle food. The cause may be food poisoning and the bacteria could easily be passed on to other people.

Questions

1. **a** What are the two golden rules of food hygiene?
b Why may food poisoning bacteria be eaten accidentally?
c What are the symptoms of food poisoning?
d What is the treatment?

2. **a** Name some types of food in which bacteria thrive.
b What happens when these foods are kept warm?

3. A collection of 1000 bacteria is just visible as a tiny speck. If a speck of dirt containing 1000 food poisoning bacteria got into a feeding bottle, and the feeding bottle was kept in a warm place, how many germs would be present after (i) 4 hours, (ii) 8 hours?

4. Name ten ways of helping to prevent food poisoning, giving one reason for each.

To do

1. Read the section 'How bacteria get into food'. List the ways shown in this Topic by which food can be contaminated.

2. **a** Find out more about the bacteria which cause food poisoning. Page 266 gives some information.
b Although bacteria in food is the most common cause of food poisoning, there are other causes. Find out about these.

3. Find out about some actual cases of food poisoning from newspaper reports or other sources.

39 Teeth

Although the teeth of a new-born baby cannot be seen, they are already developing inside the gums. They usually start to appear some time during the first year, the average age being 6 months. The mother need not worry if her baby is late in teething. The teeth will come through when they are ready and there is nothing that can be done to hurry them up.

Order of appearance

Milk teeth   There are 20 teeth in the first set which are called the milk teeth or baby teeth. The first to come through are usually the 2 teeth in the front of the lower jaw. A month or two later they are followed by the 2 teeth at the front of the upper jaw. All the milk teeth will have appeared by the age of 2½–3 years. The figure below shows the order in which the milk teeth generally appear.

Occasionally, a baby is born with a tooth that has already come through. It may need to be removed if it is so loose in the gum that it is in danger of falling out and getting stuck in the baby's windpipe. If the tooth is removed, there will be a gap in that position until the second set of teeth appear several years later.

From the age of 5 onwards, the milk teeth begin to fall out. Before they do this, their roots disappear.

Colgate Professional Dental Services

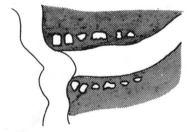

The milk teeth can be seen developing inside the jaw

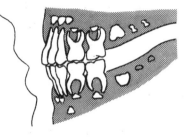

The milk teeth are all through. The permanent teeth are developing underneath

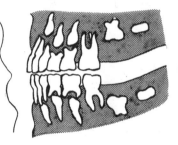

The milk teeth at the front of both jaws (the incisors) have been replaced by permanent teeth, and the first molars are also through. The roots of the remaining milk teeth are beginning to disappear

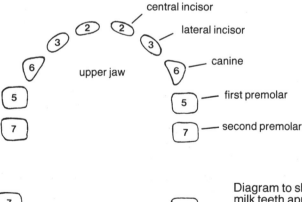

central incisor
lateral incisor
canine
first premolar
second premolar

upper jaw

lower jaw

Diagram to show the usual order in which the milk teeth appear

Permanent teeth   The milk teeth are replaced by the permanent teeth and they start to come through when children are about 6 years old. The 20 milk teeth are replaced by larger teeth of the same type. In addition, there are 12 molars — 3 on each side of each jaw. When complete, the permanent set contains 32 teeth.

The first permanent teeth to appear are usually the lower incisors and the first molars. The latter are often called the '6-year molars'. Although the new teeth may appear looking crooked, they usually right themselves in time. Otherwise they may need to be corrected by dental treatment, e.g. the wearing of a brace.

Teething

Some babies cut their teeth with no trouble at all. Other babies may be cross and irritable at such times. Babies may show one or more of the following signs that their teeth are on the way:

Sore gums   As a tooth grows, it has to pass through the gum. This process may cause the gums to become sore and painful, making the baby refuse food.

Increased dribbling   Babies seem to dribble more than usual when a tooth is about to come through.

Increased fist-chewing   Some babies seem to chew their fists more than usual when they are teething.

Red cheek   A bright red patch on one cheek is often linked with a new tooth.

Help for teething babies

A baby who is troubled by teething needs to be cuddled and comforted. Efforts should be made to divert the baby's attention, for example, by giving him something different to play with, going for a walk, some music or, if old enough, a story.

The baby may get relief from chewing something hard. For this reason, babies who are teething are given teething rings, crusts or rusks on which to chew. Teething jelly is unnecessary. It quickly washes off and, if too much is used, may poison the child.

The advice of a doctor is needed for a child who is in severe pain or very fretful at nights.

Teething does not cause illness

Although teething may make a baby feel wretched, it will not cause illness. There is no way that teething can cause bronchitis, rashes, diarrhoea, fever or convulsions. If any of these conditions appear at the time that the teeth are coming through, they will **not** be due to teething and need the prompt attention of a doctor.

Effect of diet on teeth

Items in the diet which build strong, healthy teeth are calcium, fluoride and the vitamins A, C and D.

Chewing helps to keep the teeth and gums healthy. Therefore the diet should include foods which need chewing such as crusts, apples and carrots.

Fluoride combines chemically with the enamel of the teeth, making them stronger and more resistant to decay. Children living in areas where the water supply contains fluoride have only about half as much tooth decay as those living in other areas.

When the water supply lacks fluoride, many doctors and dentists recommend that children should be given fluoride tablets daily. If the child is too young to swallow these, they can be crushed and mixed with food. The use of toothpaste containing fluoride also helps to protect the teeth.

Sweet and sticky foods   The eating of large amounts of sugar encourages tooth decay. This is especially so when sugary foods are eaten between meals and in a form which sticks to the teeth.

Tooth decay

The mouth always contains bacteria. However well the teeth are cleaned, some bacteria are always left in the mouth. The bacteria themselves do no harm, and indeed, they are essential to keep the mouth healthy.

Bacteria + sugar = tooth decay

When the bacteria in the mouth come into contact with sugar they produce acid. It is the acid which dissolves away the enamel and makes holes in the teeth. Sugar remains in the mouth for about half an hour after eating something sweet or even longer if a piece of food such as sticky toffee becomes caught up in the teeth. The longer time that sugar is in the mouth the greater the chances of tooth decay.

The chances of tooth decay are reduced if sweets, chocolates, iced lollies and other sugary foods are only given to a child on special occasions. It is also important for them to be eaten all at one go and not nibbled at over several hours.

Cleaning the teeth

Children can be taught to clean their teeth from the age of one year old. They should learn to brush them up and down and not across. Also, the inner side of the teeth and the biting surface of those at the back need to be cleaned as well. The teeth should be brushed before going to bed and preferably after meals as well.

Visiting the dentist

If children are taken to the dentist regularly from the age of 3–4 years, they get used to it. They are then likely to go more happily when they are older and the permanent teeth have come through. They will need to have these teeth checked regularly by the dentist if they want to take care of them. The dentist will be able to put right small defects before they can cause great trouble. Two words used by the dentist are:

- **caries** – the name for tooth decay;
- **plaque** – an almost invisible layer that is forming on the teeth all the time. Plaque is composed mostly of bacteria and materials from saliva. Cleaning the teeth removes plaque and leaves the teeth looking white and shiny.

Questions

1. a What is the average age at which teeth start to appear?
b How many milk teeth are there?
c By what age have all the milk teeth appeared?
d Using information from the figure on p. 150, complete the following chart to show the usual order in which the milk teeth appear.

1	Central incisors of lower jaw
2	

2. a At what age do the milk teeth begin to fall out?
b What part of a milk tooth disappears before the tooth falls out?

c What are the '6-year molars'?
d How many permanent teeth are there?

3. a Name four signs of teething shown by some children.
b Name five types of illness which are not due to teething.
c Describe ways in which a baby who is troubled by teething can be helped.

4. **a** Name two minerals and three vitamins which help to build strong, healthy teeth.
b How does fluoride strengthen teeth?
c If the water supply lacks fluoride, name two ways in which this mineral can be given to children.

5. **a** How is acid produced in the mouth?
b What effect does acid have on the teeth?
c How long does sugar remain in the mouth after eating something sweet?
d How can the chances of tooth decay be reduced?

6. **a** How should children be taught to brush their teeth?
b What is the advantage of taking a 3-year-old to the dentist?
c What is meant by (i) caries, (ii) plaque?

District General Hospital, Gorleston, Norfolk

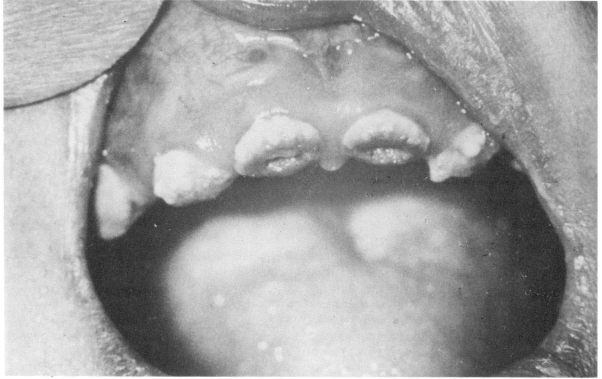

To do

The photograph shows the milk teeth of a 3-year-old girl who was very fond of sweetened blackcurrant juice. Every time she was thirsty or needed comforting, day or night, she was given this drink.
a Describe the appearance of the teeth.

b What might account for their condition? Give your reasons.
c What advice would you give to parents to prevent this situation from happening to their children's teeth?
d Are the teeth in the photograph incisors, canines or premolars?

Child study

Find out about the child's teeth. How many are there? Has there been any teething trouble? If old enough, does the child clean his teeth? or go to the dentist?

Exercises

1 a Give two reasons why milk is good for growing children.
b Suggest three ways in which milk can be made attractive to a 4-year-old.
c At about what age does a toddler have all his milk teeth? How many of them are there?
d At about what age will a child's second set of teeth begin to come through? How many of these will there be?
e What is meant by a 'deficiency disease'? Give two examples.
f Assuming that the child has not much appetite, what arrangements would you make for meals?
g What is meant by (i) weaning, (ii) malnutrition, (iii) obesity?

2 Three feeding problems with young children are: (i) Refusing to eat,
    (ii) Spitting out food,
    (iii) Throwing food around.
Possible causes of a feeding problem are that the child:

- does not like the food
- is not hungry
- is bored
- is tired
- is unwell
- has sore gums
- wants to play
- is being given food which is too hot
- is being given food in large pieces
- wants a change of flavour

a For each of the problems, give what you consider to be the three most likely causes from the list above.
b Give one other cause of feeding problems not listed above.

3 By four months of age a baby is ready to start mixed feeding.
a What essential nutrients are lacking in milk?
b What are the first foods that should be added to his diet to compensate for this?
c Describe in detail how he should be introduced to mixed feeding.
d Why is it important that he continues to get plenty of milk?
e Suggest three reasons why he should take his meals with the family as soon as he can sit up comfortably in his high chair. (*SREB*)

4 Young children are often difficult. Suggest possible reasons and the best course of action for each of the following situations.
a A 3-year-old frequently refuses to eat his mid-day meal.
b A 4-year-old defies the baby-sitter, refusing to go to bed at the time his parents instructed.
c A 2½-year-old in the supermarket with his mother, stamps his feet and screams for some sweets. (*EAEB*)

5 Explain fully how to deal with four of the following:
a temper tantrums;
b aggressiveness;
c bed-wetting;
d food faddiness;
e 'attention-getting' devices. (*WMEB*)

6 The following information appears on a packet of baby rusks.
Analysis per 100 grams

Protein	9.7 g	Phosphorus	170 mg
Fat	6.7 g	Iron	12.5 mg
Glucose	4.3 g	Sodium	185 mg
Sucrose	18.0 g	Vitamin A	1500 mg
Starch	48.0 g	Vitamin D	1.5 mg
Fibre	0.3 g	Vitamin B_1	0.3 mg
Minerals	7.0—9.0 g	Vitamin B_2	0.3 mg
Calcium	375 mg	Nicotinic acid	2.5 mg

Energy 412 calories (1729 kJ)

a Which of the items on the above list are important for each of the following?
    (i) energy production;
    (ii) blood cell formation;
    (iii) bone development;
    (iv) muscular growth;
    (v) helping the muscles of the digestive system to work.
b What is the best way to give rusks to a baby
    (i) aged 5 months;
    (ii) aged 1 year?
c State THREE precautions which should be observed when preparing home-cooked food for a baby of 6–7 months.
d Suggest TWO FOODS which would provide similar nutrients to milk for a toddler who does not like milk in any form. (*YREB*)

155

Section 6

Health

40 Infectious diseases and immunisation

Infectious diseases are caused by germs — harmful bacteria and viruses (see p. 265). Some types of germ affect people of all ages, examples being those which cause the common cold, influenza, bronchitis, tetanus and tuberculosis. Other diseases occur mainly in children — eight infectious diseases of childhood are given in the chart on pp. 160-1.

Generally speaking, the infectious diseases of childhood are less severe in children than adults. One attack usually gives long-lasting immunity to that disease so it is rare to catch it for a second time. Another way to obtain immunity against some infectious diseases is by immunisation. The diseases for which immunisation is readily available are those marked with an asterisk on the chart.

Immunity

Immunity is the ability of the body to resist infection.

Antibodies are substances made by the body to destroy germs. When a person 'catches' an infectious disease, he produces antibodies of the right type which eventually destroy the germs. The antibodies also give immunity to that disease and help to prevent the person from catching the same disease again.

Immunisation (vaccination)

Vaccines are available for certain diseases. A special vaccine is required for each disease. One or more doses of vaccine are required to make the body produce the right type of antibodies to destroy the germs which cause that particular disease.

How diseases spread

All the diseases in the chart except tetanus can be spread by droplet infection and by contact.

158

Droplet infection   Very tiny drops of moisture containing germs come from the nose or throat of an infected person when sneezing, coughing, singing and talking. If they enter the nose or mouth of another person they may give rise to infection.

Contact   It is possible to pick up infection by kissing or touching an infected person (direct contact), or by using towels, toys, or other equipment which have been in contact with the disease (indirect contact). Diseases spread by contact are called **contagious diseases**.

Tetanus germs are 'caught' in an unusual way. They can only cause disease when they enter the body through cuts or grazes in the skin. Some other types of germs, for example food poisoning bacteria, can be transferred from one person to another in food, milk and water.

When germs get inside the body

The body reacts in various ways to try to destroy any germs which may get inside it. If these fail, the germs grow and multiply and eventually produce fever and other symptoms.

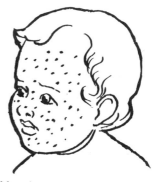

Measles

- **Incubation** is the time between the entry of the germs into the body and the appearance of symptoms.
- **Symptoms** are changes in the body which indicate disease.
- The **onset** of the disease is the point at which symptoms appear.
- The **infectious stage** is the time during which germs can be spread from one person to another. The patient becomes infectious either during the incubation period or at the end of it. Quite often, a child is infectious before anyone realises that he has got the disease.

Preventing the spread of disease

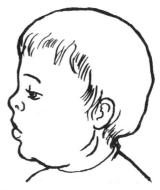

Mumps

- **Immunisation** to prevent the disease (if a vaccine is available).
- **Isolation** of anyone suffering from the disease so that germs cannot spread to other people.
- **Quarantine** — isolation of people who have been in contact with anyone suffering from a disease, because if they have caught it, they may be infectious before symptoms appear.
- **Disinfection** of clothes, bed-linen, toys and other equipment used by the patient to stop germs from being passed on to others. Also burning paper tissues which the patient has used.

Infectious diseases of childhood

Disease	Symptoms	Incubation in days	Infectious stage
Chicken pox Varicella (V)	Small red spots which turn to blisters then scabs.	10-21	2 days before the spots appear until a week after.
*German measles Rubella (V)	A mild disease with a red rash and usually with swollen glands.	10-21	From onset to end of rash.
*Measles (V)	Fever, severe cold, cough. 4–5 days later a red rash appears on the face and spreads downwards.	10-15	From onset of cold symptom until 5 days after rash appea
Mumps (V)	Painful swellings under jaw on one or both sides.	12-28, usually about 18	Until the swelling goes down
*Polio Poliomyelitis (V)	Infection of the spinal cord causing fever which may result in paralysis.	3-21	From 2 days after infection to 6 weeks or longer after onse
Scarlet fever (B)	Sore throat, fever, bright red rash.	2-4	Up to 2 weeks after onset.
*Whooping cough Pertussis (B)	Long bouts of coughing which may end with a 'whoop'.	7-12	A few days before onset to 4 weeks after onset.
*Diphtheria (B)	A white layer forms on the throat which may block the airway; it also produces a very powerful poison which damages heart and brain.	2-5	Usually for about 2 weeks af onset.

Other infectious diseases

Disease	Symptoms	Incubation in days	Infectious stage
*Tetanus Lockjaw (B)	Muscles in the neck tighten and lock the jaw.	4-21	Cannot be passed directly fr one person to another.
*Tuberculosis TB (B)	Usually coughing and damage to lungs.	28-42	Variable.

* Immunisation is available to protect against these diseases.   (B) = Bacterial infection, (V) = Viral infection.

Other information	Immunisation
mild disease in children. More severe in adults where it may cause shingles.	—
angerous in the first 4 months of pregnancy opic 49).	Rubella vaccine is offered to girls between the age of 11 and 13 years who have not already had german measles.
ore serious in infancy than in older children.	A single injection of measles vaccine is given during the second year.
umps in males over the age of 11 may amage the testes and result in sterility.	A mumps vaccine has been developed but it is not given as a routine vaccination to children in Britain.
mmunisation has almost eliminated this sease from Britain.	The vaccine is given **orally**, i.e. by mouth, often on a sugar lump. Three doses are required and are given at the same time as the triple vaccine. Booster doses are given at 5 years and again between 15 and 19 years.
carlet fever is tonsillitis with a rash. Usually ears up quickly with antibiotics.	
an be very dangerous in babies up to 1 year d. Whooping-cough vaccine does not always event the disease, but it makes it much less npleasant and the coughing less severe.	Vaccines against diphtheria, whooping cough (pertussis) and tetanus are often given together as **triple vaccine** (DPT vaccine). Three injections are needed between the age of 3 and 12 months. Sometimes whooping cough vaccine is given separately. Booster doses of vaccine for diphtheria and tetanus are given at the age of 5 years and again between 15-19 years. Further doses of tetanus vaccine may be given at 5-yearly intervals.
lthough now uncommon, it is still liable to ccur in children who have not been immunised.	
erms exist in soil, dirt and animal droppings, cluding those of horses and humans. They nter the body through cuts and scratches.	
ost people who are infected by TB germs o not develop the disease. They do however evelop natural immunity to the disease.	Between the ages of 10 and 13 years, children are given a simple skin test to find out if they are immune to TB. If not, they are given one dose of BCG vaccine so that they can develop immunity. Younger children are only immunised if they have been in contact with anyone suffering from the disease. (BCG — Bacillus Calmette-Guerin.)

Immunity of babies

Very young babies rarely catch the infectious diseases common in childhood because they are protected by antibodies obtained from the mother. When the baby was in the womb, antibodies passed across the placenta from the mother's blood to the baby's blood. Because of this the baby is born with protection against the same diseases that the mother has had or has been immunised against. If the baby is breast-fed, he will continue to get supplies of these antibodies.

Antibodies from the mother survive in the baby for several months. All that time, the baby is growing stronger and becoming more able to withstand infection. The age of three months is the recommended time to begin immunisation. The baby will then begin to develop his own antibodies to take over from those of his mother, which gradually disappear.

Whooping cough is an exception. A new-born baby has no antibodies from his mother against this disease (whooping cough antibodies are too big to pass across the placenta). It is a very dangerous disease in babies and they should, therefore, be kept well away from anyone who is infectious. Even if the baby has been vaccinated against whooping cough it takes several months for the vaccine to become fully effective. It is useful to know that the cough lasts much longer than the infectious stage.

Effects of immunisation

Until recently, most children were given the full range of immunisations. As a result, the diseases they prevented fell to a very low level, or were almost eliminated.

Nowadays, because these diseases have become rare, some parents feel it is no longer necessary to have their children immunised. Consequently, if the diseases do occur, they can easily spread and result in an epidemic.

Polio is an example. Polio vaccine was introduced in 1957, and within five years the disease was almost wiped out. Fewer children are now being immunised against polio and, when a rare case occurs, parents suddenly realise that their children are at risk and rush to have them immunised. It takes a while for the vaccine to become fully effective and, during this time, it is possible for the disease to spread rapidly.

Whooping cough is an example of a disease which is becoming more common because fewer children are being immunised. Some parents do not bother. Others decide not to have their children immunised against this disease because of the very slight risk of a severe reaction to the vaccine, for example convulsions or permanent brain damage. Doctors disagree as to how great the risk is. Some think the convulsions might have started whether the child was vaccinated or not. Whooping cough is a serious disease and may cause death or permanent damage in a young child. For the great majority of children, the risk of illness from the vaccine is thought to be very much less than the risk of illness from the disease.

Questions

1. From the chart on pp. 160-1,
a List eight infectious diseases of childhood.
b What is the technical name for (i) German measles, (ii) polio, (iii) whooping cough, (iv) lockjaw, (v) TB?
c Why is it preferable for boys to have mumps when they are young?
d Which disease may cause shingles in an adult?

2. Which of the diseases in the chart are caused by
a bacteria, **b** viruses?

3. a (i) What is the meaning of immunity? (ii) Name two ways in which long-lasting immunity can be obtained.
b For which of the diseases in the chart is immunisation readily available?

4. a (i) The triple vaccine is also called DPT vaccine. Which three diseases do these initials stand for? (ii) Sometimes only two of these vaccines are given. Which is left out?
b Which vaccine is given orally, and what does this mean?

5. a How can disease be spread by droplet infection?
b What is the difference between catching a disease from an infected person by direct contact and indirect contact?
c What is a contagious disease?

6. Give the meaning of the following terms when used to describe an infectious disease (i) symptoms, (ii) incubation period, (iii) onset, (iv) infectious stage.

To do

1. Timetable for the immunisation of children

Disease	When to give the vaccine
1	
2	3 doses between the age of 3-12 months
3	
4	
5	− 1 dose in the second year
6	
7	booster dose at the age of 5 years
8	
9	− for children of 10-13 years who have no immunity to the disease
10	− for girls of 11-13 years who have not already had the disease

Fill in the spaces with the name of the disease for which the vaccine is given.

2. Since the year 1900, the infant death rate in Britain has been reduced from about 25 % of all deaths in the whole population to about 2 %. This dramatic reduction has been due to the control and treatment of measles, diphtheria, whooping cough and other diseases. Find out
a why each of the three diseases mentioned above is dangerous,
b how each has been controlled,
c when the method of control became generally available.

Child study

1. a Has the child had any of the diseases mentioned in this topic? If so, how did they affect the child?
b Has the child been immunised? If so make out a timetable. If not perhaps the mother would be kind enough to discuss the reasons with you.

41 **Parasites**

The parasites discussed in this topic are head lice, itch mites (which cause scabies), fleas and threadworms. These parasites obtain their food from humans and they are likely to affect all children at one time or another. There is no reason for a mother to feel ashamed if her child 'catches' any of these because they so easily pass from one child to another. The treatment to remove them is simple and advice can be obtained from the doctor, health visitor or clinic.

Head lice

Head lice are tiny insects which live amongst the hairs of the head and look rather like dandruff which moves (each is called a **louse**). The lice crawl around fairly rapidly and 4-5 times a day they pierce the skin for a meal of blood, leaving little red bite marks which itch.

The eggs are called **nits** and they are easier to see than the adult lice. Nits look like tiny white specks and each is firmly cemented to a hair.

How lice spread   Adult lice can crawl from one head to another. A clean head can be infected with lice or nits when a comb, brush, hat or headscarf of an infected person is borrowed.

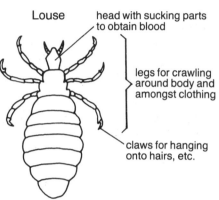

Louse

head with sucking parts to obtain blood

legs for crawling around body and amongst clothing

claws for hanging onto hairs, etc.

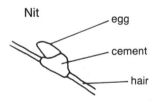

Nit

egg

cement

hair

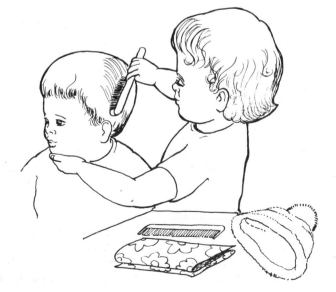

Treatment Washing hair will not get rid of head lice. They are not affected by the water as both lice and nits are waterproof. Nor do they get washed away — the nits are cemented to the hair, and the lice have claws which enable them to cling very tightly. Treatment is simple — chemists sell a special lotion which should be rubbed into the hair and left to dry naturally. After twelve hours both the lice and nits will be killed and can be washed out when the hair is shampooed in the usual way.

Scabies

Scabies is also called 'the itch' as it causes extreme irritation, especially at night, and keeps the sufferer awake. It is caused by mites which burrow into the outer layer of the skin (the keratin layer) where they spend most of their life feeding on the skin and laying their eggs.

The itch mite has 4 pairs of legs used for burrowing into skin

Scabies on the thumb of a child

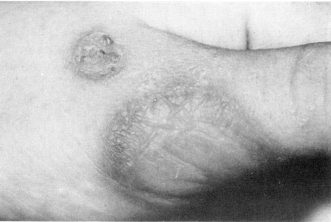

District General Hospital, Gorleston, Norfolk

An irritating rash appears on skin 3-4 weeks after infection. It looks like a scaly area with pimples and it may be possible to see the burrows of the mites. The rash makes the sufferer scratch, which can result in septic spots and boils. Scabies is most likely to occur on the palms, between the fingers, on the wrists, and sometimes armpits, groin and other places.

How scabies spreads The mites crawl from one person to another when there is close bodily contact. For this reason, scabies spreads easily between members of the same family, especially when they sleep in the same bed.

Treatment The doctor will prescribe a lotion which must be applied to all parts of the skin from the neck to the soles of the feet. The bed-linen and underclothes must be washed. The treatment only works if all the members of the family are treated at the same time so that all the mites can be killed.

Fleas

Fleas are small wingless insects with long legs adapted for jumping. It is easy to become infested with fleas as they can jump long distances from one person to another. The type of flea which feeds on human blood lives in clothing next to the skin. The human flea does not carry disease, but when it pierces the skin to suck blood it leaves small red marks which irritate. Fleas lay their eggs in dirt in buildings, furniture, bedding or clothing.

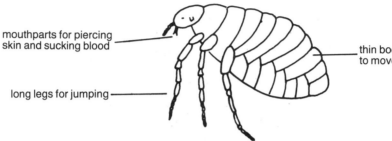

mouthparts for piercing skin and sucking blood

thin body which enables flea to move easily amongst hairs

long legs for jumping

Treatment   Cleanliness is important in the control of fleas. They do not live for long on clean people or in clothes which are regularly washed. The eggs will not survive for long in clean buildings or bedding.

Animal fleas   When young, children are often very sensitive (allergic) to fleas which live on dogs, cats, or birds. The fleas may be the cause of spots which persist for a long time. Pet animals with fleas need to be treated with an insecticide.

Threadworms

Threadworms are small white worms about 1 cm ($\frac{1}{2}$ in) long. They look like small pieces of thread which wriggle. They live in the large bowel, feeding on the contents and can sometimes be seen in the stools. It is quite common for children to have threadworms from time to time. They do little harm but are a nuisance as they cause itching around the anus. The itching occurs mainly in the evenings because this is the time that the female worms crawl out of the bowel to lay their eggs and then die.

Each of these tiny worms lays about 10 000 eggs which stick to the skin and clothes or are caught up in the finger nails. Some may eventually get into the dust of the room, where they survive for a long time. If the eggs enter the mouth of a child on the fingers or in food, they pass down to the bowel where they hatch. The worms cannot multiply in the bowel, so the number of worms depends on the number of eggs that are eaten.

166

Treatment   If necessary, the doctor will prescribe medicine to clear the worms from the bowel, but they will die out in time anyway — unless the child eats more eggs.

Helping to prevent infection   It is almost impossible to make sure that a child's hands are washed before he puts his fingers into his mouth or handles anything that he is going to eat or suck. But it helps to prevent infection to:
- teach children to wash their hands every time they use the lavatory;
- teach them to wash their hands before meals;
- make sure that the hands of the person who prepares and serves the food are washed before doing so;
- always wash fruit and raw salad vegetables thoroughly before eating.

1. Complete this chart.

Name of parasite	Where they live	What they feed on	Where they lay eggs	How a child becomes infected
Head lice				
Mites				
Fleas				
Thread-worms				

2. **a** What are the eggs of lice called?
b What is the difference between lice and nits?
c Why is it impossible to get rid of lice and nits by washing the hair?

3 **a** Where on the body is scabies most likely to occur?
b Why is scabies also called 'the itch'?
c Describe the rash.

4. Why should pets with fleas be treated with an insecticide, particularly in a household with young children?

5. What can be done to help prevent infection by threadworms?

To do

1. For each of the four parasites,
a Draw a diagram of the parasite,
b Describe treatment to remove them.

2. Find out information about other parasites, for example, bedbugs, tapeworms, bilharzia.

42 Skin problems

There are many different disorders of the skin. Some have already been mentioned. These include nappy rash (Topic 20), infectious diseases (Topic 40), and parasites (Topic 41). Other causes are dealt with in this topic and in Topic 43.

Itching and scratching

The skin usually itches (irritates) when something is wrong with it. The natural thing to do is to scratch. If the itching persists, it makes a child irritable, restless and upsets sleep. There is also a chance that scratching will damage the skin and allow germs to enter to do further damage.

Rashes

Rashes of one sort or another are extremely common in children. If a rash is not a symptom of one of the usual diseases of childhood, a mother will want to know what caused it. Is it caused by an infection? Is it caused by something the child ate? Has the child been in contact with something he might be allergic to? Whatever the cause, if it worries the child and makes him scratch, or if he is obviously unwell, then prompt treatment by a doctor is required. It is much easier to deal with a rash at an early stage rather than later when it has spread and caused more trouble.

'Nettle rash' (urticaria)   The rash looks as though it has been caused by nettle stings, with either lots of small spots or fewer, larger ones. It itches severely, but usually does not last long, and can be soothed by calamine lotion. It may be blamed on 'overheated blood', 'too rich food' or 'acid fruits', but these will not be the cause.

The rash indicates that the child is particularly sensitive (allergic) to something (see also Allergy in Topic 44). A number of substances are known to cause 'nettle rash' including:
- certain medicines such as aspirin or penicillin;
- a particular food such as strawberries;
- sensitivity to insect bites such as those from the fleas of dogs or cats, or from bedbugs.

'Nettle rash' is not dangerous, but if it occurs regularly, or persists for a long time, it needs to be investigated to discover the cause so that it can be avoided.

Heat rash   When babies get too hot, a rash may appear, particularly around the shoulders and neck. It is understandable for a rash to appear in hot weather or in hot countries — where it is known as **prickly heat**. It may also develop in cold weather if the baby is wrapped in too many clothes and kept in an overheated room.

Bathing the baby will remove the sweat — which is the cause of the rash. When the skin is quite dry, a little talcum powder or calamine lotion applied to the rash may be soothing.

Dressing the baby according to the weather will help to prevent heat rash. When it is very hot there is no reason for any clothes to be worn at all except a nappy.

Eczema   Eczema is a fairly common complaint in babies. It tends to come and go during the early years, and most sufferers grow out of it by the time they start school. It usually starts with patches of dry, scaly skin which becomes red and slightly inflamed and may weep. Eczema makes the child want to scratch the sore places and it is very difficult for the mother to stop him.

Eczema is neither contagious nor caused by poor hygiene. Although the exact cause is unknown, there is often a family history of asthma or hay fever, and it tends to be worse when the child is emotionally upset.

Skin infections

Impetigo is a skin disease caused by bacteria. It starts as little red spots which develop watery heads and then brownish-yellow crusts. It spreads quickly to other parts of the skin, and can easily infect other people when, for example, they use the same towel. Impetigo can usually be quickly cleared up by antibiotics.

Wolfe Medical Publications Ltd

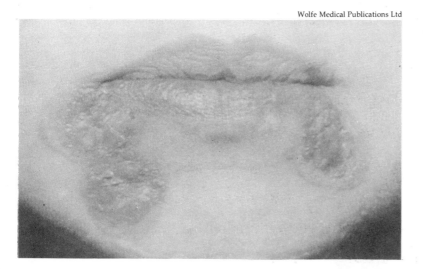

Ringworm is caused by a fungus which infects the skin and grows outwards to form a reddish patch with a ring of little pimples at the edge.

When it affects the scalp, the hairs break off to leave a bald, round patch. Treatment with antibiotic (griseofulvin) destroys the fungus and the hair will grow again.

Athlete's foot is the name for ringworm which grows on the skin of the feet. It likes the warm damp conditions encouraged by shoes and socks, especially between the toes, where it makes the skin turn white and peel off. The photograph below shows athlete's foot around the toes of a four-year-old.

Wolfe Medical Publications Ltd

Warts Although these do not cause itching and scratching, they are included here because they occur on the skin. Warts are caused by a virus infection which may spread to form a crop of warts. They are harmless and will disappear eventually without treatment.

A wart on the sole of the foot is called a **verruca** or **plantar wart**. It is very painful when pressed inwards during walking. A verruca needs to be removed because it is both painful and infectious. While waiting for treatment, it should be kept covered by sticking plaster to prevent the infection spreading to other people.

Questions

1. a Give four ways in which persistent itching may affect a child.
b When is prompt medical treatment for a rash desirable? Why?

2. a Why is urticaria given the name 'nettle rash'?
b Suggest some substances which might be the cause of 'nettle rash'.
c Name a substance which can soothe the rash.

3. a Under what conditions may heat rash develop in cold weather?
b What is the cause of eczema?
c Is eczema catching?

4. a Which of the skin infections mentioned in this topic is:
a caused by a virus,
b caused by a fungus,
c caused by bacteria,
d called athlete's foot when it grows on the feet,
e called a verruca when it occurs on the sole of the foot,
f treated with antibiotics (two answers)?

To do

There are many different disorders of the skin. A number have already been mentioned in this book. How many can you remember? The first paragraph of this topic gives some clues. What treatment, if any, was recommended for each disorder?

43  *First aid*

This topic gives a list of equipment usually kept in a first-aid box and a brief description of treatment for the more common mishaps.

First-aid box

Children often cut themselves or fall over, burn or scald themselves or get stung. Parents have to deal with these first-aid problems and it is helpful to have all the necessary equipment handy in a special box. Suggested contents for the first-aid box are:

- cotton wool } — for cleaning wounds;
- paper tissues
- adhesive plasters (sticking plasters) — to hold the sides of a cut together;
- gauze dressing, either in individual packs or a long roll — to cover wounds;
- bandages of different widths } — to hold dressings in
- roll of zinc oxide tape } place;
- safety-pins — to fix bandages;
- scissors — to cut bandages and tape;
- crepe bandage — to support a sprained ankle or other joint;
- sling or scarf — to support a damaged arm;
- tweezers — to remove splinters;
- eye dropper or eye bath — for washing the eye;
- calamine lotion or cream — for sunburn, chapped skin, or stings;
- anti-sting cream — for insect bites.

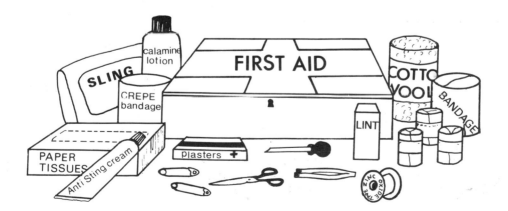

Cuts and grazes

For small cuts and grazes   Wash with clean water or soap and water; dry by patting with a clean towel. If necessary, cover with a dry dressing and hold the dressing in place with a bandage.

Bleeding from a small wound soon stops of its own accord, and the scab which forms prevents germs from getting in. There is no need for sticking plaster unless the wound keeps opening up. Also, there is no need for antiseptic ointment as a child's natural resistance deals with nearly all germs, and the ointment makes the scab soft and delays healing.

Wounds with severe bleeding   When there is severe bleeding, the aim should be to stop the bleeding immediately and to obtain medical help urgently. To stop the bleeding, pressure should be applied to the wound with the fingers. A doctor may decide that a large or deep wound needs stitches. An injection against tetanus may also be necessary.

Bruises

A bruise is caused by bleeding beneath unbroken skin. It seldom needs more treatment than a cuddle and 'kiss better'.

A bad bruise may be eased by a **cold compress** if it is applied at once. This is made by soaking some suitable material, e.g. cotton wool, in cold water and placing it on the bruise.

Nose bleeds

These are common in young children. They are more of a nuisance than a danger — the sight of blood makes them appear worse than they really are.

There are many causes, but the treatment is always the same. Sit the patient upright and leaning slightly forward. The nose should be nipped for ten minutes — do not keep taking the pressure off to see if the bleeding has stopped. If the nose is still bleeding after ten minutes of continuous pressure, then a doctor should be consulted.

Burns and scalds

A burn is caused by dry heat, for example the heat from a fire or touching a hot kettle. A scald results from contact with moist heat such as steam or hot fat.

The skin of young children can very easily be damaged by heat and the scars may last for a lifetime. Burns and scalds are also very painful. Therefore, every effort should be made to prevent them from happening (see Safety in the Home, Topic 61). In young children, especially infants, even small burns or scalds should be regarded as serious and be given immediate treatment.

For a small burn (or scald)   Put the burnt area into clean, cold water as soon as possible to remove the heat and reduce the pain. It is important to do this for a least ten minutes. Pat dry and cover with a gauze dressing or clean, non-fluffy cloth, but not sticking plaster. If the burn causes severe blistering or breaks the skin, the child should be taken to hospital.

> NEVER put ointment, cream, jelly, oil or butter on a burn — they delay healing.
> NEVER prick a blister. It lets in germs.

For a severe burn (or scald)   Wrap the child in a clean sheet and rush to hospital without waiting to call a doctor.

Sunburn

The sun's rays can easily burn the skin, so a child's skin should be exposed gradually to the sun, starting with a few minutes on the first day. The time can be gradually increased as brown pigment (melanin) develops in the skin to protect it. Special protective cream or oil rubbed on to the skin before and during sunbathing helps to protect against sunburn.

Children with fair skin or red hair burn very easily and need particular care. Children at the seaside also need special care as the sun's rays are reflected from the water and this makes them especially strong.

Sunburn only begins to hurt several hours after the actual burning has taken place. Severe burning needs medical attention. In other cases, cold water may help to soothe, as may calamine lotion or special creams or lotions sold for the purpose.

Stings

Calamine, anti-sting or anti-histamine creams give relief when rubbed on to stings from insects and nettles. They help to reduce itching.

Something in the eye

When a particle of dust, an eyelash or other small object gets into the eye it can be removed with the corner of a clean handkerchief from the eyelid but **not** the eyeball. The eyeball should never be touched because of the danger of damaging the delicate surface. Rubbing the eye can also cause damage.

Dust or other small particle on the eyeball is best removed by washing the eye. This can be done using an eye dropper or eye bath. If a little salt is added to the water (a teaspoonful of salt to ½ litre water), the water will soothe rather than sting the eye (tears are salty). If the object cannot be removed easily, it needs to be dealt with by a doctor, or at the hospital. After the object has been removed, it will still feel as though something is there if the eyeball has been scratched. When a chemical substance such as bleach gets into the eye, it should be washed out immediately by holding the face under the tap.

174

Choking

When a hard object gets stuck in the throat, it interferes with breathing, and the child chokes. In the case of an infant, hold upside down by the legs, and pat his back. For an older child, hold over the knee, head downwards, and slap three to four times between the shoulder blades.

Broken bones (fractures)

Generally, because they are still soft, the bones of a young child bend rather than break. If a bone does break, it is likely to crack on one side only. This is called a green-stick fracture because it behaves rather like a bent green twig which refuses to break off.

An X-ray is often necessary to discover whether a bone is broken or not. If a child is able to move about normally after a fall, it is unlikely that any bones have been broken.

Greenstick fracture in the forearm

District General Hospital, Gorleston, Norfolk

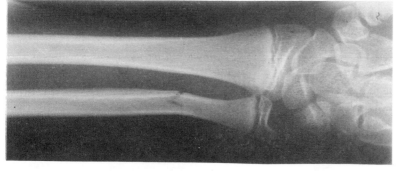

Questions

1. List the contents of the first-aid box shown on p. 171. Give a purpose for each item.

2. a Study the drawings in this topic. In each case describe the first-aid treatment that is needed or is being given.
b What is a green-stick fracture?

3. a How does first-aid treatment for a graze differ from that for severe bleeding?
b Are sticking plasters or antiseptic ointments necessary for a small cut?

4. a What is the cause of a bruise?
b What treatment is necessary?

5. a Give two reasons why every effort should be made to prevent children being burnt.
b Describe the first-aid treatment for (i) a small burn, (ii) a bad burn.
c What should never be put on a burn and why?
d Why should blisters never be pricked?

To do

Check the contents of a first-aid box. Perhaps you have one at home. There will certainly be at least one in every school and college. What items are missing? If there are any extra items, what are they there for?

44 *Common illnesses in children*

This topic gives a brief description of some of the more common ailments from which children may suffer. They are placed in alphabetical order and not in order of seriousness or frequency.

Adenoids

Adenoids consist of lymphatic tissue behind the nose which sometimes grows so large that it blocks the back of the nose. When this happens, the child has to breathe through the mouth. It may cause nasal speech, deafness, and sometimes a persistent cough. Large adenoids need to be removed.

Allergy

Having an allergy means being unduly sensitive to a particular substance which is harmless to most other people. That substance may affect the body through the skin (for example detergent), or when eaten (some people are allergic to strawberries), or when breathed in (pollen, house dust, etc).

The allergy may show itself in one or more of the following ways; hay fever, asthma, eczema, 'nettle rash', stomach upset, or other unpleasant symptoms.

Many people (adults and children) have allergies of one sort or another. Why some people are more sensitive to particular substances than others is not known. A tendency to allergy often runs in families, although it may take different forms in members of the same family. For example, a parent with asthma may have a child who suffers from hay fever.

Press Report

The news item on the right appeared in the *Eastern Daily Press.*

'Little Paul Land is nuts about his granny but every time he gave her a cuddle he burst into tears and came out in blotches.

For months doctors were baffled but now allergy experts have discovered the cause.

Two-year-old Paul of Harlington, near Mexborough, South Yorks, is allergic to peanuts — and his granny, 63-year-old Mrs Ann Land, works in a nut factory.'

Colds

The common cold is caused by a virus infection. It spreads easily, either by droplets in the air that come from an infected person, or by contact with handkerchiefs, cups, spoons or other objects recently used by an infected person. It is difficult to stop the germs from spreading between members of the same family. Colds are caused by a very large number of different viruses and as yet there is no known way of preventing them.

Young babies are more seriously affected by colds than older children. They are also more likely to suffer from complications such as pneumonia. Therefore, it is wise to try to prevent anyone with a cold from coming into contact with a new-born baby. Infants have great difficulty in feeding when the nose is blocked because they are unable to breathe and suck at the same time.

Children are particularly likely to catch colds in the first few months at playgroup or school. This is because they come into contact with a greater variety of different types of cold germs. By the time they are six or seven, they have usually built up more resistance to these germs.

Conjunctivitis ('pink eye')

This is caused by an eye infection which makes the eye look red. The infection easily spreads when other members of the family use the same towel and face flannel as an infected person. The eyes can be cleaned in the same way as for sticky eye (see p. 180); a doctor will prescribe antibiotic eyedrops or ointment.

Constipation

Constipation is the infrequent passing of very hard, dry stools. It is not a common problem in children — unless the parents worry about the child's bowels. Left to themselves, the bowels open when necessary, and usually according to a pattern. With some people (adults and children), the bowels may open once or more a day, or every other day, or once every three or four days, and any of these patterns is normal. There is no need for the bowels to open every day, or for the child to be given laxatives to make this happen. It is common for babies who are being breast-fed to go for several days without having a motion, and the stools are always soft.

Laxatives are definitely **harmful** if they are given regularly, as they interfere with the normal working of the bowels.

Bowels should be kept open by **diet not laxatives**:

- for young babies — more water;
- for those being weaned — fruit purée;
- for children — wholemeal bread, cereals, fresh fruit, vegetables.

Coughs

It is essential to cough from time to time to remove phlegm from the windpipe or lungs, especially following a cold. There is no need to consult a doctor whenever the child coughs a little more than usual. If the child coughs a great deal, it can be due to a number of possible causes and needs a medical opinion.

Cough medicine will not cure a cough, but it might comfort the back of the throat. The instructions should be read before any cough medicine is given to a child, because some are not suitable for young children.

Croup

Croup is a harsh, barking cough and noisy breathing which can occur in children up to the age of four years. It is caused by laryngitis. If it develops suddenly, a doctor needs to be consulted as soon as possible.

Diarrhoea

Diarrhoea is the frequent passing of loose, watery stools.

Diarrhoea can be very dangerous in babies. Apart from anything else, when a great deal of water is lost with the stools the baby quickly becomes dehydrated — dried out. The advice of a doctor is required.

Earache

Pain in the ears may be due to teething or a cold. It needs to be investigated by a doctor in case an infection is present in the ear itself.

Fever

Fever is when the body temperature is higher than normal. (Taking the temperature is discussed in Topic 46.) A child with a fever will feel hot and sweaty. He needs to be allowed to cool off to help his temperature to come down — not to be smothered in blankets. Sponging with tepid water will help to reduce a very high temperature and make the patient feel more comfortable.

Fever is usually a sign of infection, but not always. A high temperature is not normally a reason for asking a doctor to call. However, if it is accompanied by other symptoms (such as headache), it is wise to telephone the doctor for advice, or to call to see him.

Fits (convulsions)

When a child has a fit, his eyes roll upwards, he loses consciousness and his limbs make jerking movements. Fits are caused by a wide variety of ailments, but not by teething. In many small children they are due to fever that occurs with infections such as colds, tonsillitis or bronchitis. If a child has a fit, it should be reported to the doctor immediately.

Headaches

Headaches are common in children and may be due to tiredness, worry, infection (e.g. tonsillitis), staying indoors too much, or migraine. On the other hand, pretending to have a headache can be used as an excuse for not doing something, for example not going to school. If a child gets away with it, 'pretend' headaches can quickly become a habit.

Whatever the cause, headaches need investigation so that the right treatment can be given to stop them.

Influenza

Influenza is caused by a virus. It is a more serious infection than the common cold although the symptoms are similar.

Sore throat

There are various causes of sore throat. Often it is the beginning of a cold. Sometimes the child may have tonsillitis. It is not necessary to consult a doctor every time a child has a sore throat. If it is accompanied by earache, a rise in temperature, or if the sore throat is still getting worse after two days, a doctor should be consulted.

Sticky eye

A yellow discharge from the eye sometimes gums the eyelids together. It may result from a blocked tear duct or an infection. To clean the eye, wipe gently with cotton wool and water; always wipe from the inner corner of the eye outwards, and use a fresh piece of cotton wool for each eye. A doctor needs to be consulted if the discharge persists for more than a day or two.

Swollen glands in the neck

There are many reasons why these glands swell, and a doctor should be consulted.

Thrush

This is a fungus infection which causes white patches on the tongue and mouth. It occurs mainly in babies and makes them scream when feeding because the mouth is sore. The infection can be cleared up by an antibiotic (nystatin), or by painting the mouth with gentian violet.

Tonsillitis

Tonsillitis is an infection of the tonsils. The throat is sore, the tonsils are inflamed and it may be possible to see white spots on them. Antibiotics prescribed by the doctor usually cure the infection.

There are two tonsils, one at either side of the back of the mouth. They normally enlarge at the age of 5-6 years and shrink after the age of ten or so. Tonsils do not need to be removed just because they are large, but only if there are frequent bouts of tonsillitis which cannot be prevented by medicines.

Vomiting (being sick)

It is quite usual for young babies to bring up a little milk after a meal. This is often curdled, and it smells sour as it has been mixed with the acid in the stomach. It is not a cause for worry.

Vomiting has to be taken seriously when a child is repeatedly and properly sick. This applies to older children as well as babies, and the advice of a doctor is needed.

Vomiting and diarrhoea are often signs of food poisoning (Topic 38).

180

Wheezing

This is commonly caused by asthma or asthmatic bronchitis and can be very much helped by proper medical treatment.

Questions

1. Link each of these words with the correct description below:

adenoids   fever
conjunctivitis   sticky eye
constipation   thrush
croup   tonsillitis
diarrhoea

a body temperature higher than normal
b spreads easily when others use the same towel
c noisy breathing with a harsh cough
d white patches on the tongue and mouth
e tissue which sometimes blocks the back of the nose
f inflamed tonsils
g yellow discharge which sometimes gums the eyelids together
h loose, watery stools which are passed frequently
i the infrequent passing of very hard, dry stools

2. a What causes the common cold?
b How does it spread?
c What particular difficulty do infants have when they suffer from a cold?
d When children start attending playgroup, why are they particularly likely to catch colds?

3. a When can constipation become a problem in children?
b When and why are laxatives harmful?
c Give ways of keeping the bowels open without the use of laxatives.

4. a What can cause headaches in children?
b Why do children have 'pretend' headaches?

Child study

Has the child had any of the illnesses mentioned in this topic? If so, describe how the child was affected.

45 The sick child

A mother can usually tell when her child is ill by changes in the child's normal pattern of behaviour. It is probable that the child will show one or more of the following symptoms:
- has a fever (looks flushed and feels hot);
- will not eat;
- has a rash;
- has dark rings around the eyes, or the eyes look sunken;
- vomits or has diarrhoea;
- is fretful;
- is unnaturally quiet and limp and shows no interest in anything.

With a baby, she will also notice that he cries differently.

Consulting the doctor

When a mother feels that there is something wrong with her child, she has to decide whether to consult a doctor. There is no need to call the doctor every time the child coughs or has a rash, or vomits, or has a raised temperature. These commonly occur in childhood and are followed by a quick recovery. If the child does not recover quickly from these symptoms, or is more unwell than usual with them, or they recur frequently, then a doctor should be consulted. Early treatment often gives a rapid and complete cure.

When a mother needs the advice of a doctor, she should phone or call at the surgery or health centre, preferably before 10 a.m. She will then be told either what to do, or to bring the child to the doctor, or that the doctor will be calling to see the child.

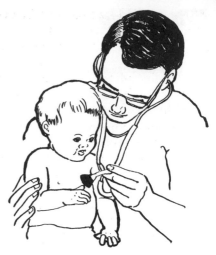

Emergencies

A child needs urgent treatment either from a doctor or the casualty department of a hospital for:
- severe bleeding;
- severe burns;
- severe pain;
- severe blow on the head;
- severe diarrhoea or vomiting (especially babies);
- difficulty in breathing;
- any type of fit or convulsion;
- swallowing poison;
- swallowing a dangerous object like a safety-pin.

Poisoning

If a child has swallowed something poisonous:
- **keep calm**; poisoning is rarely fatal in a matter of seconds or even minutes;
- **do not try to make the child sick**;
- **telephone your doctor or take the child to the nearest hospital**;
- **take a sample of the poison with you** so that it can be quickly identified.

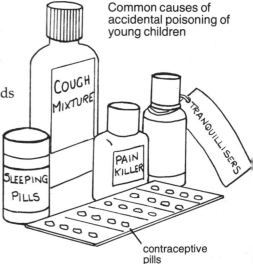

Common causes of accidental poisoning of young children

contraceptive pills

Caring for a sick child

With a few illnesses, such as rheumatic fever, it is necessary for the patient to stay in bed. Apart from these, there is no good reason for keeping a child in bed unless he is happier there. The child will get better just as well in the living room as in the bedroom, so long as he is kept warm and comfortable. He is also likely to be less bored and feel less neglected if he is near his mother, and it is easier for her to care for him and keep him amused.

When a child has to stay in bed he needs to be kept clean, comfortable and occupied.

1. Washing the face and brushing the hair helps the child to feel fresh.
2. A daily bath is unnecessary unless he is sweating a lot.
3. His hands need to be washed before eating and after using the toilet.
4. The bed-clothes and night-clothes should be changed as often as necessary.
5. The bed should be straightened several times a day and remade morning and evening.
6. The room should be kept warm.
7. The room should be kept ventilated to prevent it from becoming stuffy, especially when there is paraffin or gas heating. If the window is opened, the child should not be in a draught.
8. If the child is old enough, he needs:
   - a back rest with pillows so he can sit up comfortably;
   - to be prevented from sliding down the bed by a pillow fastened in place for his feet to rest against;
   - a bed-side table or tray for toys and play-things.

Avoiding boredom

Keeping a child happy and occupied throughout the day can be difficult at the best of times, but it requires extra thought and patience when the child is unwell. A wise mother will keep some toys and play materials tucked away, and ready to bring out when the child is ill or convalescing (getting better). Some of these things may have been given as birthday or Christmas presents, and then put aside for just such an occasion. The box in the drawing is kept by the family and taken out when a child is sick.

BED BOX

In addition to having new or different toys to play with, a child always loves having someone who will play with him, or will read or tell stories to him.

When a child has to go into hospital

Being a patient in hospital can be a big shock to a child, especially if he has to be separated from his parents and is too young to understand. When a child goes into hospital he:
- is placed in strange surroundings;
- is with strange people;
- does not understand what is happening.

In addition, he has:
- his routine changed;
- different food;
- different toys, bed, bath, etc.

When ill, a child needs more love and support from his parents than usual. Many children's hospitals now have beds for mothers so that they can stay with their babies or young children and help to nurse them. In other hospitals, parents are allowed in at all times during the day.

Hospital for an older child   If a child is old enough to understand, then it should be explained to him what is going to happen. He may even look forward to it if he is told that:
- he can take some of his toys with him;
- there will be other children to play with;
- there will be more toys in hospital to play with;
- his parents will be able to visit him;
- the doctors and nurses will look after him.

Questions

1. a How can a mother usually tell when her child is ill?
b What symptoms may the child show?
c When is it advisable to consult a doctor?

2. Name nine emergencies when the child needs urgent medical treatment.

3. a List the different kinds of poison shown on p. 182.

b What action should be taken when a child has swallowed poison?

4. How should a sick child be cared for at home?

5. a Name some changes which take place to a child's life when he goes into hospital.
b How may hospitals make life easier for a young child?

To do

1. Look at the photograph of a child in hospital with broken legs. In what ways would it be different for a child ill in bed at home?

2. Try to arrange to visit the children's ward of your local hospital. You may be able to do something useful like play with a child who does not have any visitors. Write an account.

Child study

Collect materials for a Bed Box for the child, or suggest a list of suitable items.

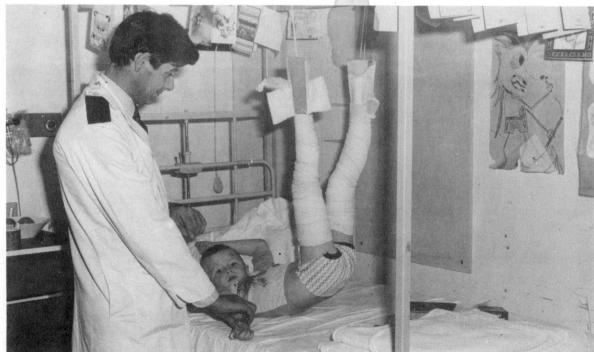

District General Hospital, Gorleston, Norfolk

184

46 *Nursing a sick child*

Taking the temperature

It is natural for the temperature of the body to vary (see also Topic 3). Most people have an average temperature in the mouth of about 37°C (98.4°F); in the armpit it is a little lower and in the rectum a little higher. A high temperature is an indication of illness, but a child can be seriously ill and yet have a temperature which is only slightly raised, or normal, or below normal.

Clinical thermometer This kind of thermometer is used for taking the temperature of the body. The arrow indicates the average normal temperature. It is not safe to put a thermometer under the tongue until the child is about five years old. For a younger child, the best place is in the armpit.

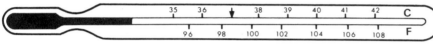

When taking the temperature:
1. Check that the mercury is well below the arrow before using the thermometer. To make the mercury fall, hold the upper end of the thermometer firmly, then flick the wrist to shake the mercury down.
2. Place the thermometer in position in the mouth, armpit or groin and hold it there until the mercury settles. This will take at least one minute (even if it is called a 'half-minute thermometer').
3. After using the thermometer, wash well in **cold** water — hot water may make the mercury expand so much that it breaks the glass of the thermometer.

Forehead thermometer An easier and quicker way of taking a child's temperature is to use a forehead thermometer. This type of thermometer is made of thin plastic which is held against the forehead. The stripes change colour to indicate the level of body temperature.

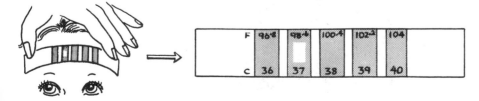

Giving medicine

Medicines usually contain drugs and they need to be used with care. When giving medicine to a child (or anyone else):

1. **Make sure it is the right medicine**   Medicine should not be given unless prescribed by a doctor. Most medicines have side-effects. Also, they can cause considerable harm if taken for the wrong reason.
2. **Follow the instruction exactly**   Too much medicine may harm and too little will not have enough effect.
3. **Ask the doctor for advice** if the medicine does not seem to be doing any good, or if it is causing troublesome side-effects.
4. **Store the medicine in a cool place and out of reach of children.**

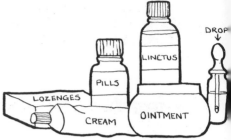

Medicine taken by mouth   Every effort should be made to get a child to take medicine willingly. Ways of persuasion include:

- making it into a game;
- pretending to have some yourself;
- bribing with a sweet afterwards.

When force is used to get the medicine into the mouth, the child will be certain to fight against it every time. It is dangerous to force medicine down a child's throat when he is crying in case he inhales it.

Generally, children under the age of five years are unable to swallow tablets, in which case they need to be crushed first and then given in a teaspoonful of milk or jam.

Antibiotics

The drawing shows three of the many different kinds of antibiotics. Antibiotics are medicines used for treating diseases caused by bacteria and fungi. It is particularly important to follow the instructions that come with this type of medicine. It is also important to complete the course of treatment even if the symptoms have disappeared, as not all the germs may have been killed and the disease can start up again.

Antibiotics must never be stored and used later as they lose their effectiveness with time.

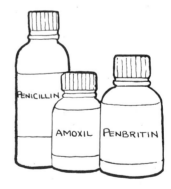

Food and drinks

A child who is not feeling well often does not want to eat. It will do no harm to go without food for two or three days. When better, the child will make up for it by eating more than usual.

While there is no point in forcing food into a child who is ill, he should be given plenty to drink, especially if feverish. This might mean offering favourite drinks, or making special fruit drinks, putting ice in, the use of a drinking straw, or flavouring milk to make it into a milk shake.

Preventing the spread of infection

If a child is suffering from an infectious disease, and the mother wants to prevent it from spreading to others:

1. The patient must be kept isolated from visitors until there is no longer any chance of spreading the infection.
2. Paper tissues used by the patient should be burnt.
3. Towels, bed-linen and clothes used by the patient should be kept separate.
4. The mother should wash her hands immediately after attending to the patient.

Attitudes to illness

Much of an adult's attitude to illness is learnt in childhood. Children learn in two ways:

- by how their mother deals with them when they are ill;
- by the parents' attitude to their own health.

All children, at one time or another, have spells of not feeling very well when they have a cut knee, sore throat, cold, headache and so on. If the mother becomes worried over every ache and pain, and keeps talking about it and making a great deal of fuss, the child will think it very important and learn to worry in the same way. If, instead of worrying too much, the mother puts her energy into keeping the child happy and occupied, then he is unlikely to grow up to be over-anxious about his health.

Questions

1. (i) Where is the best place to put a clinical thermometer when taking the temperature of a young child? (ii) Describe how to take the temperature.
(iii) Will this temperature be slightly lower or higher than the temperature in the child's mouth.

2. a What is the advantage of using a forehead thermometer?
b Describe how to take the temperature with a forehead thermometer.

3. a Name the forms of medicine shown at the top of the page opposite.
b What care should be taken when giving medicine?
c Suggest ways of persuading a child to take medicine willingly.
d What will result from forcing medicine into the child's mouth?
e What is the usual age at which children become able to swallow tablets?

4. a What is an antibiotic?
b List the different kinds of antibiotics shown at the foot of the page opposite.
c Why is it important to complete a course of antibiotics?

5. Name four ways in which a mother can try to prevent the spread of an infectious disease.

To do

1. *Discuss*: 'Do you agree or disagree that much of an adult's attitude to illness is learnt in childhood?'

2. What should a child who is unwell be given to eat and drink? Describe different ways of making drinks attractive.

Exercises

1 a If a child runs to you, crying, with a cut knee, what two things should you do immediately?

b List three signs which indicate that a child is ill.

c State two ways infection may enter the body.

d Give two ways in which infection can be passed on.

e How would you deal with a child who had been stung by a bee?

f What should you do at once if you found that a child had swallowed a poisonous substance?

g Name three precautions which can be taken to prevent an infectious disease from spreading.

h Name a deficiency disease associated with lack of (i) iron, (ii) vitamin D.

i Name four diseases which can be prevented by immunisation.

j Two of the conditions listed below do not necessarily mean that a child is ill. Which are they? Explain why the child may not be ill.

    (i) Rise in temperature shown by flushed cheeks.

    (ii) Vomiting.

    (iii) Sleeplessness.

    (iv) General irritability and poor appetite.

    (v) Stomach ache. (*SWEB*)

2 Give detailed advice to a mother concerning the care of her 3-year-old child. Use the following headings.

a Feeding,

b Rest and exercise,

c Health and hygiene. (*EAEB*)

3 A child is ill at home.

a What symptoms would suggest that a doctor should be called?

b How could you try to keep the child contented?

c What extra care should be taken in preparing and serving meals? (*EAEB*)

4 a The frequent occurrence of tooth decay in young children has caused much concern in recent years. Suggest ways in which a mother can improve her child's chances of having little tooth decay, (i) during her pregnancy, (ii) during the child's first year, (iii) later in the child's life.

b Many children are afraid of visiting the dentist. Suggest *three* ways in which a parent can help to overcome this fear. (*YHREB*)

5 a List six of the contents of a first aid box. Give a use for each item.

b Describe how to store these items safely in the home.

c Explain how to treat three of the following:

    (i) a simple cut;

    (ii) a graze;

    (iii) bruising;

    (iv) a minor burn;

    (v) a minor scald. (*WMEB*)

6 Read the following passage in which a mother describes her daughter's birthday.

'I didn't enjoy Mary's birthday at all. She was so excited. She came running downstairs when she heard the postman, and she tripped over a book and hurt herself. She had loads of cards and presents from her nannies and aunties and uncles — too many really. She refused to go to playgroup because she said she wanted to stay at home and play with her toys. She'd eaten most of her sweets by mid-morning, and the Lego bits were all over the place. She wouldn't eat her dinner so I had to give her some of the jelly I'd made for her party. Her little friends started arriving at three o'clock. We'd invited all twenty children from the playgroup. I can tell you I was glad to see the last of them at six o'clock. You never heard so much squabbling in your life — I felt I couldn't cope. Jamie tugged Mary's new doll that her nanny gave her, and it just fell apart. There was sawdust everywhere. I left the mess and washing up until the next morning, I was so worn out. It put my husband in a temper, and Mary cried herself to sleep.'

Give your views on the extract and suggest how events might have been arranged so that Mary and her parents had a happier day. (*EAEB*)

Section 7

Parenthood

Fiona Pragoff

A baby starts life with two parents — a mother and a father. When the couple make love and have sexual intercourse ('have sex'), a baby begins to develop if a sperm from the father **fertilises** (joins with) the mother's egg. 'A baby has been conceived' or 'Conception has taken place' means that an egg has been fertilised and a baby is developing and the mother is pregnant. How does this happen?

Male reproductive system

A man has two testes (each is a testis) where sperms are made, and a penis which is used to deposit the sperms inside the woman's body.

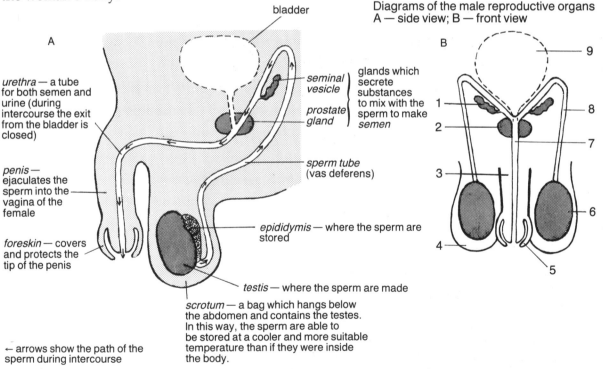

Diagrams of the male reproductive organs
A — side view; B — front view

bladder

A

urethra — a tube for both semen and urine (during intercourse the exit from the bladder is closed)

seminal vesicle

prostate gland

glands which secrete substances to mix with the sperm to make *semen*

penis — ejaculates the sperm into the vagina of the female

sperm tube (vas deferens)

foreskin — covers and protects the tip of the penis

epididymis — where the sperm are stored

testis — where the sperm are made

scrotum — a bag which hangs below the abdomen and contains the testes. In this way, the sperm are able to be stored at a cooler and more suitable temperature than if they were inside the body.

← arrows show the path of the sperm during intercourse

B

1
2
3
4
5
6
7
8
9

Circumcision The foreskin will be absent in males who have been circumcised. Circumcision is the removal of the foreskin by surgery. It is rarely necessary for medical reasons although it is widely carried out amongst some religious groups.

Female reproductive system

The female reproductive system is more complicated than that of the male because it has more things to do. It has to make eggs, receive sperm, protect and feed the unborn child, and then to give birth.

Diagrams of the female reproductive organs
A — side view; B — front view

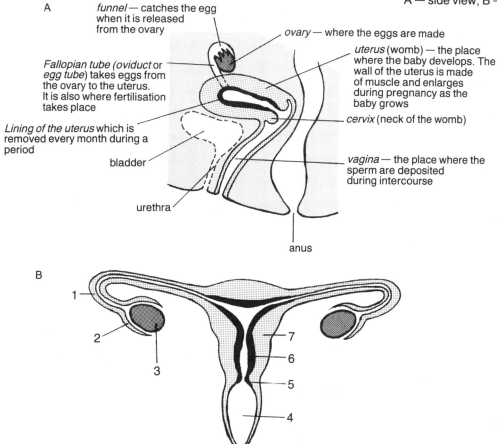

A

funnel — catches the egg when it is released from the ovary

ovary — where the eggs are made

Fallopian tube (oviduct or egg tube) takes eggs from the ovary to the uterus. It is also where fertilisation takes place

uterus (womb) — the place where the baby develops. The wall of the uterus is made of muscle and enlarges during pregnancy as the baby grows

cervix (neck of the womb)

Lining of the uterus which is removed every month during a period

bladder

vagina — the place where the sperm are deposited during intercourse

urethra

anus

B

1
2
3
7
6
5
4

Menstruation

Some time between the age of 10 and 17 girls begin to menstruate — have periods. This shows that the reproductive organs are getting into working order. It is usual for the periods to be irregular and scanty at first. It is not uncommon for a year or more to elapse between the first and second period, and for months to elapse between periods in the second year. The periods gradually become regular, although they may stop for a while during illness, poor feeding or emotional upsets.

Some time between the age of about 45 and 55, the menstrual cycle and periods cease. This stage is called the **menopause**, and the woman can then no longer become pregnant.

Menstrual cycle

The menstrual cycle is sometimes called the monthly cycle as it takes about 28 days to complete. The purpose of the cycle is to produce an egg and prepare the uterus (womb) to receive the egg if it becomes fertilised.

During the first part of the cycle, the lining of the uterus is built up into the right state to receive the egg. If the egg is not fertilised, then the lining breaks down, and is removed from the body in a flow of blood called a **period** or **menstruation**.

Although the cycle, on average, takes about 28 days to complete, it is normal for it to vary between 21 and 35 days. The cycle continues over and over again until such time as an egg is fertilised. It then stops during pregnancy and does not start again until several months afterwards.

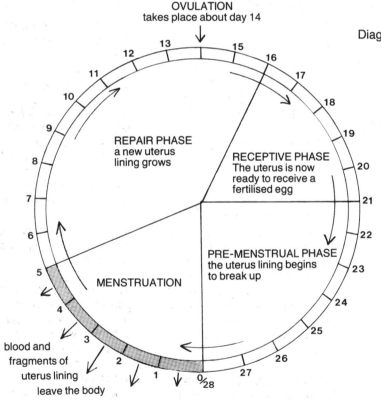

OVULATION
takes place about day 14

Diagram of a typical menstrual cycle

REPAIR PHASE
a new uterus
lining grows

RECEPTIVE PHASE
The uterus is now
ready to receive a
fertilised egg

PRE-MENSTRUAL PHASE
the uterus lining begins
to break up

MENSTRUATION

blood and
fragments of
uterus lining
leave the body

Ovulation

Generally, an egg is released every month from one or other of the ovaries. This usually happens about half-way through the menstrual cycle, that is, about the 14th or 15th day. After being released from the ovary, the egg moves slowly along the Fallopian tube.

Conception

Sexual intercourse (coitus)   Before intercourse, the man's penis enlarges and becomes hard and erect. It is now able to penetrate the vagina of the woman and semen is ejaculated there. **Semen** is a thick, milky-white substance containing millions of sperms. Once inside the vagina, the sperms use their tails to swim in all directions. Some may find their way into the womb and along the Fallopian tubes.

Fertilisation   If intercourse takes place about the time that an egg has been released from the ovary, then the egg has a chance of meeting sperms in the Fallopian tube. If this happens, the egg will be fertilised by one of the sperms, and a baby will have been conceived.

After fertilisation, the egg continues to move along the Fallopian tube towards the uterus. By the time it gets there, the uterus lining will be ready to receive it.

Implantation means the embedding of the fertilised egg in the uterus wall. The fertilised egg becomes attached to the uterus wall about six days after conception. The mother is now able to supply it with food and oxygen so that it can grow and develop into a baby.

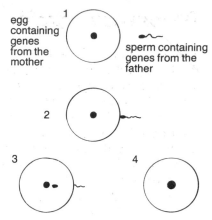

conception (fertilisation):
egg and sperm fuse (join together)

To do

1. a Copy diagram B on p. 190 showing the front view of the male reproductive system. Use the information in diagram A to add the correct labels for 1-9 on your diagram.
b Add arrows to your diagram to show the path of the sperm.

b Complete your diagram by adding the correct labels 1-7.
c Add arrows to show the path of an egg from ovary to uterus.
d Use a red crayon to colour the part called 'uterus lining'. (This is the part which is shed every month during menstruation.)

2. a Copy diagram B on p. 191 of the female reproductive system, front view.

3. Obtain information from the diagram of the menstrual cycle to complete the chart below.

Days	Phase	What happens
0—	Menstruation	
—		
—		
—28		

Questions

1. a What is conception?
b Where does conception take place?
c Copy the diagrams above showing fertilisation.

2. a Where are sperms made?
b What is the scrotum?
c Where are the sperms stored?
d What is the technical name for the sperm duct?
e Name the central tube to which both sperm ducts join.

3. a Where are eggs made?
b How often are eggs usually released?

4. a What is the function of the penis in reproduction?
b (i) Name the substance which is deposited by the penis in the vagina? (ii) About how many sperms does it contain?
c If an egg is in a Fallopian tube, how can the sperms reach it?
d After fertilisation, where does the egg move to?

5. a What is the purpose of the menstrual cycle?
b What happens to the uterus lining in menstruation?
c What happens to the uterus lining after menstruation?
d Give four reasons why menstruation may stop for a while.

193

48 Growth and development before birth

A human egg is just large enough to be seen and about the size of a full stop. After being fertilised, the egg soon starts to divide, first into two cells, then into four, then eight, and so on until it is a mass of cells. By this time is has become attached to the wall of the womb. The number of cells continues to increase and gradually a tiny embryo forms.

Besides producing the embryo, the fertilised egg also gives rise to the placenta, umbilical cord and amnion. These structures are developed for the support of the baby, and they leave the womb at birth.

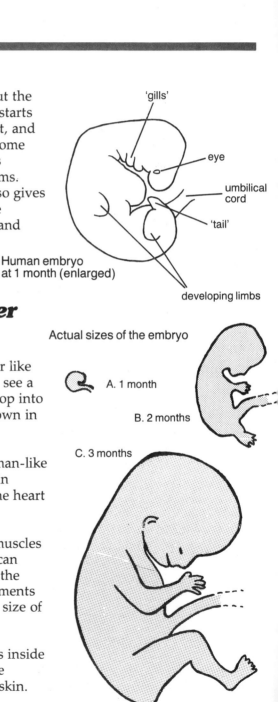

'gills'

eye

umbilical cord

'tail'

Human embryo at 1 month (enlarged)

developing limbs

Growth and development after conception

1 month At this stage a human **embryo** looks rather like the embryo of a fish or frog (tadpole). It is possible to see a tail, and parts which look as though they might develop into gills. The actual size of the embryo at this stage is shown in diagram A.

2 months The embryo has grown to look more human-like and it is now called a **foetus** (or **fetus**): see B. The main structures of the body are more or less in place and the heart is beating.

3 months During the third month the nerves and muscles develop rapidly. By the end of the month, the foetus can swallow, frown, clench the fist, and move by turning the head and kicking. The mother does not feel the movements at this stage. At three months, the foetus is about the size of a mouse and weighs about 55 g (2 oz), diagram C.

5 months The mother is able to feel the movements inside the womb as the baby practises using its muscles. The heartbeat can be heard, and very fine hair covers the skin. The foetus weighs about 350 g (³/₄ lb).

Actual sizes of the embryo

A. 1 month

B. 2 months

C. 3 months

194

7 months Development is almost complete. The baby will spend the rest of the time in the womb growing larger and stronger. It will also become more plump as a layer of fat is stored under the skin. During the next two months, the length will be doubled and the weight increased three times. The **foetal position** is shown in B below — the back is curved, head forwards, knees bent, and arms crossed over the chest.

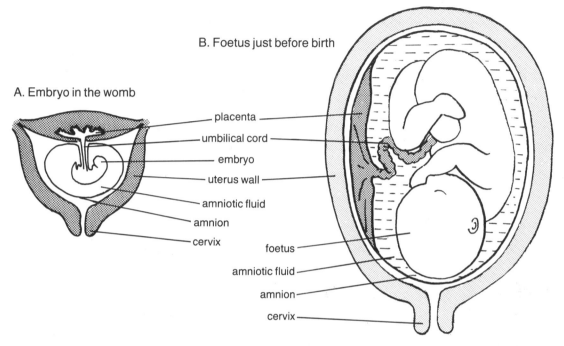

B. Foetus just before birth

A. Embryo in the womb

placenta

umbilical cord

embryo

uterus wall

amniotic fluid

amnion

cervix

foetus

amniotic fluid

amnion

cervix

Inside the womb

In the womb, the baby develops in a 'bag of waters' which remains at a constant temperature of about 37°C. The drawings above show two stages of development inside the womb and the following parts are labelled:

Uterus wall The uterus wall is made of muscle. During pregnancy the muscle tissue expands as the embryo grows. It becomes greatly enlarged, for example, a uterus weighing 30 g at the start of pregnancy, may weigh about 1 kg at the end.

Cervix This is a ring of muscle which surrounds the outlet of the uterus. It is able to expand widely during childbirth.

Amnion This is the bag which contains the amniotic fluid.

Amniotic fluid The amniotic fluid is the water in which the baby floats before birth. It acts as a cushion against shocks and so helps to protect the baby from being damaged.

Umbilical cord   This cord links the baby with the placenta. It grows to be about 50 cm long and 2 cm in width. The cord contains blood vessels.

Placenta   The placenta is a large, thick, disc-like structure firmly attached to the wall of the uterus. It is fully formed at about 12 weeks and then grows steadily to keep pace with the baby. When fully grown it is about 15 cm (6 in) across and weighs about 500 g (1 lb). When twins are developing, non-identical twins each have their own placenta. Identical twins share the same placenta (p. 226).

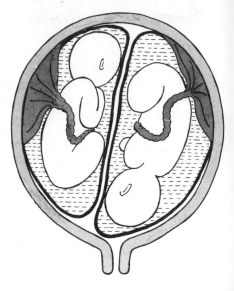

Function of the placenta

The placenta is the organ through which the baby feeds and breathes and excretes waste matter while in the womb. Blood from the baby flows continuously to and from the placenta through the umbilical cord. In the placenta, the baby's blood comes very close to the mother's blood, but they do not mix. However, they are close enough for food and oxygen to pass from mother to baby, and for carbon dioxide and other waste products to pass in the other direction.

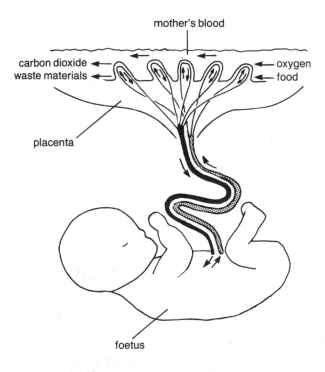

   Viruses, alcohol, antibodies, and chemicals in smoke and from medicines, can cross the placenta from the blood of the mother to the blood of the baby. Some of these substances may damage the developing child, especially in the early months of pregnancy.

196

Surviving alone

If the foetus is born before 28 weeks it will have little chance of surviving. The lungs have not yet finished developing and the baby will not be able to breathe properly.

A baby born at 28 weeks might survive with expert nursing. If born after 32 weeks, it will stand a very good chance, although it will need intensive care for a while. A **pre-term** baby is one which arrives before 37 weeks. The usual time is about 40 weeks.

Premature babies

A premature baby is one which is born before it is expected, perhaps as early as the seventh month. Any baby weighing less than 2.5 kg ($5\frac{1}{2}$ lb) is also called premature, even if it was born at full term.

Premature babies are very small and weak and need special care. Frequently they have difficulties with breathing, sucking and keeping warm, and need to be kept in an incubator for the first few days or weeks. The incubator acts as a half-way house between the womb and the outside world. The baby is kept isolated, protected and in a controlled environment. The temperature is kept constant, so is the humidity. The baby can be fed through a tube or dropper until he has the strength to suck. If necessary, extra oxygen can be supplied to help with breathing.

Premature baby in an incubator

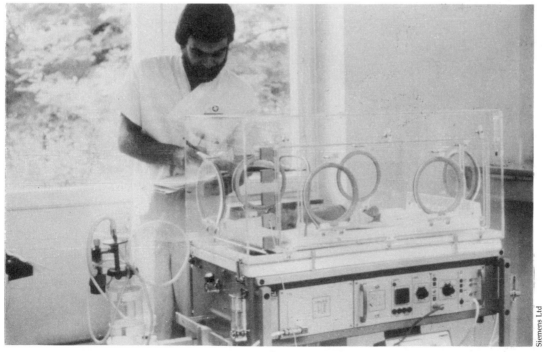

Siemens Ltd

Miscarriage

The mother has a miscarriage (spontaneous abortion) when the baby comes out of the womb accidentally and too early to survive on its own. The first sign of a miscarriage is bleeding, sometimes with pain. Miscarriages are fairly common — it is estimated that about 20 % of pregnancies end in miscarriage. The usual reason is that there is something wrong with the baby's development.

Ectopic pregnancy

An ectopic pregnancy occurs when a fertilised egg implants itself in the Fallopian tube and grows there. The tube becomes stretched, bleeds and may eventually burst. An operation is needed to remove the embryo and repair or remove the damaged tube. In rare cases of ectopic pregnancy infants have survived long enough to be born alive by Caesarian section.

To do

1. Why can an incubator be thought of as a half-way house? Name ways in which the incubator resembles
a the womb,
b the outside world. (Topic 1 may be of help.)

2. Study the photograph below of the 2-month-old foetus.
a What parts of the body can you identify?
b This photograph does not show the actual size of the foetus. What is the approximate length of a foetus at this stage?

2-month-old foetus

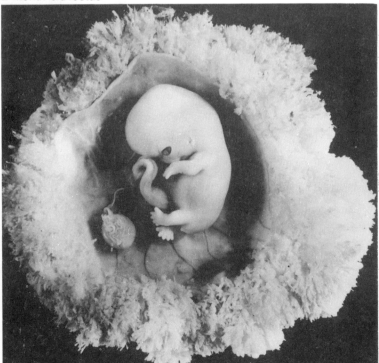

Professor W.J. Hamilton

Questions

1. **a** Describe the appearance of the embryo one month after conception.
b (i) By what age after conception does the embryo look human-like? (ii) What is it now called?
c (i) What parts develop rapidly during the third month? (ii) Give five examples of the movements the foetus is now able to make. (iii) When should the mother be able to feel those movements?
d By how many months after conception is (i) the heart beating, (ii) the skin covered with hair (can you remember the name of this hair?), (iii) development almost complete?

2. **a** Draw a diagram to show the foetus in the womb.
b Label and describe the following parts — uterus wall; amnion; amniotic fluid; umbilical cord; placenta.
c Describe the foetal position.

3. **a** Name the organ through which a baby feeds, breathes and excretes while in the womb.
b In the placenta, does the mother's blood mix with the baby's blood?
c Name one waste product which passes from baby to mother.
d Name six substances which pass from mother to baby.

4. Explain the meaning of (i) pre-term, (ii) premature, (iii) miscarriage.

49 Pregnancy

Pregnancy is the process that occurs between conception and birth.

Pre-conception care

The first three months after conception is the most important time for the developing baby. So, before pregnancy begins, the mother-to-be should:

- be in good health;
- be free from infection;
- have a good, nutritious diet;
- not be over-weight;
- give up smoking and drinking;
- not take any drugs or medicine which could be harmful.

Signs of pregnancy

For a woman whose periods are regular, and who has had intercourse recently, the first sign that a baby is on the way is usually a missed period. (Adolescent girls miss periods for other reasons, see Topic 47.)

By the time a second period has been missed, other signs of pregnancy may be noticeable. For example, enlarged breasts, darkening of the skin around the nipples, more frequent passing of urine, constipation, and possibly feelings of nausea (sickness).

When the mother is four months pregnant, it will begin to show as her waistline enlarges. At this stage, the baby is still very tiny, and the increase in size is due to the womb becoming much bigger.

Pregnancy tests   Pregnancy is controlled by chemical substances called hormones (see p. 268). These can usually be detected in the mother's urine about one month after conception. If a woman is in a hurry to know whether she is pregnant, a sample of her urine can be tested eight days after a missed period; but the result of the test is not 100 % reliable at this stage.

German measles

German measles (rubella) is a common disease in childhood and is caused by the rubella virus. It is a mild disease and once children have had it, they are unlikely to catch it again.

Unfortunately, this disease is dangerous if caught by a mother in the first four months of pregnancy. The mother will not be very ill, but the virus may kill the foetus or leave it deaf, blind, mentally handicapped, or with heart disease. **To prevent this tragedy**, girls who have not already had German measles should be vaccinated against it between the ages of 11 and 13 years. They will then have immunity for life.

Medicines, drugs and alcohol

In a strictly technical sense, medicines are drugs — a drug being any substance which has an effect on the working of the body. However, in general conversation the words are used rather differently — medicines are used for the treatment of disease and drugs are taken for their effect on the mind. We shall use the words in the latter sense.

Medicines   When medicines are taken by a pregnant woman, they are likely to cross the placenta and reach the baby. There is a chance that the medicine will interfere with the baby's normal pattern of development. If this happens the baby will develop abnormally. There is a greater chance of this occurring during the first three months after conception than later.

Medicines known to be harmful to the baby include travel-sickness pills and some antibiotics. To be on the safe side, no medicines should be taken during pregnancy, except on the advice of a doctor.

Drugs   When the word 'drug' is used, it usually refers to a habit-forming substance which affects the mind. Examples are cannabis, LSD, cocaine, heroin and some types of glue. These drugs can cross the placenta and, if taken by a pregnant woman, may cause the baby to be deformed. Another effect is that children of drug addicts may be born with the same addiction. They will suffer dreadful withdrawal symptoms shortly after birth in the same way as an adult addict suffers.

Alcohol may be thought of as a tonic, a pleasure, or a poison, but it is not usually thought of as a drug, although, like the substances mentioned above, it is both habit-forming and affects the mind. It is unlikely that an occasional drink will harm the developing baby. But the regular drinking of large amounts of alcohol can cause abnormal development of the unborn child. A pregnant mother who is an alcoholic can give birth to a baby who is also addicted to alcohol.

Smoking

When a pregnant woman smokes, some of the chemical substances in the smoke pass from her lungs into the blood stream, and soon reach the womb. At the placenta, the chemicals cross from the mother's blood into the baby's blood stream. They are then carried to all parts of the baby's body. Two of the harmful chemicals in smoke which reach the baby's blood stream are nicotine and carbon monoxide (the same poison as in car fumes).

Effects of smoking on the child
1. Mothers who smoke 20 or more cigarettes a day throughout pregnancy, generally have smaller babies than mothers who do not smoke. The average birth-weight of their babies is about 200 g less (almost ½ lb). Babies who are smaller than they ought to be are also weaker.
2. Heavy smokers are more likely to have a miscarriage.
3. Heavy smokers are more likely to have a still-born baby or one who dies in the first week of birth. It is estimated that at least 1500 babies in Britain die each year because of their mother's smoking.
4. The effect of smoking is greater during the latter part of pregnancy. Mothers who give up smoking by the fourth month, produce babies with birth-weights similar to those whose mothers had never smoked.
5. There is some evidence that in the last few weeks of pregnancy smoking damages the brain cells which are growing rapidly at this time.
6. After they are born, children who continuously inhale smoke are more likely to suffer from coughs and bronchitis.

Reducing the effects of smoking
If a pregnant mother cannot break the smoking habit, she can reduce the effect if she:
- cuts down the number of cigarettes smokes to as few as possible;
- smokes less of each cigarette;
- does not inhale;
- takes fewer puffs;
- chooses low tar brands.

1. a How does a woman know she is pregnant? Name six signs which may be present.
b At what stage can pregnancy be detected by a pregnancy test?
c What can be expected to happen to the mother's figure when four months pregnant?

2. a What causes German measles?
b (i) When is it a dangerous disease to catch? (ii) What damage may it do?
c How can this tragedy be prevented?

3. a (i) Why are pregnant women advised not to take medicines? (ii) Name two types of medicine known to be harmful to the baby.
b (i) Name five substances which are used as 'drugs'. (ii) Name two effects which drugs of this type can have on the baby in the womb.
c Name two characteristics which drugs and alcohol have in common.
d Name two effects which alcohol can have on the baby in the womb.

4. a Name two harmful chemicals in smoke.
b Use these words to complete the sentences below:
body   chemicals   womb
lungs   placenta   bloodstream
'When a pregnant woman has a cigarette, ... from the smoke in her . . . . . pass into the blood stream. They soon reach the . . . . ., cross the . . . . ., enter the baby's . . . . and are then carried to all parts of the baby's . . . . .'
c What is the cause for concern when babies are smaller than they ought to be?
d Name five ways of reducing the effects of smoking.

MY MOTHER STOPPED WHEN I STARTED

LUCKY YOU

To do

1. If the unborn child above could understand the effects which his mother's smoking might be having on him, why would he say 'lucky you'? How does smoking affect birth-weight, brain development, and health? When the child gets older, what may encourage him to become a smoker? Make a list of your suggestions.

2. What is thalidomide? Why did pregnant women take it?

What effects did it have on the unborn children? How old are these children now? Find some examples of how they are coping with life.

Child study

Are there any smokers in the child's family? Does the smoking have any effects on the life of the family?

50 *The expectant mother*

Pregnancy is a normal and natural process, and necessary for the survival of the human race. It is not an illness, and the expectant mother does not need to be treated like an invalid. Nevertheless, she does need to keep healthy for the sake of her unborn child. Also, she has to adjust to the various changes that take place in her body as the pregnancy proceeds. Changes will take place in her:

* **size**, **shape** and **weight**;
* **hormones** (the chemicals which help to regulate the way the body works);
* **emotions** (she will feel differently);
* **way of life** (at least in the latter part of pregnancy).

Morning sickness

Hormone changes are responsible for the feelings of sickness felt by some women in the early months of pregnancy, usually in the morning, sometimes in the evening, or at other times. Feelings of sickness (nausea) are much more common than actually being sick (vomiting). They may occur only on one or two occasions, or at the same time every day, but rarely last for more than a few weeks.

Diet

When a woman is pregnant, she does not need to eat much more than usual, and certainly not enough for two — she would get far too fat. The developing baby will take what food it requires, and the mother will suffer if she eats too much or too little.

It is **what** the mother eats which is important. Her diet needs to contain extra protein, vitamins and minerals for the baby, also extra fibre because expectant mothers are prone to constipation. She does not need extra carbohydrate and fat. Fried foods and spicy foods should be avoided if they lead to indigestion.

Odd tastes and cravings   It is quite common during pregnancy for a mother's tastes in food to change. She may have the urge to eat the oddest foods at the most unusual times, especially in the early months. Often she dislikes things she used to enjoy such as tea, coffee, alcohol and cigarettes.

Exercise

Exercise is good for everyone, including expectant mothers. It keeps the muscles in a healthy condition, and helps to bring restful sleep at night. The right type of exercise during pregnancy is the sort the mother **wants** to do; maybe walking, swimming, cycling, dancing. But, like everything else at this time, it should be done in moderation.

Posture

The increase in weight in the 'tummy' region alters the normal balance of the body. When walking there will be a tendency to hollow the back and to waddle and plod along. To avoid this, the spine needs to be kept upright and the head erect. It is particularly important at this time to bend at the knees and not the back when lifting a heavy weight.

Relaxation can be better than tablets for headache and backache

Rest

During the latter part of pregnancy, the increase in weight puts more strain on the legs, feet and back. A daily rest in the middle of the day helps to prevent problems like backache, varicose veins and over-tiredness.

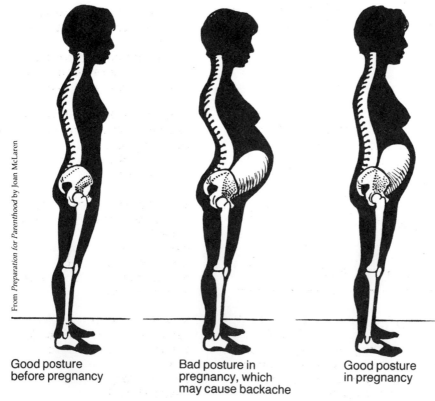

From *Preparation for Parenthood* by Joan McLaren

Good posture before pregnancy

Bad posture in pregnancy, which may cause backache

Good posture in pregnancy

Varicose veins

Varicose veins are veins which have become stretched and enlarged. This may sometimes happen to veins in the legs during pregnancy. The legs may then ache. This condition is made worse by standing still for long periods of time. Resting now and again with the feet up takes the pressure off the veins, reduces the swelling, and makes the legs feel better.

If the veins are uncomfortable or painful then it may be helpful to wear elastic tights (support tights) or stockings. They need to be put on first thing in the morning before getting out of bed so that the veins have not had a chance to swell. The elastic tights should be worn throughout the day. The tights will not cure the veins but they may relieve the discomfort. The condition of the veins almost always improves after the baby is born, although it may not completely disappear.

Visiting the dentist

Contrary to popular belief, teeth do not lose calcium during pregnancy, even when the mother's diet is short of calcium. However, they are more prone to decay and the gums may become a little swollen and spongy and may bleed more easily than usual. A visit to the dentist for a check-up at an early stage is advisable, and again after the baby is born. Dental treatment is free during pregnancy and for one year after the birth.

Clothing

During pregnancy, the breasts enlarge and the abdomen expands greatly. The mother will therefore need clothes which are loose around the waist, and a larger size of bra with good support. The bra should have wide straps, adjustable fastenings and a cup that does not squash the nipple.

Feet may ache or swell slightly in pregnancy, so it helps to wear shoes which are comfortable. They should also be designed to give support to the foot, and have low or medium heels. Shoes of this type help the mother to keep her balance as well as helping to prevent backache.

To do

1. Study the drawings opposite. Describe the difference between 'good' and 'bad' posture. How does posture affect walking?

2. Design some styles of clothes and shoes suitable for wearing during pregnancy, or find pictures of them.

Questions

1. a What is the cause of 'morning sickness'?
b Does it always occur in the morning?
c Is it likely to occur throughout pregnancy?

2. a Does an expectant mother need to eat for two?
b What substances should she make sure she eats enough of?
c What substances should be avoided in large amounts?
d Do some mothers have cravings for odd foods at this time?

3. a Give two reasons why exercise is good for expectant mothers.
b Give examples of the types of exercise that an expectant mother can do if she wants to.

4. a What parts of the body are particularly affected by the increasing weight?
b What problems does a daily rest help to prevent?

5. a What are varicose veins?
b What can make varicose veins worse?
c What is the advantage of resting with the feet up?
d What may also help to relieve the discomfort?

6. a Why should an expectant mother have a dental check-up?
b When should she visit the dentist?
c For how long is dental treatment free?

51 *Antenatal care*

If a woman thinks she is pregnant, the time to see the family doctor is when a second period has been missed. When the doctor has confirmed the pregnancy, the mother will be strongly advised to attend an antenatal clinic (**ante** = before, **natal** = birth). The mother visits the clinic once a month until the seventh month, and then every fortnight. Near the end of the pregnancy, the visits become weekly. Employers are required by law to allow women to attend antenatal clinics.

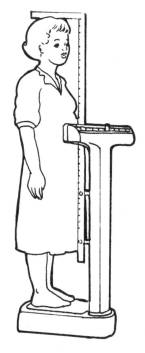

What happens at the clinic

Routine checks are carried out to make sure that all continues to be well with both mother and baby. Visits to the clinic also give the mother a chance to ask questions about anything that might be worrying her.

Weight check   Apart from the first few months, a pregnant woman gains, on average, about 450 g (1 lb) in weight per week. In total she puts on about 12 kg (2 stone). The increased weight is due to the baby plus the greatly enlarged womb, the placenta, umbilical cord, and amniotic fluid. In addition, extra fat may be stored in the layer under the skin. This fat will be used in milk production after the baby is born.

If the mother puts on too much weight, she will be advised to diet.

Blood tests
A small sample of blood is taken from the mother to test for:

Anaemia   This condition makes a person feel tired and weak. It can be easily treated by taking extra iron, usually in the form of tablets.

Blood group   Essential information in an emergency if a blood transfusion should be needed.

Rhesus factor   The Rhesus factor is a substance in the blood. Most people have this substance and are Rhesus positive (Rh+). Those who do not have it are called Rhesus negative (Rh—).

The Rhesus factor is inherited and problems can arise in families when the father is Rh+ and the mother is Rh—. If the children are Rh— like their mother there is no problem.

The first Rh+ baby will usually be all right. But a second RH+ baby may have severe anaemia and jaundice, be mentally handicapped, or die. Further RH+ babies would also suffer.

This used to be a great worry to parents, but nowadays much can be done to prevent the problem. When a Rh— mother gives birth to a Rh+ baby, a sample of blood is taken from the mother to find out if there are any of the baby's Rh+ cells in her blood. If so, the mother is given an injection which destroys these cells. This gives her a fresh start for the next pregnancy.

Immunity to German measles If the blood test shows that there are no antibodies against German measles, it means that she is not immune to the disease. Should the mother come into contact with a case of German measles, she can be vaccinated for short-term protection. After the baby is born, she will be offered a rubella vaccination for long-term protection. See also Topics 40 and 49.

Placental hormones When the placenta is functioning properly, it produces hormones which can be detected in the mother's blood. Blood tests may be carried out in the last eight weeks of pregnancy to find out if the placenta is working normally and is thus able to keep the baby well supplied with food and oxygen.

Blood pressure The mother's blood pressure is checked at every visit to the clinic. If it rises too high then she must rest, possibly in hospital. High blood pressure can lead to toxaemia of pregnancy.

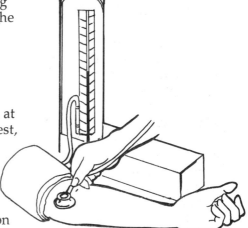

Toxaemia of pregnancy (pre-eclampsia) This condition occurs only during pregnancy, and disappears as soon as pregnancy is over. Symptoms include high blood pressure, swollen ankles, and the gaining of too much weight. One of the benefits of regular attendance at the antenatal clinic is that toxaemia of pregnancy will be diagnosed in the early stages. Steps can then be taken to prevent it from becoming worse. Should the condition be allowed to continue, the mother may develop a kind of epilepsy (eclampsia) at the end of the pregnancy. This can be fatal to the baby and also to the mother. Fortunately it rarely occurs nowadays.

Urine test At every antenatal visit a sample of urine is tested for:
- **sugar** If sugar is present it may indicate diabetes;
- **protein** (albumin) If present it may indicate (i) infection of the kidney or bladder, or (ii) toxaemia of pregnancy.

It is not very likely that either of these substances will be present. If they are, further tests will be made so that early treatment can be given if needed.

Examination of the womb   By gently feeling the outside of the abdomen, it is possible for the doctor to get some idea of the baby's size and position in the womb. Towards the end of pregnancy, it is important to know if the baby is in the best position to be born, that is, with the head downwards so that it comes out first. Should the baby be in the breech position (p. 216), the doctor will try to turn it so that the head points downwards.

Vaginal examination   On the first visit to the antenatal clinic, the mother's vagina is examined:
- **to check that there is no infection**, for example, thrush;
- **to obtain a cervical smear**. This test can detect early warning signs of cancer of the cervix. Cancer of the cervix is rare in pregnant women, but more common in later life.
Towards the end of pregnancy, the vagina is checked to make sure that the outlet will be big enough for the baby's head to pass through.

Baby's heartbeat   In the second half of pregnancy, the baby's heartbeat can be heard through a stethoscope placed on the mother's abdomen. It will be beating between 120 and 160 times per minute, which is much faster than the mother's heart.

Ultrasound scanning   Ultrasound (sound at a higher frequency — pitch — than can be heard by the human ear) is used to produce pictures of the baby in the womb. Information can be obtained about the baby's size, age, and position; also about the position of the placenta and whether twins are present.

District General Hospital, Gorleston, Norfolk

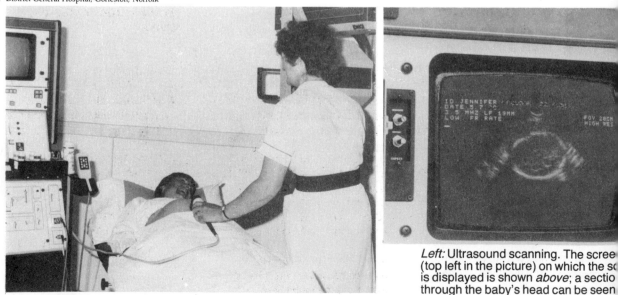

Left: Ultrasound scanning. The scree (top left in the picture) on which the s is displayed is shown *above*; a sectio through the baby's head can be seen

Preparation classes

Many hospitals and clinics hold preparation classes. They are especially useful for mothers who are expecting their first baby. At these classes they find out about:

- diet and health in pregnancy;
- how the baby develops;
- how it will be born;
- breast-feeding;
- how to look after the new baby.

Relaxation classes   The mothers may also be taught special exercises to help with breathing and relaxation for use when in labour. Being able to relax during the contractions helps to make the birth easier.

Fathers are welcome at many of these classes. The father is the person who can give the greatest help and encouragement to the expectant mother. Understanding the progress of pregnancy will enable him to be even more interested and helpful.

Amniocentesis

Amniocentesis involves pushing a hollow needle through the abdominal wall and into the uterus to remove a sample of amniotic fluid. The fluid is then used to find out information about the unborn child (see p. 268).

This test may be done at about the sixteenth week of pregnancy if there is a family history of Down's syndrome (mongolism), spina bifida, or a few other inherited diseases. Mothers over 35 may also be given this test as they are more likely than younger mothers to have children with Down's syndrome.

(see p. 268)

To do

1. Find out more about:
a The antenatal clinics in your area,
b Preparation classes,
c Rhesus problems in pregnancy and what can be done to prevent them,
d The ultrasound scan and its uses,
e Why X-rays are no longer generally used on pregnant women.

Questions

1. **a** What is the meaning of the word 'antenatal'?
b (i) Why are mothers advised to attend antenatal clinics? Give two reasons. (ii) How often do they attend?

2. **a** (i) What is the average total weight gain in pregnancy? (ii) What is the average weekly gain?
b Name six factors which contribute to this increase in weight.

3. **a** Name three tests which are carried out on the mother's blood and give a reason for each.
b (i) Name three symptoms of toxaemia of pregnancy. (ii) Why is this condition dangerous?
c Name two tests which are carried out on the mother's urine, and give reasons.

4. **a** How can the doctor tell the difference between the baby's and mother's heartbeats?

b What information can be obtained from an ultrasound scan?

5. **a** In what ways may the mother of a first baby find preparation classes useful?
b Why may breathing and relaxation exercises be taught at these classes?
c Why are fathers welcomed at these classes?

52 Arrangements for the birth

Opinions vary about whether home or hospital is the best place for a confinement. (**Confinement** is the time when the mother is confined to bed for the birth to take place.) Most doctors and midwives consider that hospital is the best place to give birth because it is the safest place to be if problems should arise. On the other hand, some people take the view that a home confinement is likely to be a happier event, and therefore better for the mother and for the future well-being of the child.

Sometimes the mother has no choice. She may have to go into hospital for the birth because of medical or other reasons, or because the local doctors will only deliver babies there. However, should a mother wish to have her baby at home, midwives are required by law to care for her there.

Hospital confinement

Confinement in hospital is definitely advised for those mothers who:
- are having their first babies;
- are under 17 or over 35;
- have had three or more children previously;
- have already had a Caesarian section;
- have Rhesus negative blood;
- have medical problems such as diabetes or high blood pressure;
- have inadequate home conditions.

Home or hospital?

Mothers who have the choice of home or hospital for their confinement should take the following points into consideration when deciding which they prefer.

Advantages of hospital confinement
- Trained staff are present all the time.
- Special monitoring equipment is there to check the baby's health and safety throughout labour.

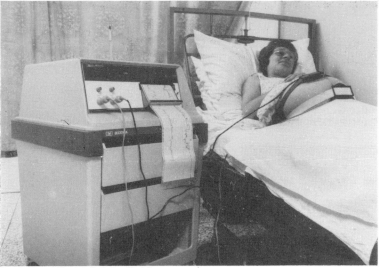

A mother in labour who has been linked to a monitor

District General Hospital, Gorleston, Norfolk

- Other equipment is immediately available in the event of an emergency.
- The mother has the opportunity to rest and relax while the nurses share responsibility for the baby.
- The mother is free from domestic responsibilities and worries.
- The mother is protected from too many visitors.
- There are other mothers to talk to and share experiences with.

Advantages of a home confinement
- The mother is in familiar surroundings.
- She will be amongst family and friends.
- She will be attended by the doctor and midwife she knows.
- Any other children in the family can be involved in the exciting event.
- She will have more privacy than in a ward with other women.
- She may find it more restful to be on her own with her baby.
- She will not have to keep to the hospital routine of meals, etc.
- She will be able to look after her baby in her own way.

Hospital and home   A scheme which aims to combine the best of both, is for the birth to be in hospital and for the mother to return home a day or two afterwards. She then comes under the care of the community midwife. This can work well provided that the full burden of housework does not fall on the mother immediately she comes out of hospital. She must have someone in the home with her, 24 hours a day, for the first 7 days after delivery.

211

Having a baby at home

The room in which the confinement will take place should have:
- a bed for the mother;
- a plastic or polythene cover over the mattress;
- a cot for the baby;
- a table for the equipment of the midwife and doctor.
- adequate light and heating;
- the carpet removed or covered to protect it;
- a wash basin or bowl and jugs of hot and cold water;
- disinfectant;
- a pail for used dressings.

The midwife will bring her own delivery pack containing items such as sterilised instruments, towels and cotton wool.

Medical staff

A midwife is a nurse who is specially trained in the care of pregnancy and childbirth.

About three-quarters of all babies born in Britain are delivered by midwives. Besides being present during labour, they undertake the antenatal care of a normal pregnancy, and also the postnatal care for up to 28 days after delivery. They either work in the maternity department of a hospital or in the community looking after mothers and babies in their own homes.

It is possible to train for midwifery in one of two ways:
1. a nursing qualification — SRN (State Registered Nurse) or SEN (State Enrolled Nurse) followed by a midwifery training, or
2. an extended midwifery training which includes some general nursing.

In both cases, it is necessary to pass examinations to become a Registered Midwife (RM).

An obstetrician is a doctor who specialises in pregnancy and childbirth. Obstetricians attend antenatal clinics to check the health of expectant mothers. They also attend the births of babies born in hospital when there are likely to be any complications such as a breech birth or Caesarian section.

A gynaecologist is a doctor who specialises in the functions and diseases of the female reproductive system. Gynaecologists are usually also obstetricians.

A paediatrician is a doctor who specialises in the care of children from the time they are born. The medical check-up given to babies born in hospital will be carried out by a paediatrician.

Questions

1. **a** Give seven advantages of a hospital confinement.
b Name eight advantages of a home confinement.
c Describe a scheme which aims to combine the advantages of **a** and **b**.
d Name seven groups of women for whom a hospital confinement is definitely advised.

2. How should a room in a home be prepared for a confinement?

3. **a** What is the job of a midwife?
b Name two ways in which midwives become qualified.
c What is the difference between an obstetrician and a gynaecologist?
d What is a paediatrician?
e Which type of hospital doctor would you expect to find (i) in an antenatal clinic, (ii) carrying out a check-up on a new-born baby?

To do

1. National Childbirth Trust: What are the aims of this organisation? There are branches in different parts of the country. Where is your nearest branch? Find out about the branch and the activities it organises (see p. 275).

53 Birth

The baby in the first drawing is ready to be born. It is lying in the correct position with head downwards. During the last few weeks, the mother may have felt her uterus (womb) contracting from time to time as it prepared for birth.

As the mother goes through the process of giving birth she is said to be 'in labour'. It is probably called 'labour' because the mother's muscles have to work hard to open the cervix and push the baby through the birth canal. Every birth follows its own particular pattern and timetable, usually taking between four and twelve hours. A midwife will be present to help the mother and assist in the birth. A doctor may also be present.

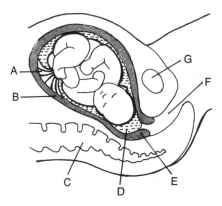

Ready to be born. A: placenta (afterbirth), B: uterus (womb), C: backbone, D: bag of water (amniotic fluid), E: cervix (neck of womb), F: vagina, G: pelvis (hip bone)

How to estimate the date of delivery

Delivery is another name for childbirth. The estimated date of delivery (EDD) can be worked out in two ways:
1. by adding 40 weeks to the first day of the mother's last period; or
2. by adding nine calendar months and one week to the first day of the mother's last period.

The mother still has to wait to find out the exact date of birth, as the baby usually arrives a little earlier or later than the estimated date.

Pregnancy lasts on average 38 weeks from the date of conception. The actual date of conception is often unknown, but is likely to have been about two weeks after the first day of the last period. So this is why the EDD is calculated on a 40 week basis, and so is the pregnancy.

Monitoring the progress of labour

The photograph on p. 211 shows a mother in labour who has been linked to a monitor by wires strapped to her abdomen. The monitor keeps a continuous check on the baby's heartbeat and the time and strength of the contractions. This information is valuable in helping to make labour as safe as possible for the baby. Apart from the inconvenience of being attached to the monitor, the mother suffers no discomfort.

THE THREE STAGES OF LABOUR

Stage 1. *The neck of the womb opens*

When the mother notices one or more of the following signs she will know that labour has started.

- **A show**   This is a small discharge of blood and mucus. It has come away from the cervix where it formed a plug.
- **The breaking of the waters**   The bag of water in which the baby has been developing breaks, and the water is released.
- **Regular and strong contractions occur**   These contractions of the womb start very slowly, perhaps every 20-30 minutes. They then become stronger, regular and more frequent.

During the first stage of labour, contractions by the muscles in the wall of the womb gradually open the neck of the womb. The bag of water bursts at some time during this stage, either at the very beginning of labour, or later on. The first stage is the longest stage of labour and it comes to an end when the neck of the womb has opened wide enough for the baby's head to pass through.

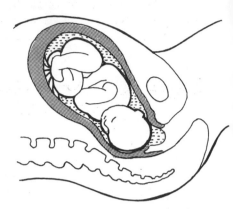

The first stage of labour

Stage 2. *The baby passes through the birth canal*

The womb, cervix and vagina have by now become one continuous birth canal. The contractions are very strong and they push the baby head-first through the birth canal. The mother must help with the pushing. When the baby's head emerges from the vagina it is called **crowning**.

When the baby's head has emerged, the midwife may clear mucus from the nose and mouth. The baby may then start to breathe, and even to cry, before the rest of the body comes out.

The midwife or doctor now eases the shoulders through the birth canal and the baby slides out into the world.

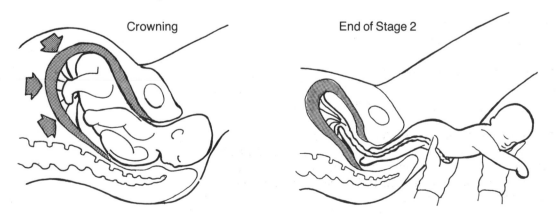

Crowning

End of Stage 2

Stitches Sometimes the opening to the vagina will not stretch enough for the head to pass through. A small cut is then made to widen the opening and prevent the skin from tearing. Afterwards, the cut is stitched together. This minor operation is called an **episiotomy**.

Stage 3. The baby becomes a separate person

Once the baby is breathing, the umbilical cord is clamped in two places and a cut is made between them. This separates the baby from the mother. Clamping the cord prevents bleeding. Cutting the cord does not hurt either the mother or the baby.

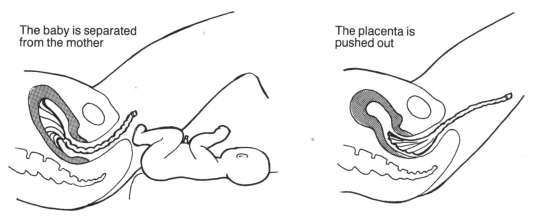

The baby is separated from the mother

The placenta is pushed out

When the baby first appears the skin is a bluish colour. As soon as breathing starts, the skin quickly turns pink (this shows that oxygen is being obtained from the air).

The contractions continue until the placenta (afterbirth) becomes separated from the wall of the womb and has been pushed out through the vagina. Labour is now completed.

Pain relief

Labour is usually painful. There are a number of ways in which the pain can be relieved including:

Relaxation and breathing exercises (taught in antenatal classes) help to make labour easier. They work well for many women, especially during the first stage of labour.

Gas-and-oxygen is often offered to the mother during the second stage of labour. A gas such as nitrous oxide (laughing gas) is mixed with oxygen. The mother inhales the mixture through the mouthpiece attached to the gas cylinder when the contractions are very strong.

Pethidine is a more powerful pain-killer. An injection of pethidine may be given if the contractions become very uncomfortable.

Epidural anaesthetic is injected into the lower part of the spine. This stops the pain by blocking the nerves that carry painful sensations from the abdomen to the brain (all pain is felt in the brain).

AFTERWARDS

The baby

The baby is handed to his mother so that she can hold him closely to her. If she wants, she can put him to the breast for a minute or two. It is comforting for the baby to be cuddled and loved, and it gives the mother her first opportunity to begin to get to know her new baby.

After being weighed, measured and cleaned, the baby will spend much of his first day sleeping.

The father

If the mother wants him to be there, many hospitals are happy to have the father present at the birth. When this happens, the mother, father and baby are all together as a family from the very first moment.

The mother

Giving birth is hard work. After it is all over, the mother will want to rest and sleep for a while to recover.

The uterus shrinks back to size in the days following the birth, and this is speeded up by breast-feeding. Eventually the uterus will be almost the same size as it was before the baby was conceived. Bleeding from the place in the uterus to which the placenta was attached continues until the wound has healed. It may take up to a month to do so.

OTHER WAYS OF BEING BORN

Breech birth

Babies are usually born head first. Occasionally, one comes out feet or bottom first and this is called a breech birth. It makes for a more difficult delivery.

Forceps delivery

Special forceps (like large sugar tongs) may be needed to help the baby out of the uterus. The forceps fit over the baby's head to protect it while the doctor gently eases the baby through the birth canal. A forceps delivery may be necessary when the contractions are not strong enough to push the baby out, or when the baby is lying in an awkward position, or there are other difficulties. The baby's head may look a little bruised afterwards but it soon returns to normal.

Caesarian section (a Caesar)

This is an operation to remove the baby from the uterus. It is carried out when the birth canal is too narrow, or the baby is very late, or the health of the baby or mother makes immediate delivery necessary.

When the mother is given a general anaesthetic she will be unconscious while the baby is being delivered. An incision is made through the abdominal wall and into the uterus so that the baby can be removed. The umbilical cord is cut, the placenta is then removed and the uterus and abdominal wall are sewn up. The operation takes about 20 minutes and the mother wakes up shortly afterwards.

Epidural anaesthetic is becoming more common for this operation. The mother remains conscious and the father can be present at the birth to support his wife.

Induction

Induction means that the process of labour is started artificially. It may be possible to do this by breaking the waters. A 'drip' may also be given to the mother through a vein in her arm. The drip contains the hormone **oxytocin** which signals the uterus to start contracting.

The birth may be induced when the baby is very late, or when the health of the mother or baby is at risk.

To do

1. a Copy the diagram of the birth position on p. 213. Add the correct labels for A–G.
b Study the diagrams on pp. 214–15. Describe what is happening in each of the diagrams.

2. A drug-free childbirth is ideal from the baby's point of view. On the other hand, drugs ease the pain for the mother. Find out more about the advantages and disadvantages of the use in childbirth of
a pethidine,
b epidural anaesthetic.

217

54 *Postnatal care*

The word postnatal refers to the first days and weeks after the baby is born. (**post** = after, **natal** = birth).

Midwife

The mother will have help from a midwife for the first 10-28 days or so after the birth. If she is in hospital, she will be looked after by the midwives there. If she is at home, a midwife calls daily.

Health visitor

The health visitor will call to see the mother and baby at home about ten days after the birth. She will call from time to time after that. The purpose of her visits is to:
- advise the mother on how to keep herself and her baby healthy;
- check that the baby is making normal progress;
- advise on feeding;
- advise the mother to attend a baby clinic;
- discuss a time-table for immunisation;
- give help and guidance on emotional problems;
- put the mother in touch with pre-school groups or child-minders.

She will also tell the mother how she can be reached when the mother wants advice, for example because the baby will not stop crying, or is vomiting, or has a sore bottom, or spots, or if there is any other matter which is worrying the mother.

Health visitors are trained nurses (SRN) with some experience in midwifery. They must also have had an extra year's training in family health and child development, and have passed examinations to obtain a Health Visitor's Certificate (HV).

Formalities after the birth

Notification of the birth   The local Health Authority must be notified of every birth within 36 hours. This is usually done by the doctor or midwife present at the birth.

Registration   A baby has to be registered by the parents within six weeks of birth (or three weeks in Scotland). The name under which the child is to be brought up must be given to the Registrar of Births. A **birth certificate** will then be issued.

If the parents are married to each other, either of them can register the child. If the parents are not married to each other, then the child is registered by the mother; should both the mother and father wish for the father's name to be shown on the birth certificate, then it is necessary for them both to be present when the child is registered.

Some hospitals arrange for the local Registrar of Births to visit the hospital so that the baby can be registered before going home. Otherwise, the parents must visit the office of the Registrar of Births.

Medical card   When a baby is registered, the parents are given a pink card to take to their family doctor. This enables the baby to be registered with the doctor and to receive an NHS medical card.

The baby

Examination of the baby   Every new-born baby is given a routine examination, usually the day after birth and in the presence of the mother. The doctor examines the baby's skin, listens to the heart, checks the mouth for cleft palate, and counts the fingers and toes to see if an extra one is present. Other checks include testing the movement of the hip joints for congenital dislocation of the hip. If a **dislocated hip** is discovered, the baby will require hospital treatment to correct the hip joint to prevent the development of a permanent limp.

PKU test (Guthrie test)   When the baby is about 7-9 days old, he is tested for a rare disorder called **PKU** (phenylketonuria). The test involves pricking the baby's heel and collecting a few drops of blood on a test card. If PKU is discovered, the baby is put on a special diet and he will then be able to develop normally. When PKU is left untreated, the brain becomes damaged and the child will be mentally handicapped. (PKU is a metabolic disorder — the baby is unable to metabolise a chemical called phenylalanine which is present in milk and other food.)

Thyroid deficiency test   This test is carried out at the same time and in the same way as the PKU test. The object is to check that the thyroid gland is producing the hormone thyroxine. This hormone is needed for normal growth and development. A baby who lacks thyroxine develops into a cretin — undersized and mentally handicapped. This condition can be prevented by giving the child regular doses of the hormone from an early age. The photographs show a baby aged three months just before thyroxine treatment began, and aged six months, now normal and healthy.

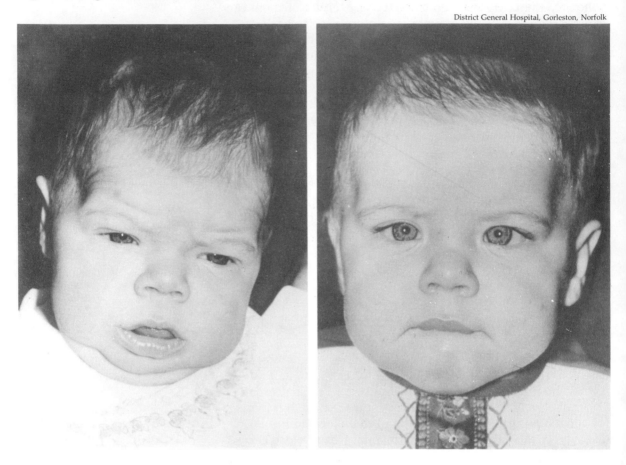

Umbilical cord   During the week to ten days following the birth, the stump of the umbilical cord attached to the baby dries and shrivels. It then drops off to leave the **navel** (belly button).

The mother

A healthy happy mother   Besides looking after the baby, the mother also needs to care for herself. The baby needs a healthy, happy mother who:
- feeds herself properly;
- does not get over-tired;
- does not worry too much about the housework;
- is able to relax for a while each day;
- has the energy to play with and talk to her baby and to take him out for walks.

Postnatal exercises   Pregnancy greatly stretches the muscles of the abdomen and afterwards they are very loose and floppy. The muscles of the pelvic floor (those in the groin) are also loosened and stretched during delivery. All these muscles will gradually improve and tighten. Special postnatal exercises will help them to regain their shape more quickly.

Postnatal examination   This takes place when the baby is about six weeks old and is carried out either at the hospital or by the family doctor. The baby is examined to make sure he is healthy and making normal progress. The mother is examined to make sure she is healthy and that the womb and other organs have returned to their normal state.

Re-starting the menstrual cycle   The time at which periods start again varies considerably and may take six months or longer after the birth. It is possible to become pregnant before the periods return. It is also possible to become pregnant whilst still breast-feeding, although breast-feeding makes conception less likely.

Baby blues and postnatal depression   During the week following the birth, commonly between the third and fifth day it is quite usual for the mother to feel miserable and depressed without knowing why. This period of mild depression is often called the 'baby blues'. Reasons for it include:

- **hormones** which controlled pregnancy and childbirth have not yet settled back into their normal pattern of activity and they are making the mother feel 'out of sorts'.
- **tiredness** due to disturbed nights and busy days.
- **reaction** to the excitement of the birth. Now it is all over, life seems to be nothing but a constant round of feeding, changing nappies and washing.

It helps the mother:

- if she can talk to someone about how she feels;
- to ask for advice;
- to know that these feelings are quite common in new mothers;
- if she can get plenty of rest.

An attack of the 'baby blues' should pass in a few days. If it develops into long-term depression (**postnatal depression**) then this is something rather different and needs the help of a doctor.

Infant Welfare Clinics (Child Welfare Clinics)

These are usually called **Baby Clinics**. They are run by the family doctor or local Health Authority and are held at regular times every week. A mother can please herself whether she goes or not, but it does have the following advantages:

- A doctor and health visitor will be present to examine the baby and check that normal progress is being made.
- A record will be kept of the baby's progress and weight.
- Advice can be obtained about any problems such as feeding, weaning and skin rashes. (The family doctor is still the person to consult when the baby is ill.)
- Advice is given about immunisation.
- Developmental checks are usually given at 6 weeks, 8 months, 18 months and 3 years.
- It is a good place for the mother to meet and get to know other mothers with children of the same age.
- It may be possible to buy baby foods at a lower price, also second-hand clothes and equipment.

To do

1. In your opinion, what are the points in favour and against (i) an expectant mother working up to the seventh month of pregnancy; (ii) returning to employment about two months after the birth.

2. **a** Draw a plan of a room which is to be used as a nursery for a young baby. Mark in the position for the cot, heater, and any furniture which you would place in the room.
b Suggest suitable wall and floor coverings.
c What other equipment would you have in the room?
Give reasons for each of your decisions.

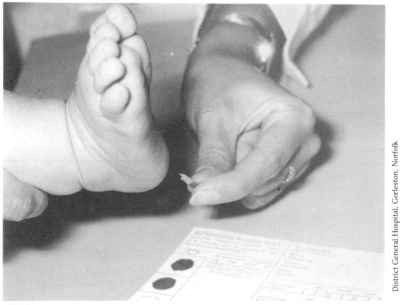

District General Hospital, Gorleston, Norfolk

Questions

1. **a** Why does a health visitor come to see the mother and baby?
b The health visitor is likely to suggest that the mother attends the Baby Clinic. What are the advantages of going to the clinic?

2. When a doctor examines a new-born baby:
a who else is also present?
b name four checks the doctor will make.
c If a dislocated hip is discovered, why is treatment necessary?

3. The photograph below shows a PKU test being carried out.
a Describe the test.
b How can PKU be treated?
c Why is it important that PKU should be treated?

4. **a** Name four ways a mother can help care for herself.
b In what way will the baby benefit from having a healthy, happy mother?
c Which two sets of muscles regain their shape with the help of exercises?
d Give three reasons why a mother may suffer from 'baby blues'.

5. **a** When does the postnatal check-up take place?
b When will the mother's periods return?
c Is it possible to become pregnant before the periods return?
d Is it possible to become pregnant while still breast-feeding?

6. **a** By what age does a baby's birth have to be registered?
b What name has to be given to the Registrar of Births?
c What two items will be issued for the baby?

55 Parenthood

Couples who hope to start a family should be reasonably happy together and fairly self-confident because child-rearing is a long, hard job. This is why it is often considered undesirable for young people still in their teens to become parents. They themselves have not finished growing up, and they may not be sufficiently mature to cope with the demands of parenthood and the changes it will bring to their lives.

Before a child is conceived, it is important that **both** parents **want** a baby. The parents should be mature enough to care for a baby, financially able to support it, and should have a home in which the child can be brought up.

How parents' lives change

Having children changes the lives of the parents in many ways.

1. **Children are hard work**. When young, they are by nature neither clean nor tidy. Also, they have to be cared for seven days a week and at nights as well.
2. **They are a long-lasting responsibility**. Children require years of care as they grow from 'dear little babies' into adolescents who are much more difficult to manage.
3. **They require sacrifices from the parents** of both time and money.
4. **They restrict the parents' freedom**, but at the same time, provide a new interest.
5. **They bring the parents much pleasure and satisfaction** — if the parents are prepared to spend time on bringing them up.

... but they bring much pleasure

Children are hard work ...

Preparation for parenthood

Preparation for parenthood begins in childhood. As children and teenagers, the parents-to-be will have been influenced by:

1. The way in which they themselves were brought up.
2. Experience gained through helping with younger brothers or sisters, cousins or neighbours' children.
3. Baby-sitting or experience of working with young children.
4. The study at school or college of subjects such as Child Care and Development or Parentcraft.

New parents

In these days of smaller families, it is quite possible that new parents will have very little knowledge of how to bring up children. If they live far away from their own families, then the grandparents will not be at hand to give help and advice.

There are a number of sources from which the parents of today can get information, advice and support.

1. Other members of their families such as grandmothers and aunts.
2. Preparation classes at the antenatal clinic.
3. The health visitor at the Baby Clinic or when she visits the baby at home.
4. Television programmes, for example those produced for parents by the Open University.
5. Pamphlets issued by the Health Education Council, the Health Visitors Association, The National Association for Maternal and Child Welfare (NAMCW), and many other organisations. A list of some of them is given on p. 274.
6. Books — there are many to choose from which have been written by parents and doctors. A suggested book list is given on p. 273.

Suggestions for parents

The following suggestions may be of help to new parents.

- **Love your baby** } to give the baby the security of
- **Cuddle your baby** } knowing he is wanted.
- **Talk to your baby** so that he can learn how to speak.
- **Listen to your baby** as well as talking to him, and you will learn how to communicate with each other.
- **Play with your baby**; he will enjoy it, and it will enable a far closer relationship to develop between you.
- **Keep your baby clean**, but not too clean.
- **Be firm with your child** when he is old enough to understand what is wanted of him.

- **Reward is more effective than punishment** in the training of children.
- **Do not over-protect**, so that the child can gradually learn to be responsible for his own life.
- **Do not spend all your time and energy on your child**. If you do not leave time for yourselves and your own interests, you will become very dull people. When the child has grown up and left home there will be the danger that you will be lonely and bored.

Questions

1. Name five ways in which having children changes the lives of their parents.

2. a Name four ways in which preparation for parenthood can begin in childhood.
b Name six ways in which new parents can obtain information, advice and support.

3. List ten suggestions which may be of help to new parents.

To do

1. Describe the preparation for parenthood that you have already gained.

2. Look at as many different books and pamphlets as you can find which deal with the bringing up of children. Comment on at least four different books and four different pamphlets. In each case, say whether you consider that the book or pamphlet would be helpful for parents, and in what ways.

Exercises

1 a Name two early signs which might indicate that a woman is pregnant.
b Give two reasons why an expectant mother needs a well-balanced diet.
c State four minor health problems which often occur during pregnancy.
d State two advantages of a mother having her baby in hospital.
e What is an antenatal clinic?
f State two reasons why a baby may need to be born by Caesarian section.
g Give two functions of the umbilical cord.
h Give two reasons for testing the blood of an expectant mother.
i Why is regular testing of urine of an expectant mother necessary?

j A pregnant mother is advised not to smoke. State two ways by which smoking can harm the unborn child.
k What is the most likely sign of a threatened miscarriage?
l How many chromosomes are there in (i) an unfertilised egg; (ii) a normal body cell?
m What is the difference between 'baby blues' and postnatal depression?
n Explain what is meant by (i) Rhesus factor, (ii) induction.
o (i) When is the postnatal examination held? (ii) Give two reasons why this examination is important.
p Name three ways in which the arrival of a baby changes the daily life of the parents.

2 a (i) Label parts 1–5 of the diagram below.
(ii) State what happens to each of the parts during childbirth.

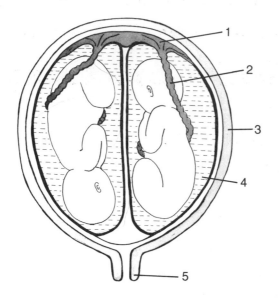

b (i) Are the twins identical or fraternal? Give a reason for your answer.
(ii) How do the twins obtain food and oxygen while in the womb?

3 a Give a clear account of the development of the foetus during the first four months of pregnancy.
b Draw a diagram to show the female organs of reproduction. (*WJEC*)

4 Maternal and child health clinics help parents before and after the birth of their baby.
a Name four benefits and services available for a pregnant woman.
b In what three ways does a woman need help during pregnancy? In each case suggest how her husband can meet these needs.
c Describe the roles of the midwife and health visitor.
d What are the values to the mother and the child of regular attendance at clinics? (*SWEB*)

5 Hormones play a very important part in controlling the menstrual cycle, pregnancy and birth.
a (i) What are hormones? (ii) How do they move around the body?
b (i) Name four hormones and give one function for each. (ii) Which two hormones help in controlling the menstrual cycle?

6 John lives in a beautiful, modern house with a garden that is the envy of the neighbours. He is four years old, strong and healthy, but very aggressive towards younger children, with the exception of his baby brother, towards whom he is very loving. His parents insist on a very high standard of cleanliness and tidiness at home. Unfortunately, because he is so rough and aggressive, the neighbours' children do not like to play with him. He hits them and breaks their toys. Recently he has taken to wandering off and playing on a nearby building site. Naturally his mother is worried by this, particularly because of the danger from lorries and machinery.
a Is there anything in this account which might explain why John is so aggressive? Give details.
b What play materials could his parents provide to encourage him to get rid of his aggressive feelings and at the same time to play in a safer place?
c In what ways could a playgroup help John and his mother? (*SEREB*)

7 It is generally agreed to be valuable for a child's father, together with the mother, to play the fullest possible part in his or her upbringing. Suggest suitable ways in which a father can become involved at each of the following times:
(i) during the mother's pregnancy,
(ii) at the delivery,
(iii) during the early weeks of the baby's life,
(iv) during the child's second and third year,
(v) when the child reaches school age.
(*YHREB*)

Section 8

The family and home

56 *The family*

During the long years of childhood, it is desirable for children to live in a family or similar group which can provide:

1. love, care, food, clothing and protection;
2. a secure home where a child matters to other people;
3. training in the skills needed for adult life;
4. knowledge of the values, standards and cultural background of the society in which the child lives;
5. the opportunity to make gradual progress to become independent adults capable of looking after themselves and others.

The extended family

The term **extended family** is used for the large family group which includes grandparents, parents, brothers and sisters, aunts, uncles and cousins. Within the extended family, are small family units of parents with their children.

   The extended family forms the traditional pattern of family life in most societies. The members of such a family have close connections with their other relations, and they help and support each other. The early development of the children is much influenced by other members of the family besides the parents. In this type of family life, there is always someone to look after the children in an emergency.

Fiona Pragoff

The nuclear family

A **nuclear family** consists of a father and mother with their children. In recent years, changes to the traditional pattern of family life have been taking place in some countries, particularly the countries of western Europe and the United States. Parents are having fewer children. The nuclear families are often separated by long distances from other members of the extended family. The parents bring up their children without the help and support (and perhaps interference!) of grandparents and other relations. Nevertheless, the family still remains of prime importance to the child.

Fiona Pragoff

One-parent families

In these families, the children are brought up by only one parent. Usually the parent is the mother, but sometimes it is the father. The one parent has to do everything that is usually shared by two parents, that is, provide the daily care, training and security. This is very hard work indeed for one person. As in any other family, the hard work continues for many years until the children are grown up.

One-parent families can vary as widely as two-parent families in terms of health, wealth, happiness and security. The family situation can also change, with a one-parent family becoming a two-parent family, and the other way round.

There are various reasons for families being 'one-parent'. These include:

- divorce;
- separation of the parents;
- the death of one parent;
- one of the parents being away from home for a long time through work, illness or imprisonment;
- unmarried mothers keeping their babies rather than having them adopted;
- women who deliberately decide to bring up their children on their own.

Step-family

In this type of family, only one of the parents is the natural mother or father. Such a family is usually the result of divorce or the death of a parent. Since the step-child will not have grown up from birth with the step-parent, it often (but not always) takes quite a long time for them to adjust to living with each other. This may be further complicated if there are other children from previous marriages to get used to, and resentments can arise.

Happy family life

When parents set up home and have a family, they naturally hope to create a happy environment in which the children can grow up. Some of the factors which can help to make a home happy are given below.

1. **Parents who love and respect each other and their children.** This helps to give all the members of the family a sense of security.
2. **Parents who consider that children are more important than the housework.** Worrying too much about tidiness or the state or appearance of the house can make for a great deal of nagging and unpleasantness. Children would rather have happy, contented parents who have time to do things with them than a spotlessly clean and tidy home.
3. **Parents who realise they are not perfect.** No parents are perfect. There are days when they are cross and irritable, particularly when they are tired, unwell or worried. It happens in all families.
4. **Parents who realise that no child is perfect.** All children go through phases of good and bad behaviour.
5. **Parents who do not expect too much of their children.** Children enjoy life more when they are praised and loved for what they **can** do, rather than criticised for what they are unable to do.

Questions

1. Why is it desirable for a child to live in a family?

2. Explain the difference between an extended family and a nuclear family.

3. Give six reasons why a family may be 'one-parent'.

4. Name five factors which can help to make a home a happy place.

Child study

Describe the family of the child and make a family tree. If this is not possible, describe and make a family tree of your own family.

To do

1. Taking each of the five factors mentioned under Happy Family Life.
a Explain what it means.
b From your own experience, describe one or more occasions when that factor was important.

2. Describe some of the changes which have taken place in the bringing up of children in Britain in the 20th century, for example, in feeding, discipline, toys, clothes.

3. Find out about the traditional patterns of life in other countries, for example, China, India, Saudi-Arabia, Mexico. Note any differences in their attitudes, values and cultures.

4. *Discuss* possible factors which may complicate life in a step-family.

57 *Family planning*

Family planning means taking action so that only wanted babies are born. When the parents want their baby, the baby will be welcomed into the family. But when the baby is unwanted, the tiny, helpless little boy or girl that is brought into the world is likely to have a very hard childhood.

Unwanted babies

It is estimated that in Britain more than 120 000 unwanted babies are born every year. Many more are aborted (**abortion** means the removal of the child from the womb before it has grown enough to survive on its own).

Many of the unwanted pregnancies happen to girls and young women because either they have been given wrong advice, or they have ignored sound advice. A girl who does not wish to become pregnant should remember the following facts.

- Pregnancy can follow first intercourse.
- Pregnancy can even occur if the penis does not enter the vagina (sperm can swim).
- Pregnancy sometimes occurs when intercourse takes place during a period.
- Pregnancy can occur even when the woman does not 'come' (have an orgasm).
- Intercourse in any position can result in pregnancy.
- Withdrawal ('being careful') can result in pregnancy.
- Douching (washing out the vagina) will never prevent pregnancy, however soon after intercourse.
- Breast-feeding does not prevent pregnancy, although it may make it less likely.

Contraception

In a long-term relationship such as marriage, it is natural for a man and a woman who love each other to want to have intercourse. But if they do not want a baby, they need to know about the various methods of contraception (**contra** = against, **ception** = conceiving). Using this knowledge, they are able to plan their family and start a baby only when they want one.

The different methods of contraception, how they work and how safe they are

Method	How it works	How safe it is
Abstention; 'Saying No' (means not having intercourse)	Because intercourse does not take place there is no danger of an unwanted child	Completely safe
Male sterilisation* (Vasectomy)	A simple operation in which the sperm ducts (vas deferens) are cut or blocked to prevent semen from containing sperm	A permanent method of birth control which is almost always 100% safe
Female sterilisation*	An operation in which the Fallopian tubes from the ovaries are blocked so that egg and sperm cannot meet	A permanent method of birth control which is almost always 100% safe
The pill*	The **combined pill** contains two hormones — oestrogen and progestogen — which stop ovulation (stop the ovaries from releasing eggs)	Almost 100% safe if the pill is taken *regularly* each day
	The **mini-pill** contains only progestogen — produces changes in the womb which make it difficult for sperm to enter or a fertilised egg to settle there	Very safe if taken regularly at the *same time* each day
Coil; IUD* (intra-uterine device)	A small plastic coil is inserted into the womb and left there. It prevents a fertilised egg from settling in the womb	Very safe. More suitable for women who have already had a baby
Cap; diaphragm* (a diaphragm is a larger type of cap)	A thin rubber device is fitted over the neck of the womb (cervix) before intercourse takes place. By covering the entrance to the womb it prevents egg and sperm from meeting in the Fallopian tube	Very safe *if* properly fitted *and* used with a spermicide
Sheath; condom (french letter; 'Durex')	A thin rubber covering is fitted over the erect penis just before intercourse. The condom prevents sperm from being deposited in the woman's vagina	Very safe *if* properly used so that no semen comes into contact with the woman's vaginal area. Spermicide placed in the vagina adds extra safety
Rhythm method ('Safe period')	Intercourse is avoided when the woman is likely to be fertile. This is usually (but not always) some time during the middle ten days of the menstrual cycle. The rest of the cycle is known as the 'safe period' — safe to have intercourse and avoid pregnancy	Unreliable because it is not always easy to be sure of the date of ovulation and therefore when the woman is, and is not, fertile

The methods of contraception marked by an asterisk* are those which require medical advice or treatment from a doctor or the Family Planning Clinic.

Method	How it works	How safe it is
Withdrawal ('Being careful'; coitus interruptus)	The penis is withdrawn from the vagina before the semen is ejaculated	*Not* a reliable method of birth control because a little semen can leak from the erect penis before the main amount is released
Spermicide (cream, jelly or aerosol foam)	Makes the sperms inactive. The spermicide needs to be placed inside the vagina before intercourse takes place	Very unreliable on its own but helps to make a cap or condom safer

The tables list the different methods of contraception and explain briefly how they work, and how safe and reliable they are at preventing an unwanted pregnancy. Deciding which of the methods to use depends on a number of factors including:
- individual preference;
- religious beliefs;
- age;
- whether a short- or long-term method is wanted.

'Morning after' contraceptive pill

'Morning after' pills are an emergency method of contraception. They may be prescribed by a doctor after intercourse has taken place and there is a risk of an unwanted pregnancy which could lead to a later abortion. These pills contain hormones and need to be taken within 2-3 days following intercourse.

'Morning after' pills are **not** recommended as a routine method of birth control.

The other method of 'morning after' contraception is the insertion of a coil (IUD).

Infertility

Sometimes couples plan to have a family and find, to their disappointment, that they are unable to produce children. Being unable to conceive is known as **infertility**.

There are many reasons for infertility and couples can obtain advice from their doctor or family planning clinic. With some couples the right advice soon solves the problem. Other cases may require treatment from a doctor who specialises in the problems of infertility.

Causes of infertility include:

1. **too few sperm are being produced** — at least 20 million sperms need to be ejaculated at any one time to ensure that one fertilises the egg.
2. **failure to ovulate** — the ovaries are not producing eggs.
3. **blocked Fallopian tubes** — the eggs cannot be fertilised.
4. **the mucus in the neck of the womb is too thick** — so the sperms are unable to enter.

Obtaining advice

Advice on contraception and family planning is provided free by the National Health Service (NHS). It can be obtained by people of all ages, married or single, male or female, from:

- **Family Planning Clinics** The address and opening times of the nearest clinic are available from places like the Health Centre, Town Hall or Post Office. The health visitor will know. The address can also be found in the telephone directory under 'Family Planning'.
- **Doctors (GPs)** Many family doctors give advice on these matters.

Questions

1. Match each of these methods of birth control with one of the statements **a-j**:
vasectomy; mini-pill; cap; abstention; sheath; withdrawal; combined pill; rhythm method; coil; female sterilisation.

a stops the ovaries from producing eggs
b prevents sperm from being deposited in the vagina
c prevents a fertilised egg from settling in the womb
d covers the entrance to the womb to prevent sperm from entering
e prevents egg and sperm from meeting in the Fallopian tube
f prevents semen from containing sperm
g allows intercourse only when an egg is not likely to be present
h is completely safe because intercourse does not take place
i does not deposit semen inside the vagina
j makes it difficult for sperm to enter the womb.

2. a Name the seven safest methods of birth control.
b (i) Which two methods are made safer when used with a spermicide? (ii) What does the spermicide do?
c Why is withdrawal an unreliable method of contraception?
d Why is the rhythm method not completely reliable?

3. a Name five methods of contraception which depend particularly on the woman.
b Name two safe methods of contraception available to men.
c Name five methods which require medical advice or treatment.

4. What do the following mean?
(i) contraception, (ii) abstention, (iii) abortion, (iv) vasectomy, (v) infertile, (vi) IUD?

5. To prevent an unwanted pregnancy, list eight facts which it might be useful to know.

To do

If more information about contraception is required, the local Family Planning Clinic, Health Visitor and Health Education Service can be approached for leaflets, films or speakers.

58 *Children in care: fostering; adoption*

Children in care

These are children who are separated from their families and placed in the care of the local authorities. They then live either with foster parents, or in special children's homes or hostels, or very occasionally, in residential nurseries. The length of time that children stay in care depends on the reason for being separated from their families.

Why children are taken into care

There are many reasons why children are taken into care. Some of these are listed below:

- Temporary illness of the parent or guardian and there is no one to look after the child at home. This is the biggest single reason.
- The child has been neglected, ill-treated or 'battered'.
- The child is beyond the control of the parents.

Children are taken into care on either a voluntary or compulsory basis.

Voluntary care is when the parents agree for their child to be placed into care. They realise it is the best thing to do for the child in the circumstances.

Compulsory care is when a court compels parents to hand over their child to the care of the local authority.

Fostering

Fostering is an arrangement for children to live in other people's homes. It is on the understanding that the children will return to their own homes to live as soon as possible. The foster parents are paid an allowance for food, clothing and general care, but they do not have any legal rights over the children.

Children stay with foster parents for varying amounts of time. It may be for many months or years, or perhaps only for a few weeks while the mother is in hospital. When the children are with foster parents for a long time they can become very attached to the family. It may then be hard for them to part when the time comes for the children to return to their own homes.

Adoption

Adoption is a legal process by which adults become parents to children not born to them. The adoptive parents are given full legal rights over the child, whom they are expected to support completely. The natural parents give up all rights to the child.

Children are adopted for a number of reasons. Some are adopted by couples who are unable to have children of their own. Others are adopted by grandparents or other relatives if both the parents die. In other cases, a mother may marry a new husband and they jointly adopt her child so that all the family share the same surname. Foster parents can also apply to adopt a child whom they have fostered for five years or more.

People who adopt must be over 25 years of age, and 21 years older than the child. Adoption orders are usually granted jointly to married couples, although in some cases a single person may be allowed to adopt.

Adoption societies   When a childless couple wish to adopt, it is usual for them to do so through an adoption society. There are a number of different societies, and they each have their own particular rules and regulations. So, if one society is unable to help the couple, then another might. But there are usually long waiting lists these days because fewer unwanted babies have been born since abortion became more readily available. Also, single mothers are now tending to keep their babies.

Information about adoption can be obtained from the local Social Services department, or from British Agencies for Adoption and Fostering (p. 274), or from any of the adoption societies.

How adoption takes place   The couple who wish to adopt are interviewed by the adoption society:
- to find out if they would be suitable parents;
- to make sure that they are healthy, happy, have a stable marriage, and can manage financially;
- to ensure that they really **want** to adopt a child.

When a suitable child becomes available he lives with the adoptive parents for a probationary (trial) period of three months. A social worker from the adoption society visits the home from time to time to make sure the arrangement is working well. The probationary period cannot start until the child is six weeks old. This is to give the natural mother time to be sure of her decision to part with her child. During the probationary period, the child does not legally belong to the adoptive parents, and the natural parents can claim him back.

If the probationary period has been satisfactory, the adoption can then be made legal. This is usually done in a juvenile or county court. From that moment, the child belongs to the adoptive parents. The natural parents no longer have any claim to the child. Adopted children who want to, are entitled to see their full birth certificates when they reach the age of 18 years. If they wish, they may then apply to make contact with their natural parents. This is not always possible, for example the natural parents may refuse to have any contact, or their whereabouts may be unknown.

Questions

1. a List some of the reasons that children are taken into care.
b What is the difference between voluntary care and compulsory care?

2. What are the differences between fostering and adoption?
a Which is a temporary arrangement?
b Which involves legal rights over the child?
c Which provides payment for the child's care?

3. a Give three reasons why children are adopted.
b Can only married couples adopt?
c How old must people be in order to adopt?
d Give two reasons why there are fewer children for adoption these days.

4. a Why are people who wish to adopt first interviewed?
b What happens during the probationary period?
c What happens when the probationary period has been satisfactory?

To do

1. *Discuss* the 'tug-of-love' case below from the point of view of
a the child,
b the foster parents,
c the natural parent.

2. Find out more about
a fostering,
b adoption shops,
c children in care.

3. *Discuss* ways in which you think a change of environment due to fostering, adoption or being taken into care could affect the child's health, development and character.

Tearful Debbie aged 7 clung to her foster parents Joan and Geoff Taylor before being taken by car from the house in Balesham Road which has been her home for the last four years. 'We are heartbroken — it's so cruel,' said Geoff, 'especially as we were hoping to adopt her soon, and this came out of the blue a month ago.'

Debbie was taken to her new home with her mother Sue Neil who had had to give up Debbie when she lost her job and became ill. 'It was a very sad time, but that's all in the past', she said. 'I'm now in a steady job and have a nice flat. Having Debbie back completes my happiness, and I think I can be a mum she will be proud of.'

The social worker dealing with Debbie's case said, 'We are confident Sue Neil can give her a good home and upbringing. It is her legal right to have Debbie back.'

Yesterday evening, Mr and Mrs Taylor contemplated life without Debbie: 'She was such a joyful child, we can only hope she doesn't lose that. We're keeping her room just as she left it.'

59 Children with handicaps

A handicapped child is one who suffers from a long-term disability which interferes with growth and development, or the normal function of the body, or the ability to learn.

Most babies are born perfectly healthy and with no problems, but defects do occasionally occur. It is important to know about them because it may be possible to:

- **prevent them**, e.g. German measles damage, Rhesus damage and birth injuries.
- **have treatment to remove them**, e.g. hole-in-the-heart, and cleft palate and hare lip (at birth the top of the mouth and lips are not joined together in mid-line).
- **have treatment to relieve the condition**, e.g. some cases of spina bifida.
- **control the handicap with drugs**, e.g. epilepsy.
- **lessen the handicap by early training**, e.g. Down's syndrome, cerebral palsy and deafness.
- **prevent the development of a secondary handicap**, e.g. early treatment of deaf children will make it possible for them to speak, and correct treatment at an early age for squint will prevent blindness in the squinting eye.

Handicapped children are either born with their handicap or acquire it later because of accident or infection.

Congenital handicaps

A congenital handicap is one which is present at birth. With some children, the handicap is obvious from the moment they are born, for example, Down's syndrome or spina bifida. In other cases, for example, deafness or mild cases of cerebral palsy, the handicap only becomes apparent as the child develops, or rather, fails to develop in the usual way.

Congenital handicaps can arise in three ways. They can be due to:

1 Genes which the child inherits from his parents. Examples include Down's syndrome, haemophilia (severe bleeding from minor wounds) and muscular dystrophy.

2 Brain damage during development or birth. This may be caused by lack of oxygen or a number of other reasons. The handicap which results depends on the part of the brain which is damaged. For example, if a part controlling movement is damaged the result is cerebral palsy (spasticity). If a part controlling intelligence is damaged the result is a mental handicap.

3 Failure of development of particular parts of the body. Examples include 'hole in the heart', cleft palate and hare lip, and damage caused by German measles virus, drugs, smoking and alcohol.

Accident or infection during childhood

A serious accident, particularly a blow or fall on the head, may lead to a handicap. Some infections may also do the same, for example, polio can cause paralysis, and meningitis may cause deafness or mental handicap.

Physical handicaps

A physical handicap affects the body. Normal growth and development are prevented and the result is a physical handicap, for example,

- cerebral palsy;
- muscular dystrophy; see p. 241
- spina bifida;
- cleft palate and hare lip;
- hole in the heart;
- deformed limbs such as dislocated hip (p. 219);
- blindness (visual handicap);
- deafness (auditory handicap);
- speech difficulties;
- damage to the body caused by accidents.

Mental handicap

Mental handicap affects the intelligence. It is caused by an abnormality of the brain which results in a low level of intelligence. The handicap can be mild, moderate or severe. Many mentally handicapped people also have physical handicaps as well. Children who are mentally handicapped progress at a much slower rate than is normal and do not grow up to meet average standards.

Causes of mental handicap   Mental handicap can have a wide variety of causes including:

- Down's syndrome (see p. 241);
- brain damage in the womb from the German measles virus;
- brain damage during birth;
- brain damage caused by an accident to the head;
- brain damage due to an infection such as meningitis;
- lead poisoning from chewing toys or furniture coated with lead paint;
- autism (see p. 241).

Intelligence Quotient (IQ)   One way of measuring a person's intelligence is by finding his IQ. This is worked out from the results of intelligence tests. The average IQ is 100. A person is considered to be mentally handicapped if the IQ is less than 70. An IQ below 35 indicates severe mental handicap.

Training   Once brain damage has occurred, it is impossible to repair the damage and remove the handicap. However, much can be done to help by proper care and training. The training of the mentally handicapped is aimed at developing as much independence as possible. Those with a mild handicap can learn to live independent lives. The more severely handicapped will always need to be cared for to a greater or lesser degree by the community.

Catherine

Effects on the family

Most handicapped children are cared for at home by their families. Generally, this is the best place for them as they have the same need for a happy family life as other children. They also need to be treated in the same way — that is, cuddled, smiled at, talked to, played with, taken for outings, meet new people, and so on.

   Having a child with a severe handicap undoubtedly puts stress on the family. It often means a great deal of extra work and expense, especially if the child is unable to feed himself or be toilet trained, or is unable to move around unaided, or requires special equipment.

   If the other children in the family are not involved in caring for the handicapped child, they may feel left out and behave badly to try to get more attention. If the mother devotes all her time to the handicapped child, her husband may feel neglected, which will not be good for the marriage. It may lead to breakdown of the marriage and the extra problems of a one-parent family.

David   ASBAH

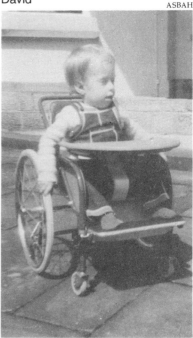

Help for families

Families with a handicapped child need lots of outside help including:

- practical advice for day-to-day care;
- advice on the right way to train a handicapped child from babyhood onwards to lead as full a life as possible;
- contact with other families with similar problems — to find out how they overcome difficulties;

- financial help for special equipment and other necessary expenses;
- help with the extra laundry;
- child-minding help so that the mother can have a break;
- transport for outings;
- help with holidays.

The help can come from relations, friends, neighbours, health visitors, the family doctor, social workers, schools and teachers. There are also a large number of voluntary societies which help both the handicapped and their families. A list of some of them is given on pp. 274-5.

Handicapped children

Catherine has **Down's Syndrome**. She is very small for her age and, although she is growing slowly, she will not reach full adult size. Her intelligence is limited and learning is a slow process. Catherine is much loved by her family. The care and training they give her means that she will learn to do far more than if she was in a family where they had no time or love for her.

David is now almost five years old and was born with **spina bifida**. His backbone did not develop properly, so part of the spinal cord was left unprotected and became damaged. This caused David to be paralysed from the waist downwards so that he is unable to walk.

Nigel has a severe form of **muscular dystrophy**. This disease weakens muscles and makes movement difficult.

Wendy is **autistic**. Children with this handicap do not make emotional contact with other people and find it very difficult to communicate in any way. They appear to live in a world of their own and often the only emotion shown is occasional rage.

Cerebral palsy This results when the part of the brain which controls muscle co-ordination is damaged at birth. The muscles go into spasms (contractions) or jerky movements and it is impossible to control them. It is a severe handicap. The face and limbs are constantly making jerky, uncontrolled movements and the speech is difficult to understand. It is important that people still talk to sufferers in the same way as they would an ordinary child.

Special schools

Special schools are for handicapped children who require more individual care than is available in ordinary schools, or who require specialised training. Physical handicaps prevent

Nigel   Maria Bartha

Wendy

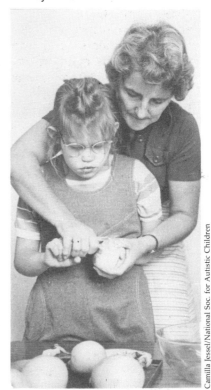

Camilla Jessel/National Soc. for Autistic Children

241

children from learning in the usual way, and mentally handicapped children will be slow to learn. Special schools differ from ordinary schools in that they have:

1. teachers who are specially trained to teach handicapped children;
2. assistants who are specially trained to care for handicapped children;
3. a higher ratio of teachers to children so that the children can have more individual attention;
4. physiotherapists to train the children to make as full a use of their muscles as possible. This helps mobility and increases independence;
5. occupational therapists to help with training in the skills of daily living activities — dressing, feeding, toilet management;
6. speech therapists to help those with speech difficulties;
7. suitable buildings — corridors and doorways wide enough for wheelchairs, no stairs, specially designed chairs, lavatories, washing facilities and so on.

The trend these days is for handicapped children to be educated in ordinary schools, although perhaps in a special class. This has the advantage of bringing handicapped children more into contact with normal children. The normal children learn to accept the handicapped as part of the community.

Questions

1. Name two types of handicap which can be
a prevented,
b treated,
c lessened by early training.

2. a A handicap which is present at birth is called a ..... handicap.
b Name three ways in which such handicaps can arise.

3. a What is the difference between physical and mental handicap?
b Give some examples of each.

4. Describe the types of help which families with a handicapped child often need.

To do

1. For each of the four handicapped children in the photographs on pp. 240 and 241:
a Describe the handicap.
b Is the handicap mainly physical or mental or both?
c Do you think the child will benefit more from attendance at an ordinary school or a special school?
d Where are the special schools in your district?

2. The Warnock Report (1980) recommends that, wherever possible, handicapped children should be educated in ordinary schools.
a What are the advantages of such a scheme?
b What extra facilities would the schools need for the proper care and education of handicapped children?

3. Make a list of the different voluntary societies which aim to help the handicapped and their families (see pp. 274-5).

60 *Prevention of accidents*

Accidents are the biggest cause of death and injury in children over the age of one year. Every year more than 2500 children under the age of five years die as a result of accidents. Many more are injured.

Training for life in a dangerous world

The world is a dangerous place and children have to learn to cope with the dangers.

Parents are responsible for their children. At the same time, they are responsible for training them to become independent people who can take care of themselves. Throughout childhood, parents have to judge between the amount of protection their child needs for safety and the amount of freedom the child needs and wants. Children **need** to be given freedom so that they can learn to make judgements for themselves. Children often **want** more freedom than is safe for them because it is a natural part of growing up to react against parents' wishes.

Learning about danger

During the first 18 months of life, infants have no understanding of danger and therefore need complete protection. However, during this time they are beginning to learn what is unpleasant and can hurt, for example, a child will remember for a while touching something which was too hot.

By the time they reach the age of 18 months, children are beginning to learn the meaning of 'NO'. They can now start to be taught that there are some things that should not be done.

Between 18 months and 2 years, children are beginning to understand a great deal of what the parents say and their memory is improving. They start to realise that certain actions have certain consequences. For example, if something hot is touched it will hurt. They still need a great deal of protection by parents, but they are just beginning to learn to protect themselves.

From this age onwards, the amount of supervision can be gradually relaxed as the children acquire more sense about what is dangerous and how to avoid it. At times, parents have to take calculated risks when they allow children a little more freedom. But if complete protection continues too long, children suffer the consequences of over-protection.

The type and amount of supervision changes as the children get older. It gradually becomes less and less, but even as adults they will need to be protected by Health and Safety rules at work and Regulations for Safety Standards of equipment, tools, etc.

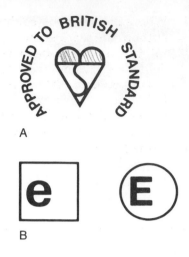

A

B

When accidents are more likely to happen

Accidents to children are more likely to happen:

1 At times of stress   These are the times when people (both parents and children) are more careless and forgetful. For example, when in a hurry, when afraid, during an argument, or when very worried — about health, friendship, jobs, money.

2 When parents are less alert   Their senses may be dulled by medicines such as tranquillisers, or by alcohol, or drugs, or perhaps because they are just very tired (parents do get very tired at times).

3 To children who are over- or under-protected
Children who are under-protected are not made aware of dangers, so fail to take care. Children who are over-protected may either:
- be made so aware of danger that fear makes them nervous and unsure and therefore unsafe;
- rebel against their parents by taking more risks than would otherwise be the case.

THE MARK OF SAFETY

C

Samples of appliances bearing this label have been subjected to rigorous tests for SAFETY

BEAB APPROVED
YOUR ELECTRICAL SAFEGUARD

Reducing the risk

All children have accidents, however safe the home and however careful the parents. It is neither possible nor desirable to watch a child every minute of the day. Nevertheless, parents can help to reduce the possibility of accidents by the following means.
1.   Set a good example — children copy the behaviour of adults.
2.   Make the home and garden as accident-proof as possible.
3.   Teach children to be aware of dangers and how to cope with them.
4.   Never leave children alone in the house.

D

5. Where possible, buy equipment which has the appropriate mark showing that it has been approved for safety. Some of these marks are shown opposite.
  A The Kitemark of the British Standards Institute. Items with a kitemark have been checked for safety.
  B European markings.
  C The BEAB Mark of Safety. This is the sign of the British Electrotechnical Approvals Board. The BEAB mark is attached to domestic electrical appliances which meet the Government Safety Regulations.
  D The British Gas Seal of Service. All gas appliances with this label have been tested and approved for safety.

Questions

1. Why are accidents more likely to happen
a at times of stress,
b when parents are less alert,
c to children who are under-protected,
d to children who are over-protected?

2. Name five ways that parents can help to reduce the possibility of accidents to their children.

3. Draw or describe four marks which may be found on different pieces of equipment to show that they have been approved for safety.

4. a During what stage of life do children need complete protection?
b When can the amount of supervision be gradually relaxed, and why?

To do

1. Study the tables below showing home accidents to children under the age of five years.
a Table 1. Describe in words the figures shown in this table and suggest reasons for them.
b Table 2. (i) Compare the types of injury of the two age groups. (ii) For the age group 0-8 months, suggest one reason for each type of injury, and suggest an action which might have prevented it. Do the same for the types of injury to the older children.

2. What is the meaning of RoSPA? Find out more about this organisation and the work that it does.

3. Read the booklet 'Play it safe'. Add to your notes any information you consider to be useful.

HOME ACCIDENTS TO CHILDREN UNDER THE AGE OF FIVE YEARS

Table 1 The age groups of the children who attended hospital because of a home accident

Age group	Number per 1000 children who attended hospital
0–8 months	40
9–12 months	44
1 year	278
2 years	288
3 years	199
4 years	151
	1000

Table 2 Types of accident of the children taken to hospital

Type of injury	For every 1000 children 0–8 months	For every 1000 children 9 months–4 years
Cuts	100	373
Bruises	213	115
Dislocation/ fractures	48	59
Burns	76	38
Scald	94	52
Poisoning	22	73
Concussion	57	21
Suffocation	5	0
Electric shock	0	2
No injury found	251	103
Others	134	164
	1000	1000

61 *Safety in the home*

Homes are for people of all ages to use and to live in and it is impossible to make them completely safe for children. Nevertheless, much can be done to prevent accidents.

1. Dangerous objects can be kept away from children.
2. Children can be kept away from dangerous situations.
3. Those items with which the child has contact should be made as safe as possible.

Dangerous objects

The following objects should be kept from children until they are old enough to use them sensibly.

Plastic bags   There is the danger of suffocation if a plastic bag is put over the head. Plastic material is airtight and clings to warm surfaces, therefore a plastic bag over the head will be very difficult to remove.

Small, hard objects such as sweets, peanuts, or pieces from a toy can cause choking if swallowed. Choking is one of the commonest accidents of infancy because children of this age put everything into their mouths.

Medicines can be poisonous and should be locked in a cabinet which needs adult hands to open it. Pills and tablets in child-resistant containers are difficult for a child to get at. Blister or strip packs make it less easy for a child to swallow a lot of pills at once. On the other hand, a child may find these packs attractive to play with, especially if he sees an adult using them.

Poisons   Poisonous substances include cleaning materials, alcohol, weedkillers and other garden chemicals. Empty drink bottles should never be used to store poisonous liquids to avoid the possibility of mistakes.

Dangerous objects   There are quite a number of these in the average home, for example, sharp knives and scissors, razor blades, needles, matches, lighters, petrol, paraffin, methylated spirits and, occasionally, fireworks.

Dangerous situations

This section applies particularly to toddlers. At this stage, children are able to move around but are not yet old enough to understand about safety.

Safety barrier (safety gate) prevents a young child from wandering to a part of the house the parents consider dangerous. Safety barriers are often fitted across the bottom of the stairs and across the kitchen doorway (the kitchen is the most dangerous room in the house). The barrier should be too high for a small child to climb over. It should also have locks which he cannot undo and bars in which he cannot get his head, hands or feet trapped.

If a safety barrier is required at the top of the stairs, it needs to be high enough so that it cannot be climbed over. If a child should climb over the barrier, the fall can be more serious than a simple fall down the stairs.

Electrics

Young children should be kept away from electrics because of the risk of:

A Electric shock   If electrical equipment is damaged or live wires are touched, it can give rise to a shock. So too can a worn or damaged flex. Modern sockets are designed to prevent tiny fingers or small objects from being poked inside. Electrical equipment should never be touched when the hands are wet, as this increases the likelihood of an electric shock.

B Injury from moving parts   Items such as electric mixers or wringers can cause nasty accidents.

C Fire hazards   Electric irons are examples of equipment which, if misused, can be the cause of fire.

Tablecloths

These can be a danger, for example, if a young child pulled at this tablecloth, he could be badly scalded by hot tea. Liquids do not need to be very hot to damage the skin of a young child.

Fire

There are two good reasons for keeping children away from fire. There is the danger that:

1. they may burn themselves;
2. some action by them, either accidentally or in play, may cause the furniture and the building to catch fire.

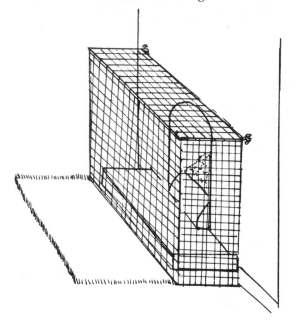

A Fireguards In England and Wales, it is illegal to leave a child under the age of twelve years in a room where there is a fire without a fireguard. In Scotland and Northern Ireland this law applies to children under the age of seven years. A good fireguard is one which:

- is strong and sturdy and has a cover on top;
- has no sharp edges;
- is firmly fixed to the wall by hooks which cannot be undone by a small child;
- has mesh small enough to prevent a baby from pushing his arms or toys through;
- has a door (if there is one) which fastens securely.

When a fireguard is in front of a fire, it should never be used as a clothes dryer.

B Mantelpiece Objects on the mantelpiece tempt children to reach for them. This can be a danger if there is a fire underneath. A mirror over the mantelpiece may also tempt children to go too close to a fire.

C Paraffin heaters (oil heaters) can be the cause of dangerous house fires, particularly the older types which do not meet modern safety standards. Children should be kept from paraffin heaters in the same way as for any other type of fire.

The following precautions should also be observed when the heater is in use:

1. Place the heater on a level surface.
2. Place in a position where it is unlikely to be knocked over.
3. Do not fill with paraffin when the stove is alight.
4. Do not move when alight.
5. Do not place in a draught.
6. Do not place near to flammable objects such as curtains.

Making the home safe

There are some parts of any home which it is impossible to keep children away from or to keep out of their reach. The only thing to do is to try to make them as safe as possible. Three examples are dealt with here — floors, windows and cookers.

Floors

Children can hurt themselves when they slip. To reduce this danger:
- always wipe up spilt grease or liquid;
- it is safer to have a heavy mat than a light-weight one;
- if floors have to be polished, non-slip polish should be used;
- never polish under mats.

Windows

A   Falling out of windows   To prevent this from happening:
1. Young children should not be left alone in a room with an open window through which they could fall, unless there are safety bars.
2. Catches need to be securely fastened on all windows that children can reach.
3. Keeping chairs and tables away from windows helps prevent children from climbing onto the window sills.

B Glass   Toddlers have accidents with glass (windows and drinking glasses) because they are unsteady on their feet and fall over easily. Older children are at risk when they play rough games.

Ordinary glass is very brittle and breaks with sharp, jagged edges which can cause serious cuts. Therefore, in houses with children, it is safer to have toughened glass (safety glass) in any windows or glass doors which are in danger of being broken. Another way to make glass safer is to cover it with a film of clear plastic specially made for this purpose.

Cookers

Ideally, a cooker should have controls which are difficult for a child to reach and switch on. When the cooker is in use, it can be made safer by a cooker guard. Turning the handles of pans inwards makes them more difficult to reach and tip over.

Questions

1. Name objects which should be kept away from children because of the danger of
a suffocation,   **c** poisoning,
b choking,   **d** injury.

2. a Name three possible dangers when children touch electrics.
b Give two reasons for keeping children away from fire.
c What safety features will a good type of fireguard have?
d Name three features which are essential for a good type of safety barrier.
e Give one reason for not putting a safety barrier at the top of the stairs.

3. a Give four ways of making floors safer.
b Name three safety precautions which help prevent dangerous situations involving windows.
c Name two ways of making the glass in windows and doors safer.

4. a Name three ways of making the cooker safer if there are young children in the home.
b When can tablecloths be a danger?
c Give one advantage and one disadvantage of having pills in a blister pack.

To do

1. Draw or find pictures to illustrate your answers to the questions.

2. If a young child came to stay in your home, what would need to be done to make it safer?

3. List the safety points you can remember from previous topics (or look them up), particularly the topics which dealt with clothing, nursery equipment and toys.

62 *Outdoor safety*

Children love to be independent, to explore and experiment. This makes it difficult to foresee all the dangerous situations which might occur, especially when outside the home. However, there are precautions which parents can take and some of the more obvious ones are mentioned here.

Playing outside

Parents can help to prevent accidents by making sure that:

1. Children never play on the road.

2. Young children, when playing outside, are supervised by an adult or responsible older child.

3. The garden is a safe place for playing.

4. Children do not have dangerous toys such as bows and arrows, air guns and catapults until they are old enough to understand the dangers and behave responsibly.

5. Children do not play with gardening or other equipment stored outside, e.g. tools, lawn-mowers, chemicals. They should not be allowed to play in gardens where chemicals such as slug pellets, weedkiller, or rat poison have been put down.

6. Children do not run around with sticks or other sharp objects in their mouths. If they fall, they may perforate the palate (a hole may be made in the top of the mouth).

7. Children should be discouraged from eating plants in the garden as many are poisonous to a greater or lesser degree.

8. Dog droppings in the garden should be cleared away as they can spread worm infections and other illnesses.

9. Children do not play with fireworks.

Tetanus   When children play, they are likely to graze their skin occasionally. Those children who have been immunised against tetanus will be in less danger from tetanus germs in the soil.

Safety near water

Special care is needed when children are near or on water because of the risk of accidental drowning. Parents should make sure that:

1. Paddling pools containing water are not left unguarded. Babies have been known to drown in 7.5 cm (3 in) of water.
2. Garden pools or swimming pools are completely fenced off or emptied when young children are around.
3. Children are taught to swim as soon as they are old enough.
4. Children always wear a life-jacket when in a boat or canoe.

Types of restraint in cars

A

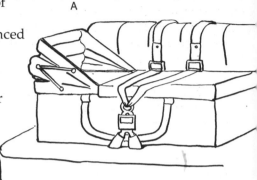

Safety in cars

Every year, as many as 60 000 child passengers are in car accidents and 120 are killed. The following precautions should be taken when travelling with children:

1. The doors must be safely secured. Child locks can be fitted to the rear doors. It may be possible to reverse the handles on the doors so that they can only be opened by pushing upwards.
2. Try to prevent a child from leaning on the door at any time.
3. Doors should be shut with care so that a child's fingers are not trapped.
4. An adult holding a baby must sit in the back of the car. Even if wearing a seat belt, an adult in the front would not be able to keep hold of the baby in a crash.
5. A child in a car should always be restrained by a belt or placed in a safety seat to prevent him from being thrown around. Children who are safely restrained are less likely to:
   - distract the driver;
   - be injured by the movement of the car;
   - be seriously injured if the car is in a crash.

B

Types of restraint

The type of restraint used depends on the age of the child. Whatever the type, it should be approved by the British Standards Institute and carry the British Standards Kitemark.

A Babies Babies in a carry-cot should be in the back of the car with the carry-cot securely held in place by belts. The cot cover (apron) should always be used, or a net or secure bedding, so that the baby cannot be thrown out.

C

B   Toddlers   When babies become too big for a carry-cot, they should be placed in a car safety seat which is firmly fastened to the back seat of the car. The buckle should be too difficult for young fingers to undo, but simple for an adult to release quickly.

C   Young children   When children become too big for the car safety seat, they should sit in a child harness on the back seat of the car. If it is necessary to use an adult seat belt, a cushion should be provided to raise the child up so that the belt can work properly.

D   Older children   When children reach the age of about ten years they can use adult seat belts in the front or the back of the car.

To do

1. How would you change the numbered items shown in the garden scene below in order to make it a safe place for children, and why is each action necessary?

2. Draw or find pictures to accompany your notes of the different types of car restraints for children.

3. Look outside your own home and make a list of the safety hazards for a young child. How would you recommend dealing with each if a young child came to stay?

Questions

1. Give ways in which parents can help prevent accidents to children playing outside.

2. What four precautions can be taken against accidental drowning?

3. Name five ways of helping to prevent accidents to children in cars.

4. What type of car restraint is suitable for
a babies,
b toddlers,
c young children,
d older children?

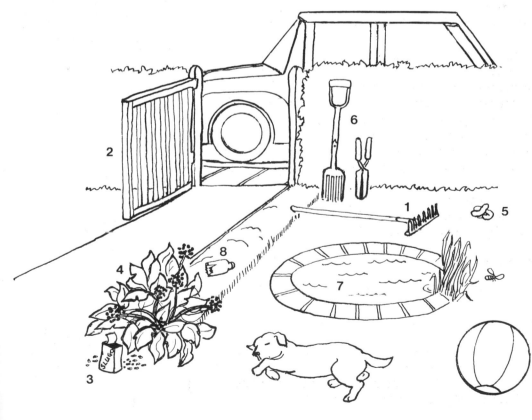

63 *Safety on the roads*

Accidents on the roads are the most common danger outside the home. Every year, about 500 children under the age of 15 years are killed on the roads of Britain and as many as 50 000 are injured, many of them seriously.

How parents can help

Parents can help prevent their children becoming involved in road accidents when they follow these instructions:

1. Set a good example by always crossing roads in a careful way.
2. Use walking reins for toddlers. Never rely on holding a toddler's hand — he can pull free in an instant.
3. Do not let young children out on the roads by themselves until they are reliable.
4. Insist that a young child holds the hand of an adult when crossing a road.
5. Make sure the child can be seen. When out in the dark, children should always wear light-coloured or reflective clothing, or carry a reflective bag.
6. Make sure their child knows the Green Cross Code. Go through the code every time the road is crossed until the child knows it.

Why crossing the road is difficult for young children

Young children cannot cross roads safely because:
- being small, they cannot see over stationary cars, etc;
- they do not remember instructions for very long;
- they have not yet learnt to be good judges of distance or of the speed at which the vehicles are travelling;
- they do not yet understand how traffic behaves.

Learning about road safety

The under-5s   Children begin to learn about road safety as soon as they are old enough to sit up in a pram or push-chair and take notice. They watch what goes on and sense when their parents are aware of danger.

As children become able to walk and talk, they learn that pavements are for people and roads are for traffic. All the while, they are learning to cross roads by copying their parents' behaviour.

5-6 years Children of this age are not yet old enough to be out on the roads by themselves. They should be taken to and collected from school. They have reached the stage when they can begin to be taught how to cross quiet roads on their own. They will need to be taught and then to be reminded often to:

STOP;
LOOK for traffic;
LISTEN for traffic *BEFORE* THEY CROSS THE ROAD.

7-9 years Children over the age of seven should be able to cross quiet roads alone. They should now begin to be able to learn, understand and remember the Green Cross Code. When they have done so, they will be better able to cross busy roads safely.

The Green Cross code✗ and how to use it.

1.
First find a safe place to cross, then stop.

2. Stand on the pavement near the kerb.

3.
Look all round for traffic and listen.

4.
If traffic is coming, let it pass. Look all round again.

5.
When there is no traffic near, wallk straight across the road.

6.
Keep looking and listening for traffic while you cross.

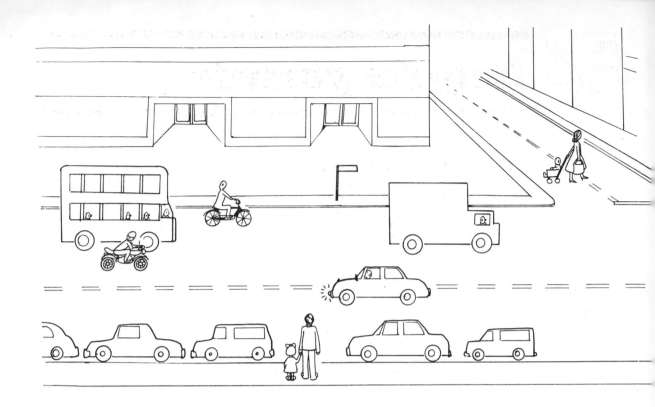

Questions

1. Name six ways that parents can help to prevent their children from being involved in road accidents.

2. Give four reasons why it is difficult for young children to cross roads safely.

3. a Write out the six rules of the Green Cross Code.

To do

1. a Study the picture above showing Sally and her father waiting to cross the road. (i) What can Sally see? (ii) What can her father see? (iii) Suggest possible reasons for the flashing indicator.
b Sally's father is making crossing the road into a game by letting Sally tell him when it is safe or unsafe to cross. Imagine a conversation between them.
c Why is it generally safer for a pram or pushchair to be pulled rather than pushed across a busy road?

2. Describe how a child from babyhood onwards can learn about road safety.

3. Many leaflets and booklets are produced on safety matters. List as many as you can, saying which aspects of safety each deals with and who it is published by.

Child study

If the child is old enough to talk to you, find out what he knows about road safety.

64 *Help for parents*

A great deal of help is available to parents in the form of advice, assistance and money from many different sources. Therefore parents may have difficulty in knowing where to go and whom to ask. In addition, government departments and the rules by which they work are likely to change from time to time.

Sources of help

1. **Social Security benefits** — financial help during pregnancy and afterwards.
2. **National Health Service** — for health care.
3. **Social Services** — for advice and assistance but not money (except in rare cases).
4. **Voluntary organisations**.

The DHSS (Department of Health and Social Security) is the government department responsible for **1** and **2**. The Social Services are the responsibility of the local authorities.

Voluntary organisations work independently of the government and local authorities, but often co-operate with them. Some of these organisations are listed on pp. 274-5.

Social Security benefits

Financial help from benefits, grants and allowances can be obtained in the following five ways:

1 Benefits which every mother receives

Child benefit   The mother receives a weekly sum from the government for every child in her family under the age of 16, or 19 if still a full-time student at school or college. She can also obtain:

- free dental treatment for herself
- free doctor's prescriptions for herself

  } during pregnancy and for 12 months afterwards;

- free dental treatment for her child;
- free doctor's prescriptions for her child.

2 Benefits which depend on National Insurance contributions

National Insurance contributions are paid to the government by employees and their employers. Employees who have paid contributions may be entitled to claim:

Maternity grant   This is a lump sum paid to the mother to help with the expenses of having a baby. It can be claimed 14 weeks before the baby is due and up to three months afterwards. The grant depends on National Insurance contributions having been paid either by the husband or the wife. Almost all mothers qualify, but not schoolgirl mothers (as they will not have paid any contributions), unless they have a husband who has paid.

Maternity allowance   Mothers who have paid full National Insurance contributions while they were working may qualify for this allowance. It is paid weekly to help make up for the earnings which the mother loses when she stops working to have her baby. It is normally paid for 18 weeks, starting 11 weeks before the baby is due, so that the mother can give up working in good time and not start again until 7 weeks afterwards.

Earnings related supplement   This is an extra weekly amount which may be added to the maternity allowance, depending on the mother's contributions.

3 Benefits for families on low incomes

Families whose incomes are below a certain level may be entitled to:

Family income supplement (FIS)   People who are in full-time work, but with a low income, and have at least one dependent child may be entitled to receive extra money each week. A single parent may also be able to claim FIS if working part-time. Families receiving FIS also get:
- free milk   } for expectant mothers and children
- free vitamins ∫   under 5 years;
- free school meals for each child at school;
- free glasses;
- free prescriptions.

Playgroup fees may also be paid.

4 Supplementary benefit

Supplementary benefit is money which is given to unemployed people, or those with a part-time job, to help cover their necessary living expenses. Parents who are on supplementary benefit will also be able to get similar benefits to those on FIS — free milk, vitamins, etc.

5 Child's special attendance allowance

This is available for children of two years and over who are severely disabled and require a great deal of care for six months or more.

National Health Service (NHS)

The NHS aims to help people keep well and to help care for them when they are ill. Doctors, dentists and health visitors are all part of the NHS. In addition, the NHS provides a number of other services specially for parents and children, for example:
- antenatal clinics, p. 206;
- preparation (parentcraft) classes, p. 209;
- midwives, p. 212;
- maternity hospitals or wards;
- baby clinics, p. 222;
- family planning clinics, p. 234;
- genetic counselling, p. 268;
- school health service.

School health service

When children start school, at five years or earlier, they will be given a medical examination. Parents are asked to be present when this takes place. The school doctor tests eyesight, hearing and speech. Checks are also made on health and development — height, weight, posture and co-ordination of movements when walking, using the hands, etc.

Any child who is found to have a particular problem which affects health or learning will be checked regularly and, if necessary, referred to a specialist for treatment.

Places which give help to parents

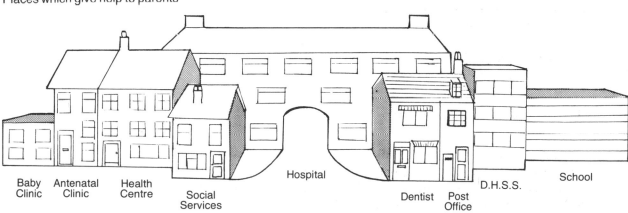

Baby Clinic Antenatal Clinic Health Centre Social Services Hospital Dentist Post Office D.H.S.S. School

Social Services

Every local authority has a Social Services Department with social workers to help and advise people with their problems. They aim to support parents in difficulties and to prevent children from coming into care. Parents who need help should get in touch with their local Social Services Office. The address can be found in the same way as for the Family Planning Clinic, p. 234. The Social Services can be of assistance in a number of ways, for example, by providing:

- day nurseries;
- home helps;
- fostering services;
- adoption services;
- supervision of children in care;
- children's homes and hostels;
- hostels for unmarried mothers;
- registration and supervision of playgroups;
- registration and supervision of child-minders.

It is also the duty of the Social Services to investigate any cases of suspected child abuse.

Child abuse

Child abuse is the term which is used to describe any injury to a child which is not the result of an accident. This includes:

- physical injury (child battering — see below);
- mental cruelty;
- severe neglect;
- sexual abuse.

Signs of child abuse are:

- injuries to the child for which there is no satisfactory explanation;
- bruises which indicate that a child has been tightly gripped and possibly shaken;
- failure of the child to thrive for no particular reason;
- delay by the parents in seeking advice or medical help.

Child abuse can happen in any kind of home and any type of family. Social workers from the local Social Services office investigate and deal with cases which come to their attention. In severe cases it may be necessary for them to remove the child from the family and take him into care for his own safety.

Child battering (baby battering)   Parents are said to 'batter' their children when they damage them in anger or give cruel punishments. Besides bruises, battering may take the form of burns, bites, damage to the mouth region, or other types of injury. Injuries caused in this way may be referred to as **non-accidental** injuries.

Babies may be battered because they cry continually. The parent cannot stand the noise any longer, loses self-control and shakes or beats the baby. Toddlers may be attacked because they have been 'naughty' and are being 'taught a lesson'. For example, a young child may be beaten because he wet his pants or got his clothes dirty.

All parents feel angry with their children occasionally. Those who batter their children at such times often do so because, for one reason or another, they are deeply depressed and cannot cope. They lose self-control and attack their children. In some cases, the parents themselves were beaten as children and have grown up to think that it is all right to do the same.

Any parent who feels in danger of battering a child needs to talk to someone about it. Family doctors, health visitors, social workers, Samaritans and the National Society for the Prevention of Cruelty to Children (NSPCC) are always ready to help and advise parents on how to avoid cruelty to children.

Questions

1. **a** Name four sources of help for parents.
b What is the main difference between the help given by the Social Services and by Social Security?
c Which two sources of help are the responsibility of the DHSS?
d Who is responsible for the Social Services?
e How are the voluntary organisations financed? See p. 274.

2. Which of the Social Security benefits
a does every mother receive,
b can be claimed by almost all mothers,
c depend on National Insurance contributions,
d is for low-income families,
e is for unemployed people,
f is for disabled children?

3. Name nine ways in which the Social Services can be of assistance to parents and children.

4. When a child is given a medical examination on starting school, what does the school doctor test and check?

5. What do the following mean
a DHSS,
b NHS,
c FIS?

6. **a** What is the difference between child abuse and child battering?
b Name types of child abuse other than physical injury.
c Name four signs which might indicate child abuse.
d Give a reason which might lead to the battering of (**i**) a baby, (**ii**) a toddler.
e To whom can parents turn for advice if they feel in danger of harming a child?

261

1. The following is an extract from a report of one case dealt with by the NSPCC:

When the local Inspector first called on Mary, he met with a dejected young woman, seven months pregnant and who could not have weighed more than six stone.

Her three young children (aged 4, 3 and 2) by a much older man, demanded constant attention — something which Mary just could not give them.

Help was desperately needed — for Mary's sake as well as the children's. The father of her next child, a man named Joey, was serving a six-month jail sentence.

Meantime, Mary had just moved into a house for which she was paying an exorbitant rent even though it was very damp and in poor repair. She had no friends or relations nearby and lived in constant fear of eviction.

Though the odds were very much against the family staying together once they were reunited, their trust in the inspector in helping them to build up a home and plan for the future was such that after two years all is well. Joey has not returned to prison, and the children are all fit and happy. Mary has put on some weight and smiles once more.

a What does NSPCC stand for?
b Suggest reasons why (i) Mary was dejected, (ii) her children demanded constant attention.
c What advice might the Inspector have given Mary and Joey about applying for help from (i) Social Security benefits, (ii) Social Services, (iii) National Health Service?
d Can you suggest any other voluntary organisations (see pp. 274-5) which might be able to help this family?

2. Study newspaper reports of cases of child battering. From the information given, what appears to be the likely cause, or causes, in each case?

Exercises

1 a Give three ways of securing babies and children in a car.
b Suggest two causes of electrical accidents in the bathroom and ways of avoiding them.
c The Green Cross Code has six rules. Write down those you can remember.
d State two differences between fostering and adoption.
e Name two ways in which the Social Services may provide for the care of babies of working mothers.
f Name one handicap known to be of genetic origin.
g State two ways a child may become handicapped after birth.
h Of the methods of contraception in common use, name two which are (i) efficient, (ii) unreliable.
i Give three ways in which a Special School differs from an ordinary school.

2 The kitchen is an obvious source of danger to a young child. Name eight hazards which may exist in other parts of the home, and describe the precautions which should be taken in each case. *(EAEB)*

3 A hundred years ago there were no clinics or welfare services. Many children died in infancy.
a Describe what is being done today to improve child health by:

(i) health visitors;
(ii) infant welfare clinics;
(iii) school health inspections.

b What financial help is available to mother and baby?
c What can other members of the family do to contribute to the health and well-being of mother and baby? *(SEREB)*

4 a What is contraception and why is it used?
b Explain fully the following methods:
   (i) intra-uterine device;
   (ii) oral contraceptive pill;
   (iii) condom or sheath;
   (iv) rhythm method.   (*WMEB*)

5 What particular difficulties would each of the following face, and how might they be helped?
a A four-year-old child with a pronounced stammer.
b Parents of a baby with spina bifida.
c A six-year-old child who is afraid of the dark.
        (*EAEB*)

6 Mary is four years old. She lives in a small flat with her mother, father and baby sister. She spends most of her time indoors because the flat is on the fourth floor and the street below is crowded with traffic. There is no lift. Mary sits all day, holding her doll and rocking it, but she does not have any other toys or games. She does not talk or run about and is very thin and pale. The family is trying to get a house, but there is a long waiting list.
a Why do you think Mary does not talk or play?
b How could her parents make things better for Mary?
c In what ways could a playgroup help Mary and her mother?
d Name *two* organisations, or people other than family, who would be able to help.   (*SEREB*)

7 Peggy and her husband have three children under five, the youngest being fifteen months.

She has not been really well since the youngest was born. She never takes them out, scarcely ever goes out herself, except to the corner shop, and seems to avoid her neighbours and former friends. When her best friend, Alison, went to see her, Peggy would not even let her into the house. The children were crying and a quick glimpse of the youngest showed Alison that he had two black eyes. Alison does not believe that the injury was accidental.
a Make a list of five possible causes for Peggy behaving in this way and write in detail about *two* of the causes, giving full explanations.
b Suggest three possible courses of action that Alison could take, bearing in mind that she is Peggy's friend and wants to help her.   (*SEREB*)

8 Imagine that on a hot sunny afternoon a mother has asked you to look after her two young children aged 12 months and 4 years. She has suggested that you take the children to a nearby public park.
a Explain how the children should be got ready for their outing and suggest plans that should help you all to have a happy afternoon.
b What precautions should be taken throughout the afternoon to ensure the safety of the children in your care.   (*EAEB*)

9 Give an account of the support which is made available to families by:
a the State,
b the local community,
c voluntary organisations.   (*LREB*)

Supplement

This section contains additional information amplifying some items mentioned in the main text and which may be required by certain examination syllabuses.

GERMS

Microbes which cause disease are often called germs (or **pathogens**) and they can only be seen with the aid of a powerful microscope. Germs are usually either bacteria or viruses, but a few fungi and other microbes are also able to cause disease.

Bacteria

Bacteria are found almost everywhere — in the air, soil, water, food, and both on and inside the bodies of plants and animals. There are many different types of bacteria and each has its own special shape, size, and conditions in which it can live and grow. Only a small proportion of the total number of bacteria are able to cause disease in humans.

Each tiny bacterium consists of a single cell. After growing to its full size, it reproduces by dividing into two. In the right conditions, this may take place about every twenty minutes, so large numbers of bacteria can be built up very quickly.

Bacteria cause disease when they damage the tissues of the body in which they are living, or when they produce **toxins** (poisons). The toxins may travel in the blood stream to harm other parts of the body.

Viruses

Viruses are even smaller than bacteria. They only become active when they get inside the living cells of plants or animals. There are many different types of virus including those which can live inside human cells. When the virus gets inside the right type of cell, it feeds, grows and multiplies. The cell then bursts and the virus particles are released to infect other cells. As the virus spreads, it damages the cells and causes disease.

Food poisoning bacteria

Types of bacteria responsible for food poisoning include:

(a) Salmonella   These bacteria usually live in the bowel. They get into food from the excreta of humans or animals or from water which has been polluted by sewage. Illness is caused by eating large numbers of these bacteria. If food containing them is thoroughly cooked, the bacteria are killed and will not be harmful.

(b) Staphylococcus   Bacteria of this type are found in many places including the nose, throat, boils and the pus from an infected wound. These bacteria produce toxin as they grow and multiply in food. It is the toxin and not the bacteria which causes food poisoning. The bacteria are readily killed by cooking but the toxin is only gradually destroyed.

(c) Clostridium   These bacteria are frequently found in human and animal excreta and they thrive when they get into the right types of food.
    When conditions become unfavourable for the bacteria (for example, they become short of water) they produces **spores**. The spores are very hardy and can survive for long periods of time in dust, dirt and soil. They may even survive normal cooking processes. When they find themselves in warm, moist food, the spores turn into active bacteria again and multiply rapidly.
    Clostridium welchii gives rise to a common type of food poisoning. Bacteria of this type produce toxin when they get inside the intestines. So, if the food is cooked thoroughly before eating, the bacteria will be killed and there will be no food poisoning.

CHROMOSOMES AND GENES

The human body is composed of vast numbers of tiny cells and each normally contains 46 chromosomes. Of the 46, 23 are exact copies of the chromosomes which came from the mother in the egg: the other 23 are exact copies of the chromosomes which came from the father in the sperm. They can be matched together in 23 pairs.
    The only cells of the human body which do not contain 46 chromosomes are the sex cells (the eggs and sperm) and they only contain 23.

Sex chromosomes   The sex of a baby is determined by one pair of chromosomes — the sex chromosomes. One of the sex chromosomes is called X, the other is called Y. A female has two X chromosomes (XX). A male has an X and a Y (XY).

Boy or girl?   Each egg contains an X chromosome. Some sperm contain X and some contain Y. Whether the child is a boy or girl depends on whether the egg is fertilised by a sperm containing an X or a Y chromosome.

Genes

A chromosome contains thousands of tiny parts called genes and each gene contains an instruction for building a part of the body. Working together, the genes control all the characteristics which are inherited from parents (see also p. 11). Children resemble parents, grandparents and other relatives because some of their genes are the same.

Dominant and recessive genes   Genes can be either strong (dominant) or weak (recessive). Strong genes mask the presence of weak genes. For example, if a child inherits a gene for dark hair from the father and a gene for red hair from the mother, he will have dark hair because the gene for dark hair is dominant to that for red hair. However, the child will be a 'carrier' for red hair and may pass the gene on to his children. Recessive genes can only have an effect when they are inherited from both parents, for example, two genes for red hair are necessary to produce a red-headed child.

Inherited disease

Very occasionally a slight change (mutation) takes place to the chromosomes or genes and is the cause of illness or abnormal development. (If a major change takes place, the embryo does not survive.) When the fault is able to be passed on from parent to child it may result in inherited disease, for example:
- haemophilia
- muscular dystrophy } due to faulty recessive genes;
- phenylketonuria
- Down's syndrome results from having 47 chromosomes instead of 46;
- an inherited factor is thought to play a part in spina bifida, congenital dislocation of the hip, and diabetes.

Genetic counselling

Genetic counselling is the giving of expert advice on the likelihood of disease passing from parents to children by inheritance. People may ask for genetic counselling:

1. when there is a history of inherited illness or abnormality in their family;

2. when the father and mother are closely related, for example, cousins. If there are harmful recessive genes in the family, they may both be carriers. Any children they have may then inherit a double dose of these genes;

3. when there is a possibility of an abnormal condition which can be detected in early pregnancy by tests such as amniocentesis and the mother may wish to consider terminating the pregnancy by abortion.

Amniocentesis can detect:

*   the number of chromosomes in the cells of the foetus — important in detecting Down's syndrome;

*   the sex of the child — important when there is a high risk that a male child may inherit muscular dystrophy or haemophilia;

*   the amount of AFP (alpha-foeto-protein) in the amniotic fluid — a high level indicates spina bifida or other severe defect of the nervous system.

HORMONES

Hormones are substances which act as chemical messengers. They are produced in glands called **endocrine glands** and then circulate in the blood stream, carrying messages to various parts of the body. There are many different hormones and they help control the way the body works.

Hormones play a very important part in controlling the menstrual cycle, pregnancy and birth. Examples are:

*   **oestrogen**, the female sex hormone. At puberty, it is responsible for the development of the womb, breasts and other female characteristics;

*   **progesterone**, the pregnancy hormone. It helps to prepare the womb to receive the fertilised egg and maintain a state of pregnancy. Progesterone interacts with oestrogen and other hormones to control the menstrual cycle;

*   **oxytocin**, stimulates the womb to contract during childbirth;

*   **prolactin**, controls milk production.

ENERGY IN FOOD

The body needs a continuous supply of energy to keep alive. Energy is used for breathing, circulation, growth, keeping warm and other activities. It is required to enable the body to move and the more energetic the person, the more energy will be used. This energy all comes from food.

The amount of energy a particular food contains can be measured in either kilocalories (kcal) or kilojoules (kJ):

1 kcal = 4.2 kJ (approx)   1000 kJ = 1 MJ (megajoule)

In everyday language the 'kilo' part of kilocalorie is often left off. So, when the word calorie is used it usually means kilocalorie. The same often happens to the word kilojoule. It is technically inaccurate to use calorie and joule in this way and can be confusing. The 'Manual of Nutrition' (HMSO) describes these terms in the following way:

'1 kcal is the amount of heat required to raise the temperature of 1 kilogram of water by 1°C. The SI unit, the joule, is hard to define in familiar terms, but 1 kilojoule (kJ) may be visualised as the amount of heat required to raise the temperature of 239 grams of water by 1°C.'

Energy content of food

All food contains energy. Different foods contain different amounts of energy per unit weight, that is, they have different energy values. Foods which have a high energy value are those which contain little water and a high proportion of fat or sugar. Examples of high-energy foods are shown on p. 131.

Daily intake of energy

It has been estimated that, on average, the daily intakes of energy shown in the table are required. These figures apply to boys; girls require slightly less. The average daily intake for women is 9.2 MJ (2200 kcal). When pregnant they require 10.0 MJ (2400 kcal) and when breast-feeding 11.3 MJ (2700 kcal).

(Recommended daily amounts of nutrients for population groups, DHSS, 1979.)

	MJ	kcal
Birth to 3 months	2.3	550
3 to 6 months	3.2	760
6 to 9 months	3.8	910
9 to 12 months	4.2	1000
1 year	5.0	1200
2 years	5.75	1400
3 to 4 years	6.5	1560
5 to 6 years	7.25	1740

BIRTH-WEIGHT

Average birth-weight

Average birth-weight at 28 weeks — 1.5 kg (3¼ lb)
at 32 weeks — 2.0 kg (4½ lb)
at 36 weeks — 2.6 kg (5¾ lb)
at 40 weeks — 3.5 kg (7½ lb)

Low birth-weight

Low birth-weight babies are those who weight 2.5 kg (5½ lb) or less at birth. The reason is likely to be one or more of the following:

1. **The baby inherits a small size**, probably because one or both of his parents are small. These babies are perfectly normal and present no problem.

2. **The baby is born prematurely** and therefore has not had time in the womb to grow to full size.

3. **Shortage of food in the womb** prevents the baby from growing at the normal rate. A baby who grows more slowly than is normal is said to be **'small for dates'** or **'light for dates'**. This may be due to:

    a **the mother being starved** — rare in Europe nowadays, but sadly still common in other parts of the world;

    b **the mother smoking** during pregnancy (p. 201);

    c **toxaemia of pregnancy** (p. 207);

    d **regular drinking of alcohol** in large quantities;

    e **drug addiction**.

Low birth-weight in babies in groups 2 and 3 indicates that they need special care. They will be weaker and less able to cope with the stress of being born, and then of living an independent existence outside the womb. These babies may therefore need to be kept for a while in an incubator.

Graph to show the average weight of boys and girls from birth to 7 years

(Boys, on average, continue to weigh more than girls except during the years of 11 to 14.)

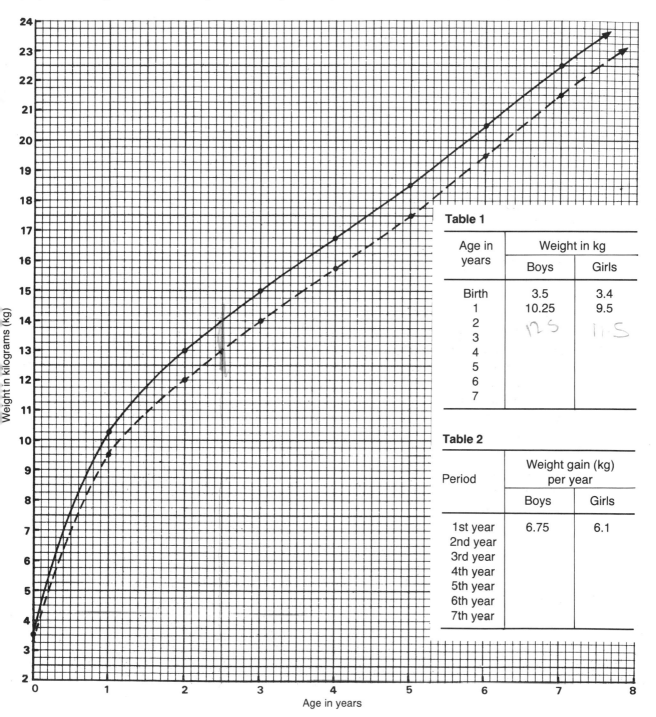

Table 1

Age in years	Weight in kg	
	Boys	Girls
Birth	3.5	3.4
1	10.25	9.5
2	12 S	11 S
3		
4		
5		
6		
7		

Table 2

Period	Weight gain (kg) per year	
	Boys	Girls
1st year	6.75	6.1
2nd year		
3rd year		
4th year		
5th year		
6th year		
7th year		

Weight in kilograms (kg)

Age in years

Questions

1. Use information from the graph above to complete Table 1.
2. Use Table 1 to work out how much weight is gained on average each year, and complete Table 2.

The graphs above and on p. 272 are based on charts by J.M. Tanner and R.H. Whitehouse, with the measurements slightly modified for easier calculation.

Graph to show the average height of boys and girls from birth to 7 years

Boys, on average, continue to be taller than girls except for about two years during puberty between the ages of 11 and 13.

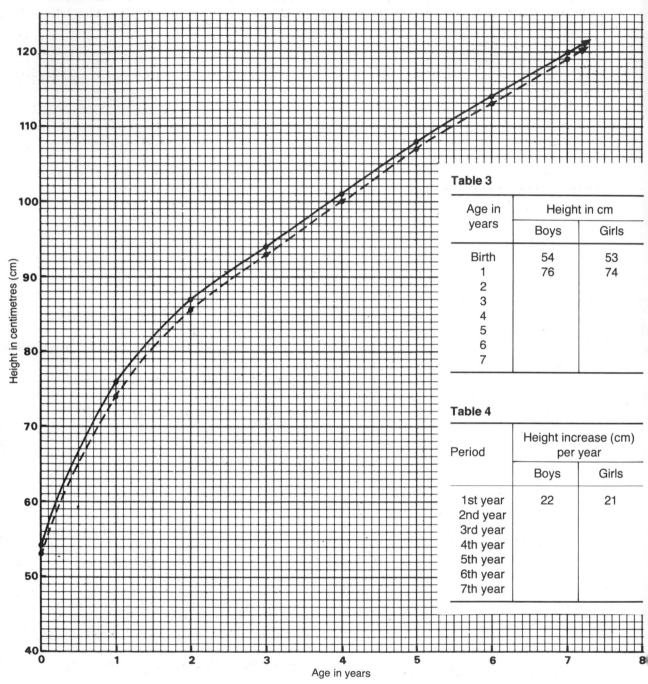

Table 3

Age in years	Height in cm	
	Boys	Girls
Birth	54	53
1	76	74
2		
3		
4		
5		
6		
7		

Table 4

Period	Height increase (cm) per year	
	Boys	Girls
1st year	22	21
2nd year		
3rd year		
4th year		
5th year		
6th year		
7th year		

Questions

1. Use information from the graph above to complete Table 3.
2. Use Table 3 to work out the average yearly increase in height, and complete Table 4.

BOOK LIST

The author has found the following books, pamphlets and leaflets useful.

Babies and Young Children, Ronald and Cynthia Illingworth (Churchill Livingstone)

Baby and Child, Penelope Leach (Penguin)

The Complete Book of Babycare, Edited by Barbara Nash (Marks and Spencer)

Book of Child Care, Hugh Jolly (Sphere)

Baby and Child Care, Dr Spock (New English Library)

Developmental Progress of Infants and Young Children, Mary Sheridan (HMSO)

The First Years of Life, Open University and Health Education Council (Ward Lock)

The Pre-School Child, Open University and Health Education Council (Ward Lock)

Child Care and Development, Catriona Hood (Bell and Hyman)

Toys and Playthings, John and Elizabeth Newson (Penguin)

Pyjamas Don't Matter, Trish Gibbon (John Murray)

Manual of Nutrition, Ministry of Agriculture and Fisheries (HMSO)

Play It Safe, The Health Education Council and Scottish Health Educational Group

You and Your Baby, Parts 1 and 2, Family Doctor Publications (British Medical Association)

New Baby, Health Visitors Association Publication

Babyboots, a catalogue issued by Boots

Mothercare, a catalogue issued by Mothercare

Also information published by:

Pre-School Playgroups Association, Alford House, Aveline Street, London SE11 5DH (This organisation has other branches in many large cities.)

Clarkes Shoes, Clarkes Ltd., Street, Somerset

Johnson & Johnson Ltd., Slough, Berks.

National Dairy Council, John Princes Street, London W1M 0AP

Robinsons Baby Foods Ltd., Colman Foods, Norwich NR1 2DD

Wyeth Nutrition, Wyeth Laboratories, Taplow, Maidenhead, Berks (for information on infant feeding and breast feeding)

Health Education Council, 78 New Oxford Street, London WC1A 1AH

National Association for Maternal and Child Welfare (NAMCW), 1 South Audley Street, London W1Y 6JS

AUDIOVISUAL AIDS

This is only a small selection of the large number of films, videos and slides which are available for use in Child Care and Development courses. Most can be borrowed through the Health Education Service.

Hello Baby — about the methods of communication between parents and their children (Health Education Council).

Immunisation (Health Education Council).

Through the Eyes of a Child (CTVC, Foundation House, Walton Road, Bushey, Watford, Herts.).

Parents in Playgroups (CTVC).

Facts of Life — ten programmes on pregnancy, childbirth and the early years of parenthood (ITV for Schools and Colleges, Granada Television, Query Street, Manchester M60 9EA).

With a Little Help — illustrates the adjustments needed when a new baby arrives in the family (Farley Health Products Ltd, Torr Lane, Plymouth, Devon PL3 5UA).

Give Us a Chance — shows how more interest, fun and a greater meaning can be given to the lives of people who are mentally handicapped (Town and Country Productions Ltd, 21 Cheyne Row, Chelsea, London SW5 5HP).

Play it Safe — a series of ten programmes on accident prevention (BBC, Villiers House, Ealing Broadway, London W5 2PA).

Nobody Told Me — shows 25 typical accidents which take place in the home (BIA, Aldermany House, Queen Street, London EC4N 1TU).

Voluntary organisations

There are a large number of voluntary organisations dealing with particular aspects of child welfare and some of them are listed below. Each organisation has its own aims and rules and most are financed by voluntary contributions although, in some cases, the government may give a grant or subsidy towards running costs.

   The organisations listed have indicated that they will provide further information on their work. When they have asked for a large stamped addressed envelope (s.a.e.) this has been mentioned.

Association for Spina Bifida and Hydrocephalus (ASBAH)
Tavistock House North, Tavistock Square, London WC1H 9HJ

Gives support and advice to those with spina bifida and/or hydrocephalus and to their families. Further information from the Director of ASBAH.

British Agencies for Adoption and Fostering (BAAF)
11 Southwark Street, London SE1 1RQ

Gives information and advice on adoption and fostering.

Child Poverty Action Group (CPAG)
1 Macklin Street, London WC2B 5NH

Works with and on behalf of poor families. Helps to sort out which benefits parents and children are entitled to. Send s.a.e. for further information.

Disabled Living Foundation
346 Kensington High Street, London W14 8NS

Is concerned with those aspects of ordinary life which present particular problems to disabled people.

Down's Children's Association
41 Oxford Street, London W1R 1PA

Helps parents with the care, treatment and training of children with Down's syndrome.

Invalid Children's Aid Association (ICAA)
126 Buckingham Palace Road, London SW1W 9SB

Aims to improve the quality of life for handicapped children and their families. Runs a residential school for sufferers from eczema, asthma and cystic fibrosis, and three schools for children with language disorders.

MENCAP, Royal Society for Mentally Handicapped Children and Adults
MENCAP National Centre, 123 Golden Lane, London EC1Y 0RT

Aims to increase public awareness and understanding of mental handicaps. Provides specialist advice and support for parents of mentally handicapped children.

MIND (National Association for Mental Health)
22 Harley Street, London W1N 2ED

Gives advice and guidance to the parents of handicapped children.

Muscular Dystrophy Group of Great Britain
Nattrass House, 35 Macaulay Road, London SW4 0QP

A national charity raising funds for medical research into neuro-muscular diseases. S.a.e. for leaflets. This organisation regrets that they have insufficient staff to deal with project enquiries.

National Association for the Welfare of Children in Hospital (NAWCH)
Exton House, 7 Exton Street, London SE1 8UE

Aims to promote unrestricted visiting and better play facilities for children in hospital.

National Children's Bureau
8 Wakely Street, London EC1V 7QE

Organisation for research into children's needs. Links together the many organisations concerned with the welfare of children. Prefers requests for information to come from teachers.

The National Childbirth Trust
9 Queensborough Terrace, London W2 3TB

Helps women to prepare for childbirth to make birth a satisfying experience. Provides antenatal classes, breast-feeding advice and postnatal support. Send s.a.e. for further information.

National Council for One-parent Families
255 Kentish Town Road, London NW5 2LX

Free advice, information and help given to lone parents and single pregnant women. Send s.a.e. for details and publication list.

The National Deaf Children's Society
45 Hereford Road, London W2 5AH

Represents deaf children's interests nationally and locally and supports parents through a large network of self-help groups.

The National Autistic Society
276 Willesden Lane, London NW2 5RB

Runs centres for the care, education and training of autistic children and arranges meetings for parents. Send s.a.e. for more information.

National Society for the Prevention of Cruelty to Children (NSPCC)
1 Riding House Street, London W1P 8AA
The NSPCC exists to prevent child abuse and provides immediate help for children in need.

In nearly one third of the cases dealt with, it is the parents themselves who ask the society for help and advice.

Pre-School Playgroups Association (PPA)
Alford House, Aveline Street, London SE11 5DH

The PPA exists to help parents understand and provide for the needs of their young children. It advises on the running of playgroups and mother and toddler groups. Publishes two magazines 'Contact' and 'Under-5'.

Royal National Institute for the Blind
224 Great Portland Street, London W1N 6AA

Provides education, training and many other services for the blind of all ages including schools for blind children.

The Royal National Institute for the Deaf (RNID)
105 Gower Street, London WC1E 6AH

Advice and information is freely given on all aspects of deafness.

Spastics Society
12 Park Crescent, London W1N 4RQ

Provides services for children with cerebral palsy including care, education and training. Promotes public awareness of the handicap.

Play Matters (Formerly the Toy Libraries Association)
Seabrook House, Wyllyotts Manor, Darkes Lane, Potters Bar, Herts EN6 2HL

To promote and advise on toy libraries for both the handicapped and non-handicapped.

Save the Children Fund
Mary Datchelor House, 17 Grove Lane, London SE5 8RD

This organisation works to raise the standard of child care and welfare both in Britain and abroad. It runs playgroups in many urban areas and is working for a better organised service of child-minders.

Index

Page references in bold type indicate where topics are given their principal treatment.